ADA:
An Introduction

Countess Ada Augusta Lovelace aged nineteen, painted by Margaret Carpenter, soon after Ada's marriage to Lord King in 1835.

ADA:
AN INTRODUCTION

Sabina Saib

HOLT, RINEHART AND WINSTON
New York   Chicago   San Francisco   Philadelphia
Montreal   Toronto   London   Sydney   Tokyo
Mexico City   Rio de Janeiro   Madrid

To my husband, Ihsan,
and my sons,
David and Joseph

Ada is a trademark of the U.S. Department of Defense. (Ada Joint Program Office)
The frontispiece photograph is courtesy of National Physical Laboratory, Teddington,
England.

Library of Congress Cataloging in Publication Data
Saib, Sabina.
    Ada : an introduction.
    Includes index.
    1. Ada (Computer program language)   I. Title.
QA76.73.A35S25 1984   001.64'24   84–27987

ISBN 0-03-59487-1

Printed in the United States of America

Published simultaneously in Canada

5 6 7 8   039   9 8 7 6 5 4 3 2 1

CBS COLLEGE PUBLISHING
Holt, Rinehart and Winston
The Dryden Press
Saunders College Publishing

CONTENTS

CHAPTER 13 DISCRIMINANTS   191

CHAPTER 14 LIST PROCESSING   199

CHAPTER 15 PRIVATE TYPES   219

CHAPTER 16 USING ADA FOR DESIGN   226

CHAPTER 17 FILES   241

CHAPTER 18 TASKING   253

Chapter 19 Exceptions   275

Chapter 20 Real Time Interfaces   287

Chapter 21 The Ada Environment   306

Appendix A Predefined Identifiers   309

Appendix B ASCII Character Set   311

Appendix C Input Output Packages   314

Appendix D Attributes   322

Appendix E Pragmas   333

Appendix F Package Standard   336

Appendix G Package System and Package Calendar   342

Glossary   344

Index   351

PREFACE

This book provides an introduction to Ada, a modern computer programming language. The book assumes some background and familiarity with computers but not with Ada itself. Central to this text are the many examples and problems. Besides being helpful in learning Ada, these illustrations and exercises can serve as models for you to create your own programs. The examples have all been tested using an Ada compiler. An introductory class may omit the later chapters on more advanced programming techniques while an intermediate programmer may prefer to skim the first chapters.

SOME BACKGROUND ON ADA

The programming language Ada was named after Countess Ada Augusta Lovelace (1815–1852) of England. The frontispiece shows a picture painted when she was nineteen, shortly after her marriage to Lord King.

Ada was born into a notable English family. Her father was Lord Byron, the poet, who spent much of his time away from his family. Her mother, Lady Noel Byron, encouraged Ada to develop her talents, one of which was an aptitude for mathematics. Ada studied mathematics and became a friend and collaborator of Charles Babbage (1792–1871), who designed and attempted to build a mechanical digital computer or what he called an "analytical engine."

Ada is best known for her translation of an article about Babbage's computer. She not only translated the article but added her own notes to the paper that included the instructions for a computer program to calculate a table of Bernoulli numbers used in the solution of differential equations. As a result, Ada is known as the world's first computer programmer.

Ada is a high-level programming language with roots in a research language called LIS. Certain features were also borrowed from such modern programming languages as Pascal. The first Ada compiler was developed for a Digital Equipment Corporation computer, the VAX 11/780, by the Courant Institute, New York University in 1983. This compiler, called Ada/ED, was used to test the programs in this book. There are Ada compilers available today for mainframe and minicomputers and also for the most popular microcomputers.

A well-supported language, Ada has been designated by the U.S. Department of Defense as its official computer language. The U.S. government intends to make Ada compilers available on many computers at a nominal charge through the National Technical Information Service. The Ada compiler will be supported with numerous tools to aid in the design, preparation, testing, and maintenance of computer programs written in Ada.

Ada is an American National Standards Institute language, and there is a reference manual available from the U.S. Printing Office. After you have mastered Ada, you may want to order this manual to help you in writing your programs.

To learn more about Countess Ada Augusta Lovelace:

Moore, Doris Langley. *Ada, Countess of Lovelace* New York: Harper & Row, 1977.

Ada's program:

Menabrea, L. F. "Sketch of the Analytical Engine Invented by Charles Babbage (with notes by the translator Ada Augusta, Countess of Lovelace)," in *Babbage's Calculating Engines,* New York: Dover, 1961.

The official Ada reference manual:

U.S. Department of Defense, *Reference Manual for the Ada Programming Language,* ANSI/MIL-STD-1815A (February 1983).

More about LIS:

Ichbiah, J. D., and G. Ferran "Separate Definition and Compilation in LIS and its Implementation." In *Lecture Notes in Computer Science, Cornell Symposium on the Design of Higher Order Languages,* New York: Springer Verlag, 1977.

CHAPTER
❖ 1 ❖
INTRODUCTION

❖❖ Ada is a high-level programming language used to communicate instructions to computers. It would be ideal if we could communicate with computers in English, but computers are not yet as smart as we are, so we need special languages to talk to them. Ada is one of many such special languages.

We call Ada a high-level programming language—this implies that there must also be some lower level programming languages. And indeed there are. While many programmers work with these lower level languages, they have several drawbacks.

One drawback is that working with them is tedious, time-consuming, and error-prone; the languages themselves are often not very meaningful unless you are a programmer trained in one computer's specific *machine language,* the lowest level programming language and the language that speaks directly to the computer's hardware. Programmers communicate with a computer in machine language with a stream of numbers,

```
1000  10  07  00002
1001  20  03  02002
1003  04  03  02003
```

which the computer interprets as an instruction to add, print, store, or so forth.

Another drawback to machine language and other low level languages is that they are machine-specific; a program written for one kind of computer cannot be used on any other. This also holds true for assembly language, which is the next level above machine language.

Assembly language is a step removed from machine language in that you write your commands using numbers, letters, and short words:

```
ORG 1000
LDA 2
ADD C
STA X
```

Each assembly language command translates into one machine language command, which is made up of the stream of numbers we saw before. The computer program that performs this translation is called an *assembler*.

While an assembly language command such as ADD is more meaningful than the machine number 20, which might also mean *add*, the program is still far from readable. Another drawback to assembly language is that each computer has its own assembler program and machine language. Programs written in assembly language cannot be moved from one kind of computer to another.

There are many higher level languages such as FORTRAN, the forerunner of most of these languages. These languages use commands that are more readable than assembly language, looking something like English and mathematical notation. As with assembly language, these languages also need translators to turn their commands into machine language; these translators are called *compilers*.

Ada is a higher level language similar to FORTRAN. However, because Ada is an American National Standards Institute standard and is designed to be used on a variety of computers, it will be the same across all these computers. There will be no omissions or enhancements in Ada compilers, which

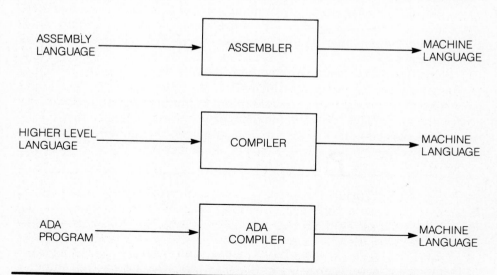

Figure 1.1   Levels of Languages

is not the case with most other programming languages. These enhancements, sometimes called *supersets*, and the omissions, called *subsets*, have made transporting programs across computers difficult.

Another Ada advantage over other high-level programs is that Ada programs use complete English words instead of cryptic abbreviations. This means that programmers can use meaningful names in writing their programs instead of being limited to using very short names. It's still up to programmers to make the programs comprehensible to their colleagues, but Ada at least provides a means for them to do so.

Ada can also detect errors very early in the preparation and testing of a computer program, a process known as *error-checking*. It also possesses powerful constructs for writing programs that programmers previously could write only in assembly language.

Even higher level languages than Ada exist. However, these languages are designed for special application areas such as surveying or structural analysis—Ada was designed for general rather than special applications.

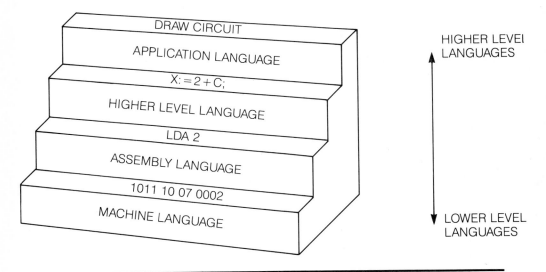

Figure 1.2 Computer Programming Languages

COMPUTER PROGRAMS

A computer program is made up of a series of commands written in a language understandable by a computer. Analogies to computer programs are the instructions you see on the back of a shampoo bottle, the steps in a recipe, or the directions to a friend's house. The shampoo analogy is a good one because the instructions on a shampoo bottle usually ask you to repeat all the steps.

The English instructions that you see on the shampoo bottle make up what is called an *algorithm*, a specific sequence of steps you use to solve a

Figure 1.3   Algorithms

problem. You can think of an algorithm as a computer program written in English.

Creating an algorithm is considered more difficult than actually writing the program once the algorithm is given. To design an algorithm, the problem is first divided into relatively large steps, each of which is further subdivided into smaller steps. This subdivision or refinement of the algorithm is very important in developing large programs—this way individual programmers can each work on a small part of the problem and their efforts are then combined. In most algorithms for computer programs, there is a great deal of repetition in the instructions—repetition is something that computers are able to handle very nicely.

The data for the program are also a part of programming. You will have many choices as to how to represent, store, and operate on the information needed by a computer program—the way data are handled in the computer is very important. We will see that decisions on how data are stored and operated on using computer algorithms can make a program easier to understand, can cause a program to compute faster, and can help prevent programming errors, especially when the program is changed.

SIMPLE ADA PROGRAMS

Although you may not be using the same compiler as the one used in the preparation of this text, the programs given in this chapter and throughout the book should word on your computer just as they did when they were prepared. Enter the programs exactly as they are shown. Your computer terminal probably has a TVlike display and a typewriterlike keyboard. You will prepare your Ada program using an editor and the Ada compiler and then execute or run your program and view your results on the display.

A very simple Ada program that you should type into your terminal, translate with the Ada compiler, and execute on your computer is shown below:

```
with TEXT_IO;
use TEXT_IO;
procedure SIMPLE_ADA is
--This is a simple Ada program
begin
--It displays the message within quotes on the terminal
    PUT_LINE('' Hi there, I am a very friendly computer! '');
end SIMPLE_ADA;
```

When compiled and executed this simple program will cause the computer to display, "Hi there, I am a very friendly computer!" on your terminal. Out of the eight lines in the program, only one line causes this to happen. Lines that cause the computer to do something are called *executable lines*. The line that started with PUT_LINE is the single executable line or statement in the program. The remaining lines set up the program.

You'll note that the program was written using a combination of upper- and lowercase letters. Ada does not differentiate between upper- and lowercase in interpreting the program commands. A bold typeface differentiates some important words to Ada called *keywords*. Since you do not have boldface on your terminal, you will type the keywords just like all the other words in your program. The keywords are sometimes called *reserved words*; they have a special meaning to Ada and must be used according to its rules. There are only 63 keywords in Ada, this program used six of them: **with, use, procedure, is, begin,** and **end.**

The first two lines in the program, **with** TEXT_IO and **use** TEXT_IO, appear so often in programs that some Ada compilers assume they exist even though you have not typed them in. These lines tell the compiler that you want to input some information into the computer and receive some output from the program. Almost any program you write will input some information and output some results. This program's output was the message displayed on the terminal, "Hi there, I am a very friendly computer!"

Ada uses programs that have been written and stored in a *program library* for input and output. A program library is made up of library units, each of which is a previously prepared program or, more likely, a collection of previously prepared programs. The **with** statement (the first line in our example) names one or more program library units—we can use these programs in our program merely by naming them. The name of the program library unit in our example is TEXT_IO. The semicolon following TEXT_IO ends the statement. If a program has a **with** statement, it will always be the first statement to appear in the program. The simple form of the **with** statement is:

with *program library units;*

where the italicized portion of the statement stands for something that must be filled in. We filled it in with one of the standard program library units available with Ada compilers, TEXT_IO. We will learn more about the **with** statement in chapter 10.

The program's next line is the **use** statement, which names a package of programs in the program library unit named in the preceding **with** statement. A package is a collection of related programs and data; packages can also contain packages for organizing programs together in a large collection. For example, think of a law library, which might be part of a larger library system, as a package. A law book from that library would be considered a package in the library. As with the books in a law library, the packages that are part of a larger package should all be related.

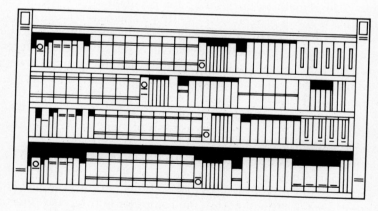

with *a_library*;--Ada library of packages
use *a_book*;   --Ada package in program library

with LAW_LIBRARY;
use LAW_LIBRARY.TORTS;

Figure 1.4   Law Library

In our example, we want to access all the packages in the library, so we name the entire package in the **use** statement. The **use** statement is not confined to the beginning of the program and can appear in several places. Until we learn more about it in chapter 10, however, we will employ **use** for input and output and keep it separate in front of the program. The simple form of the use statement is:

use *package name;*

As we saw, semicolons end statements. You can type more than one statement on a line if you wish, but most programs look better if you just type one statement per line. You can also spread out statements across several lines; for example, the first two lines in our program could have been written on one line:

```
with TEXT_IO;  use TEXT_IO;
```

But again your program will be more readable if you keep statements to just one line wherever possible.

The third line in our example names the program SIMPLE_ADA. We could have given it any name as long as we started the name with a letter and used only letters, digits, and the underscore in the name. For example, we could have named the program EXAMPLE_1 or FRIENDLY_COMPUTER_ PROGRAM or any other name conforming to Ada's rules. It is better to pick meaningful names for your programs than names such as PROGRAM_1 or TODAYS_JOB. The name of your program can be as long as you like so long as it fits on one line of your terminal (usually 80 characters).

In Ada, the instructions that tell the computer what to do and the data used in the program make up a computer program. The instruction or executable part of the program is contained after the keyword **begin** and before the keyword **end.** The data declaration is contained after the keyword **is** and before the keyword **begin.** Thus the usual layout of any Ada program after the statements that tell it which library and packages to use is:

```
procedure program name is
   declaration part
begin
   executable statements
end program name ;
```

The program we wrote is also called a *main program*, a *procedure*, or a *main procedure*. When we write a single procedure, it is always the main procedure. When we write a collection of procedures, we will place them in a package and have a main procedure that will use the package. It is good practice to line up the keywords **procedure, begin,** and **end** as shown in the example. An Ada compiler will still run your program if you don't line them up, but people who read your program will rely on your nice layout. In chapter 8, we will see how to write procedures that work together.

The top part of our simple example had no data declaration statements. We had, instead, a *comment*, special text set off with two hyphens. Comments can contain English text to explain what the program does—such information is called *program documentation*. Comments in Ada do not need to end with a semicolon because the end of the line ends a comment. Some good things to put in a comment are your name, the date, the version of the program, and of course what the program does. Comments can be placed anywhere in an Ada program, even on the same line as a statement, but that makes the rest of the line a comment. A well-commented program will be more understandable because you can explain what you are doing in the program in plain English. The general form of a comment is:

```
-- English text
```

Note that the second comment in our example tells what the program does—that it displays the message within quotes on the terminal.

The only output statement in this program—PUT_LINE (" Hi there, I am a very friendly computer! ");—causes output to a terminal, or for those computers without terminals, causes output to a printer. PUT_LINE is actually another program prepared for your use and put in the TEXT_IO package. To use PUT_LINE, you give its name and place what you want to be displayed within parentheses. Text messages such as were used in the example require quotes around the message. The statement ends with a semicolon. The general form of the PUT_LINE statement for messages is:

PUT_LINE (" *message* ") ;

The message must be able to fit on one line. If your message takes more than one line, all you have to do is use more than one PUT_LINE statement.

In our second example, we will use several PUT_LINE statements to form a picture.

```
with TEXT_IO;
use TEXT_IO;
procedure VALENTINE is
-- A program to draw a heart
begin
   PUT_LINE ("    xxx    xxx    ");
   PUT_LINE ("   x   x x    x   ");
   PUT_LINE ("   x     x    x   ");
   PUT_LINE ("   x          x   ");
   PUT_LINE ("     x       x    ");
   PUT_LINE ("      x     x     ");
   PUT_LINE ("       x   x      ");
   PUT_LINE ("        x x       ");
   PUT_LINE ("         x        ");

end VALENTINE;
```

While this may not be the most elegant heart in the world, it should give you the idea how you can draw Snoopy, ET, or happy faces for the calendars or schedules that you will learn to program. As with the first program, you should enter this program and compile and execute it on your machine. If you are ambitious, you could add an arrow or initials to the heart. Note that this program executes statements one at a time, from top to bottom. This is the normal order of execution for an Ada program.

Some things to watch out for when you enter your program:

—do *not* put a semicolon after **procedure, is,** or **begin.**

—do put a semicolon after the end of the program and after each statement in the program.

The reason you do not put a semicolon after **procedure, is,** or **begin** is that the procedure statement does not end until the **end** that names the procedure. Statements inside a procedure have their own semicolons.

The two programs that we have looked at are good introductions to Ada and to your computer, but they do not demonstrate any of the computer's ability to compute. Our next example causes the computer to add together two numbers that you enter on the terminal, and display the result.

```
with TEXT_IO;
package INTEGER_IO is new TEXT_IO. INTEGER_IO (INTEGER);
with TEXT_IO, INTEGER_IO;
use TEXT_IO, INTEGER_IO;
procedure ADDITION is
-- This program reads in 2 whole numbers
-- and sums them to form the result.
-- It echos the data read in as well as displaying the result.
  FIRST_VALUE, SECOND_VALUE, RESULT : INTEGER;
begin
  PUT_LINE (" The addition program has started to execute. ");
  PUT_LINE (" Type two whole numbers separated by spaces, ");
  PUT_LINE (" and followed by a carriage return. ");
  GET (FIRST_VALUE);  -- Bring in the first number
  GET (SECOND_VALUE); -- Bring in the second number
  -- Display what was read into the computer
  NEW_LINE;
  PUT (" First_value = "); PUT (FIRST_VALUE);
  NEW_LINE;
  PUT (" Second_value = "); PUT (SECOND_VALUE);
  NEW_LINE;
  -- Perform the calculation of adding the two numbers
  RESULT := FIRST_VALUE + SECOND_VALUE;
  -- Display the result
  PUT (" Result from addition = "); PUT (RESULT);
end ADDITION;
```

When this program compiles and executes, it will display on your terminal:

```
The addition program has started to execute.
Type two whole numbers separated by spaces,
and followed by a carriage return.
```

You should then type in two numbers. For example you might type:

```
5    20
```

in which case you will then see displayed on the terminal:

```
The addition program has started to execute.
Type two whole numbers separated by spaces,
and followed by a carriage return.

>5    20

First_value =            5
Second_value =          20
Result from addition =            25
```

This program starts out with

```
with TEXT_IO;
package INTEGER_IO is new TEXT_IO. INTEGER_IO (INTEGER);
```

These two statements prepare the program to input and output whole numbers, which are called integers in Ada. The program library unit TEXT_IO is a package containing the package named INTEGER_IO. The second line causes the program to create a new package named INTEGER_IO that contains programs to input integers from the keyboard into the computer and to present integers on the display. This is called *generic instantiation*; we'll cover it more fully in chapter 12. The general form of an instantiation for programs in TEXT IO is

package *new package name* **is new** *generic package name* (*data type name*);

Until chapter 12, we will use generic instantiation just to allow input and output for the various data types.

After the instantiation, we see a group of **with** and **use** statements. These statements allow the program that follows to use both the TEXT_IO and INTEGER_IO packages. The package we just created—INTEGER_IO—is used for integers, and TEXT_IO is used for messages.

The name of the program is given after the keyword **procedure** and a group of comment lines describes what the program does. The line following these comments describes the data that are used in the program.

There are three data items in this program: FIRST_VALUE, SECOND_VALUE, and RESULT. After naming each data item, you specify the data type and separate the list of data items from the data type with a colon. The data type, INTEGER, used in this program is one of Ada's four predefined data types—the INTEGER data type is used when working with whole numbers. You will learn about the other three predefined data types in chapter 3 and learn how to define your own data types in later chapters.

The general form for defining a group of integers is:

list of data names : INTEGER;

where *list of data names* is the names you've given the data. Each name in the list is separated from the others by a comma.

A data name is also called a *variable* or a *variable identifier.* The best way to think of data at this point is to visualize a box labeled with each name. In Ada these boxes are set aside when the data definition for the name is reached in the program. The concept of setting aside space for variables during execution of a program is termed *dynamic allocation.* Each box is also given a data type. In our example, the data types are all integers or whole numbers. In Ada, each data type has a set of values and a set of operations. In many small machines today, the set of values for integers is between −32767 and 32767.

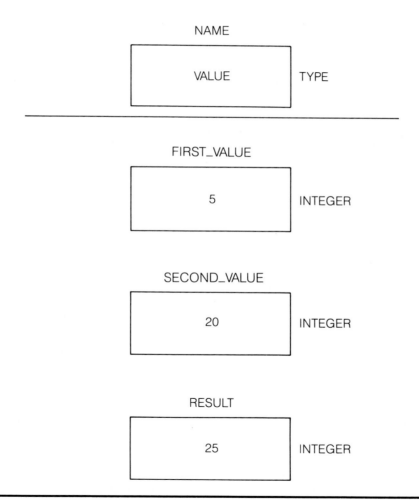

Figure 1.5   Ada Variables

Larger machines allow integers between −1,073,741,823 and 1,073,741,823, and the largest machines allow even greater integers. You can find the largest integer value on your computer by including the following statement in your program

```
PUT (INTEGER'LAST);
```

The value INTEGER'LAST is called an *attribute* of the INTEGER type. Attributes are very useful in computer programs and we will be meeting some of them throughout this book. All the attributes are contained in Appendix D. Included in the set of operations on integers are addition, +; subtraction, −; multiplication, *; and division, /. In the program, the addition operator adds the two numbers read into the program.

The executable portion of the program starts off with two messages using PUT_LINE. The first message merely lets us know that the program has gotten through the data portion. It is good practice for you to have a similar message in your first programs to let you know the program has begun to execute, especially if your computer is slow. The next message instructs the program's user to take action. It is also good practice to let the user in on this—even when you wrote the program yourself.

At this point in the program, spaces or boxes have been set aside that are named FIRST_VALUE, SECOND_VALUE, and RESULT, but the contents of these boxes are undefined. In Ada, these named spaces are called *objects*. It is not until we set the contents of the boxes by means of computing or reading in data from the terminal or some other equipment that the contents will be known. The next line in the program, which reads

```
GET (FIRST_VALUE); --  Bring in the first number
```

causes the computer to wait until you type in an integer, and it records the value of that integer in the box named FIRST_VALUE.

For example, if you typed the number 5, it would record the value 5 in FIRST_VALUE. However, if you typed the letter x or a number such as 0.1, it would give you an error message. If you type a carriage return instead of a number, the computer will wait for a number to be typed. Ada always checks that the data you type in are proper for the data type of the variable that is to receive the value. These checks, which are done while the program executes, are called *run-time checks*.

We now have one of the three boxes defined. The next line in the program:

```
GET (SECOND_VALUE); -- Bring in the second number
```

works in the same manner as the previous statement to set a value into the box named SECOND_VALUE. Again the computer waits until a number is entered into the terminal. In some Ada compilers the computer also waits for a carriage return. The number is checked against the correct values for integers and if acceptable, it is then stored into the box named SECOND_VALUE. We could continue in this manner to set 100 or 1000 or even 1000000 numbers, but when we work with large quantities of data, we will see there are better methods than naming each variable individually. Chapter 7, on data structures, presents methods of handling large quantities of data.

The general form of the GET statement to bring in values from the terminal is:

GET (*data name*);

where *data name* is the name of a variable such as FIRST_VALUE.

The next line positions the following output at the start of a new line. This keeps the output more readable. The general form of the NEW_LINE statement is:

NEW_LINE;

The following line shows an example of putting more than one statement on a line. The first statement places a message on the display that will read:

" First_value = ".

The second statement will then place the value that is stored in FIRST_VALUE on the *same* line as the preceding message. By not placing quotes around the name, FIRST_VALUE, we obtain its value via the PUT statement.

The PUT statement differs from the PUT_LINE statement in that it displays its output but does not go to a new line. In this case it will place the value in FIRST_VALUE immediately after the message " First_value = ". If FIRST_VALUE contains a 5, the display will read:

```
First_value =          5
```

Similarly, the line with the two statements that reads

```
PUT (" Second_value = "); PUT (SECOND_VALUE);
```

will display the value stored in SECOND_VALUE along with the message " Second_value = ". If SECOND_VALUE contains a 20 at this point in the program, the display will read:

```
Second_value =         20
```

When the data you typed into the computer are played back to you in the program, it is called *echoing the data*. You should echo your data unless you have an interactive environment. An interactive environment lets you enter data as you execute the program. Even though Ada provides a great deal of protection against mistakes, it is still possible to make errors, and a major source of errors is incorrect input data. By echoing your data you will protect yourself from letting erroneous data enter your programs undetected.

The general form of the PUT statement to display values on a terminal is:

PUT (*data name*);

When this form is used the value will be placed on the display immediately after the previous display. To place the value and then go to a new line use

PUT_LINE (*data name*);

The line following the next comment is called an *assignment statement* because it assigns a value to a data name. The general form of an assignment statement in Ada is

data name : = *expression* ;

In our statement, the data name was RESULT and the expression was

FIRST_VALUE + SECOND_VALUE

Ada will cause the value of the expression to be computed and store the value in the data name. Hence, if FIRST_VALUE was 5 and SECOND_VALUE was 20, the value of the expression would be 25 and the value of RESULT would be also 25 after the execution of the assignment statement.

The final executable statements in the program display on the terminal a message and the value in RESULT.

At this point you should enter this program and execute it with several values. This is also a good program to try with some deliberate errors such as leaving out semicolons, misspelling key words, and misspelling the names of your data. Don't try to put in any deliberate errors until you get the program correct. Then put in one error at a time to see the messages that your compiler gives you. When you see these messages again, you will have some idea as to what you may have done wrong.

WHAT HAVE YOU LEARNED?

How to name programs.

  general form : **procedure** *program name* **is**
  example   : **procedure** ADDITION **is**

The basic structure of simple Ada programs.

  with TEXT_IO;
  use TEXT_IO;

  procedure *program name* **is**
      declaration part
  begin
      executable statements
  end *program name;*

The basic structure of Ada programs that input or output integers.

```
with TEXT_IO;
package INTEGER_IO is new TEXT_IO.INTEGER_IO (INTEGER);
with TEXT_IO, INTEGER_IO;
use TEXT_IO, INTEGER_IO;
procedure program name is
        declaration part
begin
        executable statements
end program name ;
```

How to write comments.

```
general form : -- text
example      : -- This is a comment
```

Some of Ada's keywords.

with use procedure is begin end package new

How to display messages.

```
general form : PUT_LINE (" message ");
               PUT       (" message ");

example      : PUT_LINE (" Hi there ");
               PUT       (" Hi there ");
```

How to enter data into a program from your terminal.

```
general form : GET (data name);
example      : GET (FIRST_VALUE);
```

How to start a new line on the terminal.

```
general form : NEW_LINE;
```

How to compute an expression.

```
general form : data name + data name
example      : FIRST_VALUE + SECOND_VALUE
```

How to assign a value to a data object.

```
general form : data name := expression;
example      : RESULT := FIRST_VALUE + SECOND_VALUE;
```

How to display data on your terminal.

```
general form : PUT (data name);
example      : PUT (RESULT);
```

PROBLEMS

1. Write a program to display a friendly message on your terminal.

2. Write a program to display your initials on your terminal in letters that take up several lines. For example, the initials SHS would appear as

```
SSSSSS    H         H         SSSSSS
S         H         H         S
S         H         H         S
 S        H         H          S
  S       H         H           S
   S      HHHHHHHHHH             S
    S     H         H             S
     S    H         H             S
      S   H         H              S
       S  H         H              S
SSSSS     H         H         SSSSSS
```

3. Change the addition program to a subtraction program that reads into the computer two numbers and takes the difference between them. Use the minus sign ($-$) for subtraction.

4. In Ada multiplication is done with a *. The program is designed to read two numbers into the computer, multiply them together, and display the result. After stating what is wrong with the program, rewrite it to execute correctly.

```
program FAILURE is ;
      -- This is a very bad program X, Y, Z : INTEGER
      -- It reads in numbers into X and Y
      -- and computes the area Z by multiplying X times Y
      GET (X)
      GET (Y)
      Z = X * Y
      PUT (Z)
   end.
```

5. State in your own words what happens as a result of a GET statement and a PUT statement.

6. In the program you wrote in response to problem 4, underline the keywords with one line, underline the assignment statement with two lines, and underline the comments with three lines.

7. What is wrong with each statement? Rewrite each statement to be a correct Ada statement.

```
PUT X;
PUT_LINE (' HAVE A NICE DAY ! ');
PUT (X, Y);
X = 5 + 25 ;
FIRST_VALUE is INTEGER;
GET (" the best one ");
- What a fantastic program !!!
comment anything you want;
```

CHAPTER
❖ 2 ❖
NAMES IN ADA

Identifiers

In Ada, both programs and data have names, or *identifiers*. You have almost complete freedom to choose any name you want for Ada identifiers, but there are just a few rules to observe and a few suggestions for making your work easier.

First, a name must start with a letter. Hence the names

Ada
Batman
Julie
Navigation
United
Steel
Velocity

are all good Ada names.

Second, a name may contain underscores to be more readable because blank spaces are not allowed. Hence the names

New_York_City
Santa_Barbara_California
Time_of_day
Height_above_sea_level
Time_to_go

are all good names too. An extension of this rule is that two underscores in a row or a name ending in an underscore are not allowed. Hence the names

Very_very__big_number   —Two underscores together
Distance_from_Seattle_   —An underscore at the end

are not valid Ada names.

Third, after the first letter, names may have numbers in the name or at the end of the name. Hence the names

Car_1
X2
R3_72
L1011_Airplane

are valid Ada names.

A fourth rule is that the use of capital letters or lowercase letters makes no difference in the name. Hence:

Ada
ada
ADA

are all the same name to Ada.

Fifth, only letters, numbers, and underscores may be used in Ada names. Hence, names using punctuation marks

Who_is_this?   —   ? is not allowed
X.3   —   . is not allowed
Amos&Andy   —   & is not allowed

are not valid Ada names.

A suggestion is to use descriptive names as much as possible in the application instead of such names as

A
X100
BXy_35
KC_Jones

which may mean something to you, but may not have much meaning to anyone else.

KEYWORDS

Now that you are convinced that you have almost perfect freedom in giving names to programs and data objects, you should be aware of one major restriction: You must not use the Ada keywords as names. The 63 keywords shown in table 2.1 are reserved for special use in Ada programs. If you use such a name as an identifier, the Ada compiler will give you an error message.

TABLE 2.1
TABLE OF ADA KEYWORDS

abort	exception	private
abs	exit	procedure
accept	for	raise
access	function	range
all	generic	record
and	goto	rem
array	if	renames
at	in	return
begin	is	reverse
body	limited	select
case	loop	separate
constant	mod	subtype
declare	new	task
delay	not	terminate
delta	null	then
digits	of	type
do	or	use
else	others	when
elsif	out	while
end	package	with
entry	pragma	xor

PREDEFINED NAMES

There are also a sizeable number of predefined names that you should avoid using as identifiers. (See Appendix A for a complete list of these predefined names.) You've already met these predefined names: INTEGER, GET, PUT, PUT_LINE, AND NEW_LINE; you'll learn others as we go along, so it's not important to check every name you use against the list in the appendix. Some of the most common names are given in table 2.2.

TABLE 2.2
TABLE OF COMMON PREDEFINED NAMES

ASCII	GET	RESET
BOOLEAN	GET_LINE	SET_COL
CALENDAR	INDEX	SET_INDEX
CHARACTER	INTEGER	SET_LINE
COL	LINE	SET_PAGE
CREATE	LINE_LENGTH	SEQUENTIAL_IO
CURRENT_INPUT	MODE	SIZE
CURRENT_OUTPUT	MODE_ERROR	SKIP_LINE
DATA_ERROR	NAME	SKIP_PAGE
DELETE	NAME_ERROR	STANDARD
DEVICE_ERROR	NATURAL	STANDARD_INPUT
DIRECT_IO	NEW_LINE	STANDARD_OUTPUT
DURATION	NEW_PAGE	STATUS_ERROR
END_ERROR	OPEN	STRING
END_OF_FILE	PAGE	SYSTEM
END_OF_LINE	PAGE_LENGTH	TEXT_IO
END_OF_PAGE	POSITIVE	TRUE
FALSE	PUT	USE_ERROR
FLOAT	PUT_LINE	WRITE
FORM	READ	

COMMENTS

Feel free to use many comments in your programs, you can use any name or symbol available on your keyboard in a comment—you can even use reserved words in a comment. Ada ignores comments, so it will not find any errors in your comments. The only rules for comments are:

1. Comments start with two hyphens placed together (--).

2. Comments end at the end of the line.

This means that once you've started a comment on a line, the rest of the line is treated as a comment.

```
--   A well-commented Ada program
-- will be almost self-explanatory
-- comments will be after many statements
AREA := WIDTH * LENGTH; -- area in square meters
-- to better explain the program --
---* --<><><><><><><><><> ><><><><> ----*---
--**--** --**--**--**--** --**--**
------------------------------
```

These are eight examples of comments; remember that you have complete freedom to put anything in a comment after it starts. Three of these comment lines are designs that might be used to highlight a section of the program. Three others are full-line text comments, one of which ends with two hyphens just to look symmetrical. One of the comments follows an assignment statement and explains the units used in the expression.

Some examples of incorrect comments are:

```
- - This is not a comment. The hyphens must be together.
AREA -- in square meters -- := WIDTH * HEIGHT;
```

In the first example, a space between the hyphens would cause an error. In the second example, the rest of the line after the identifier AREA would be treated as a comment. If it was intended that it be an assignment statement instead of a comment, the statement would be in error.

STRUCTURE OF AN ADA PROGRAM

An Ada program is made up of two parts: a data declaration part and an executable part as shown in figure 2.1. The first part of the program contains a list of data declarations. The second part of the program starts after the keyword **begin.** This second part contains the executable statements for the program. All the identifiers that appear in the program must be declared in

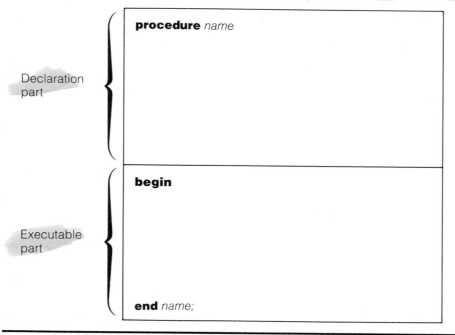

Figure 2.1   Ada Program Structure

the declaration part of the program or in previously compiled packages.

You'll recall that the first two programs in chapter 1 do not contain any declarations. The declaration part of the program contained only comments. All the identifiers in those programs were predefined in the package named TEXT_IO. In our third program, we used three identifiers: FIRST_VALUE, SECOND_VALUE, and RESULT. These identifiers were listed in the declaration part of the program. Besides giving the names in the declaration part of the program, we stated that the type of these names was INTEGER. This allowed us to put whole numbers, or integers, in space associated with these names. The declaration also allowed us to perform integer arithmetic on these named data.

Types are very important in Ada, and we will learn about types in chapters 3 and 6. Not only will we learn about the predefined types such as INTEGER, but we will learn how to define our own data types.

WHAT HAVE YOU LEARNED?

Ada identifiers begin with a letter and may contain digits and/or underscores. An identifier can end with a letter or a digit and may be as long as a line (but will usually be much shorter). Keywords may not be used as identifiers. Identifiers should have meaningful names but not be one of the predefined names.

Some examples of Ada identifiers are:

Ada	Speed	Height	Distance
Money	Bank_account	Name	

Some thought should be given to the use of case in names. It does not matter what style is chosen as long as the case structure is uniform. Names can also be too long as well as too short. For example, the identifier

Seconds_remaining_to_charge_a_battery_on_a_cold_morning

is probably too long to be useful.

Comments begin with two hyphens and end at the end of a line. Comments may contain special characters that are not normally used in Ada programs. It is permissible to use keywords in comments. Feel free to use as many comments as necessary, they can provide good program documentation.

Some examples of comments are:

```
-- Waiting time
-- This program calculates the odds in the daily double
-- f = ma
```

An Ada program is made up of two parts: the declarative part and the executable part. Data are described in the declarative part. Executable statements are contained in the executable part.

PROBLEMS

1. State which identifiers are legal and which are illegal. For the illegal identifiers, state why they are illegal.

   a. Nancy_Drew

   b. Old Orchard

   c. 1500_Holiday_Hill

   d. Time_or_Distance

   e. x

   f. procedure

   g. "identifier"

   h. integer

   i. Friends—always

   j. Jack&Jill

2. The following identifiers are legal but not recommended. Using the comments beside each identifier select a name that would be better to use.

   a. x33 — height above runway

   b. t — execution time

   c. David_1 — student with highest grade

   d. book_43 — Bears by Ben East

   e. flt_123 — flight between Reno and Las Vegas

   f. twt -- waiting time

   g. no_sts — number of seats

   h. cost — cost of a computer second

   i. bat_crg — time to charge a battery

   j. no_st_barb — number of people in Santa Barbara

3. State which of the following comments are legal. For those that are illegal, state why they are illegal, and transform them into legal comments.

   a. - - - Is this legal or not?

   b. -_-_-_-_-_-_-_-_-_-_-_-_

   b. -1--1--1--1--1--1--1--1--1

   c. get -- the time of day -- (time);

   e. ---   A good program is a readable program   ---

4. State what is wrong with the following program. Fix the program and execute it. State which lines are executable, which lines are declarative, and which are the keywords used in the program.

```
with TEXT_IO;
use  TEXT_IO;
program SAMPLE;
A, B, C : INTHEGER;
V : INTEHGER;
start
-- this program inputs three numbers which represent the size of
the sides of a room in feet and computes the volume of the room
in square feet by multiplying the three numbers together.
GET (A, B, C)  -- read in the three numbers
V = A*B*C   -- multiply the three numbers together
PUT (V)      -- display the answer
end;
```

CHAPTER

❖ 3 ❖

PREDEFINED DATA TYPES

❖ Ada has predefined data types as well as user-defined data types. In this chapter we will examine four data types: INTEGER, CHARACTER, BOOLEAN, and FLOAT. Ada uses types to make programs reliable, and you will use types to make programs readable. Ada uses type information to check that your program is correct even before you run your program. Ada also checks the values you compute using type information, and, if you calculate inappropriate values for the type, will report on errors when you run your program. You will also learn how to define your own data types based on the predefined data types and how to give meaningful names to your data types to make your program readable by others.

A type is a set of values and the operations that are possible on the values. For example, we have seen a sample program that used the predefined data type named INTEGER. Associated with this data type are the basic arithmetic operations of addition, subtraction, multiplication, and division. There are also available some arithmetic operations which are not used as commonly such as exponentiation, negation, modulo, and remainder.

The four predefined data types are *scalar data types,* which means they describe a single data item. You can visualize a scalar data type as taking up one unit of space such as the box described in chapter 1. In subsequent chapters we will study data types that take up many units of space.

Most Ada programs will have a combination of scalar data types and other data types available for you to use. Your Ada programs should have user-defined data types defined in terms of the predefined data types described in this chapter.

INTEGER

The integer data type is used for whole numbers. The set of possible numbers that belong to the integer data type will vary from machine to machine, but you can expect to have at least a range from -32767 to $+32767$, and perhaps a much larger range. As we learned in chapter 1, the value INTEGER'LAST will tell you the largest number of the integer data type that can be represented in your computer. If you try to use a number beyond your computer's range, the computer will tell you that an error has occurred.

The following program demonstrates many of the integer operations that are available in Ada. We declare three objects of the integer data type with the declaration

```
FIRST_NUMBER, SECOND_NUMBER, RESULT : INTEGER;
```

in the declaration part of the program. These objects are also called *variables* because different values can be placed in them. For example, at one point in the program, FIRST_NUMBER can contain the value 0, and at a later time it can contain the value 3.

The general form of an integer declaration is:

list of data names : INTEGER;

where the list of data names or variables is made up of legal Ada names separated by commas.

In the executable part of the program, Ada assignment statements demonstrate many of the possible operations on the integer data type.

```
with TEXT_IO;
package INTEGER_IO is new TEXT_IO.INTEGER_IO (INTEGER);

with TEXT_IO, INTEGER_IO;
use  TEXT_IO, INTEGER_IO;
procedure INTEGER_OPERATIONS is

  FIRST_NUMBER, SECOND_NUMBER, RESULT : INTEGER;

  --  A program to demonstrate integer operations
  --  integer operations include +, -, *, and /
  --  as well as **, mod, and rem

begin
PUT_LINE (" The integer operations program has started to execute.");
```

```
FIRST_NUMBER := 3;   -- assign 3 to first_number
SECOND_NUMBER := 2; -- assign 2 to second_number

RESULT := FIRST_NUMBER + SECOND_NUMBER; -- integer addition
NEW_LINE; PUT (" 3 + 2 = "); PUT (RESULT);

RESULT := FIRST_NUMBER - SECOND_NUMBER; -- integer subtraction
NEW_LINE; PUT (" 3 - 2 = "); PUT (RESULT);

RESULT := FIRST_NUMBER * SECOND_NUMBER; -- integer multiplication
NEW_LINE; PUT (" 3 * 2 = "); PUT (RESULT);

RESULT := FIRST_NUMBER / SECOND_NUMBER; -- integer division
NEW_LINE; PUT (" 3 / 2 = "); PUT (RESULT);

RESULT := - FIRST_NUMBER; -- integer negation
NEW_LINE; PUT (" - 3 = "); PUT (RESULT);

RESULT := FIRST_NUMBER ** SECOND_NUMBER; -- integer exponentiation
NEW_LINE; PUT (" 3 ** 2 = "); PUT (RESULT);

RESULT := FIRST_NUMBER rem SECOND_NUMBER; -- integer remainder
NEW_LINE; PUT (" 3 remainder 2 = "); PUT (RESULT);

RESULT := FIRST_NUMBER mod SECOND_NUMBER; -- integer modulo
NEW_LINE; PUT (" 3 modulo 2 = "); PUT (RESULT);

end INTEGER_OPERATIONS;
```

The program sets FIRST_NUMBER to be 3 and SECOND_NUMBER to be 2. Next, the program demonstrates each integer operation. For addition, Ada uses the plus (+) sign, so the result of adding the two numbers will be displayed as

$3 + 2 = 5$

The result of adding two integer values together results in an integer value that may be stored in another integer variable. In this example, the integer variable named RESULT is set to the sum of two other integer variables in the assignment statement:

```
RESULT := FIRST_NUMBER + SECOND_NUMBER;
```

The part of the assignment statement in which the addition is performed is called an *expression*. It is an *arithmetic expression* if arithmetic is being performed; it is an *integer expression* if the values in the expression are of the integer data type. The general form of an assignment statement is:

data name := *expression* ;

For subtraction, Ada uses the minus (−) sign, so the result of subtracting the two numbers will be displayed as

$3 - 2 = 1$

For multiplication, Ada uses the asterisk (*). The result of multiplying the two numbers will be displayed as

    3 * 2 = 6

For division, Ada uses the slash (/). In integer division, the answer is in whole numbers so the result will be displayed as

    3 / 2 = 1

You will rarely want to use integer division because of the unexpected answers that result from working with whole numbers. For instance, the expected answer of 1.5 in the division example becomes 1 due to truncation. However, some algorithms make use of the peculiarities of integer division, and it is available to you for wise use.

The general forms of simple integer expressions for the four common arithmetic operations are:

> *integer data name* + *integer data name*
> *integer data name* − *integer data name*
> *integer data name* * *integer data name*
> *integer data name* / *integer data name*

For example,

    FIRST_NUMBER + SECOND_NUMBER

is a simple integer expression.

Most of your programs will probably use only the four operations listed so far. Ada provides some additional operations that are often useful in computer programs. These include exponentiation, negation, modulo, and remainder.

For exponentiation, Ada uses two asterisks typed together with no space between them (**). Integer exponentiation is equivalent to the first number being multiplied by itself as many times as specified by the second number. In our example, the result will be displayed as

    3 ** 2 = 9

For negation, Ada uses the minus (−) sign. Hence the result for negation will be displayed as

    − 3 = −3

Negation is called a unary operator because it has one operand—an *operand* is defined as the value an operator works on. The other operators ($+$, $-$, $*$, $/$) we have seen so far are called binary operators because they work on two operands.

The modulo operation, **mod**, is particularly useful in counting time and in counting the number of days in the month. In time, the value of 59 seconds is followed by 1 minute 0 seconds. Such counting is also called circular counting because the counts can be placed in a circle such as on the face of a clock. We will also show the use of the modulo operation in counting amounts of input data. In modulo arithmetic, a number is specified as a *modulus*. For instance, if 2 is the modulus, we count 0, 1, and then start over again. As an example, we will take 3 modulo 2. Since 2 is the modulus, the result is 1. Hence the display will show

3 modulo 2 = 1

The **rem** operation results in the true remainder for integer division. For positive numbers, the **rem** operation will give the same result as the modulo operation. For example, the display will show

3 remainder 2 = 1

For negative numerators, the **rem** operation will result in a negative value. Thus,

-3 rem 2 = -1

CHARACTER

The CHARACTER data type in Ada is used for individual characters. There are 128 different characters in Ada, which correspond to the 128 characters in the standard character set known as the ASCII character set (ASCII stands for American Standard Character Information Interchange). Individual characters will usually be used to process messages read into a program. Examples of the ASCII characters are the capital letters A to Z, the lowercase letters a to z, the digits 0 to 9, and special characters such as ;, #, and +. All the ASCII characters are listed in Appendix B, including the control characters such as BEL, which will cause ASCII terminals to ring a bell. If your terminal does not have some of the special characters or the lowercase letters, it is still possible to write a program that uses these characters because each one has a name, as shown in Appendix B. For example, the lowercase letter a has the name LC_A and # is named SHARP.

The individual characters in Ada are written normally but with single quotes surrounding the character. In order to write a single quote or apostrophe, for instance, it is necessary to write it as '''. Each of the characters has an ASCII value associated with the character that is one of the integers from

0 to 127. The order of the characters is as shown in the table in Appendix B so that 'A' comes before 'Z' and '0' comes before '9'.

Instead of arithmetic operators on characters, there is a special set of operations called *attributes*. These attributes for the CHARACTER data type are used in the next program.

The characters' attributes have names and operate on just one character. This program shows four of the possible operations on characters: CHARACTER'SUCC, CHARACTER'PRED, CHARACTER'POS, and CHARACTER'VAL.

The general form of these operations is

CHARACTER'SUCC (*character data name*)
CHARACTER'PRED (*character data name*)
CHARACTER'POS (*character data name*)
CHARACTER'VAL (*integer data name*)

```
with TEXT_IO;
package INTEGER_IO is new TEXT_IO. INTEGER_IO (INTEGER);

with TEXT_IO, INTEGER_IO;
use  TEXT_IO, INTEGER_IO;

procedure CHARACTER_OPERATIONS is

   FIRST_CHARACTER, SECOND_CHARACTER, RESULT : CHARACTER;

   INTEGER_RESULT : INTEGER;

-- A program to demonstrate character operations

-- Character operations include SUCC, PRED, POS, and VAL

begin
   PUT_LINE (" The character operation program has started. ");

   FIRST_CHARACTER  := 'C';   --assign C to first_character;
   SECOND_CHARACTER := 'B';   --assign B to second_character;

   -- Character successor operation

   RESULT := CHARACTER'SUCC (FIRST_CHARACTER);
   NEW_LINE;  PUT (" successor of 'C' is "); PUT (RESULT);

   -- Character predecessor operation

   RESULT := CHARACTER'PRED (SECOND_CHARACTER);
   NEW_LINE; PUT (" predecessor of 'B' is "); PUT (RESULT);

   -- Character position operation yields an integer

   INTEGER_RESULT := CHARACTER'POS (FIRST_CHARACTER);
   NEW_LINE;  PUT (" position of 'C' is "); PUT (INTEGER_RESULT);
```

```
-- Character value operation on previous result

RESULT := CHARACTER'VAL (INTEGER_RESULT);
NEW_LINE;  PUT (" character value of 'C' is "); PUT (RESULT);
```

    end CHARACTER_OPERATIONS;

A general form of any attribute in Ada is

    type name'attribute name

A complete list of all the attributes in Ada is found in Appendix D. We will meet most of these attributes in succeeding chapters.

    CHARACTER'SUCC is called the *successor function*. When applied to a character value, the SUCC operator yields the next character in the list of ASCII characters. Hence when applied to an object in which the value of 'C' is stored, the value of 'D' results. When applied to an object in which the value of 'Z' is stored, the value of '[' is obtained since this character follows 'Z' in the list of ASCII characters. When applied to an object in which the value of the control character named DEL is stored, an error will result. This is because DEL is the last character in the list of ASCII characters and as such it has no successors.

    CHARACTER'PRED is called the *predecessor function*. When applied to a character object, the PRED operator yields the previous character in the list of ASCII characters. Hence when applied to an object in which the value of 'B' is stored, the value of 'A' results. When applied to an object in which the value of 'A' is stored, the value of '@' is obtained since this character precedes 'A' in the list of ASCII characters. When applied to an object in which the value of the control character named NUL is stored, an error will result because NUL is the first character in the list of ASCII characters and as such it has no predecessors.

    CHARACTER'POS is an operation that yields the position of the character in the list of characters. The position of the character 'C' is 67 in the ASCII list of characters, so a value of 67 will result from the operation CHARACTER'POS('C'). Note that the first position is 0. We need to use the INTEGER_IO procedures to display the result of this attribute, which is of the integer data type.

    The opposite of CHARACTER'POS is the operation CHARACTER'VAL, which takes an integer that is meant to represent the position of the character in the list of characters. Hence CHARACTER'VAL(67) will result in the value 'C'. CHARACTER'VAL(0) will result in NUL.

    Most of the character operations are used in processing groups of characters called *strings*. We will see some applications of character handling and strings in chapter 7.

    Although characters and integers seem very different, they are actually members of the same class of data types called *discrete data types* that share many of the same operations. While we cannot add characters together, integers can have successors and predecessors. For example, the successor of 3 is 4 and the predecessor of 10 is 9. Hence, we can write a statement such as

```
FIRST_NUMBER := INTEGER'SUCC (SECOND_NUMBER);
```

or

```
SECOND_NUMBER := INTEGER'PRED (FIRST_NUMBER);
```

BOOLEAN

Data of the BOOLEAN data type have only two values, TRUE and FALSE. Although the BOOLEAN data type may be used for performing logical operations, it is usually used to store the results of comparisons and to combine the results of comparisons. The comparison operations in Ada are:

=	for equality
/=	for inequality
>	for greater than
<	for less than
>=	for greater than or equal to
<=	for less than or equal to

For example, 3 > 5 has the value FALSE and 2 < 10 has the value TRUE.

These operations may be applied to the three data types that have been covered so far : INTEGER, CHARACTER, and BOOLEAN. In the case of characters, the order is as it appears in the ASCII character list so that 'A' is less than 'B'. In the case of Booleans, the order is defined so that FALSE is less than TRUE.

The comparison operations are also called *relational operations*. When a Boolean value results, the expression is often called a *logical expression* to differentiate it from expressions that result in integer values or in character values.

```
with TEXT_IO;
package BOOLEAN_IO is new TEXT_IO.ENUMERATION_IO (BOOLEAN);

with TEXT_IO, BOOLEAN_IO;
use  TEXT_IO, BOOLEAN_IO;

procedure BOOLEAN_OPERATIONS is

-- A program to demonstrate the use of the comparison operations
--  and the Boolean operations

  FIRST_NUMBER, SECOND_NUMBER : INTEGER;
  FIRST_CHARACTER, SECOND_CHARACTER : CHARACTER;
  FIRST_RESULT, SECOND_RESULT, RESULT : BOOLEAN;

begin
```

```
   PUT_LINE (" The Boolean operations program has started. ");

   FIRST_NUMBER := 3;
   SECOND_NUMBER := 5;
   FIRST_CHARACTER := 'B';
   SECOND_CHARACTER := 'C';

-- compare for equality

   FIRST_RESULT := FIRST_NUMBER = SECOND_NUMBER;

   NEW_LINE; PUT (" 3 = 5 ? "); PUT (FIRST_RESULT);
   SECOND_RESULT := FIRST_CHARACTER = SECOND_CHARACTER;
   NEW_LINE; PUT (" 'B' = 'C' ? "); PUT (SECOND_RESULT);

-- compare for greater than or equal to

   FIRST_RESULT := FIRST_NUMBER >= SECOND_NUMBER;
   NEW_LINE; PUT (" 3 >= 5 ? "); PUT (FIRST_RESULT);

-- compare for less than or equal to

   SECOND_RESULT := FIRST_CHARACTER <= SECOND_CHARACTER;
   NEW_LINE; PUT (" 'B' <= 'C' ? "); PUT (SECOND_RESULT);

-- combine comparisons

--      first with not operation

   RESULT := not FIRST_RESULT;
   NEW_LINE; PUT (" the not of 3 >= 5 is "); PUT (RESULT);

--      and operation results in a true
--      only if both operands are true

   RESULT := FIRST_RESULT and SECOND_RESULT;

   NEW_LINE; PUT (" 3 >= 5 and 'B' <= 'C' ? "); PUT (RESULT);

--      or operation results in a true
--      if one of the operands is true

   RESULT := FIRST_RESULT or SECOND_RESULT;

   NEW_LINE; PUT (" 3 >= 5 or 'B' <= 'C' ? "); PUT (RESULT);

--      xor operation results in a true
--      only if both operands are different

   RESULT := FIRST_RESULT xor SECOND_RESULT;

   NEW_LINE; PUT (" 3 >= 5 xor 'B' <= 'C' ? "); PUT (RESULT);

--      and then operation is the same as and as far as results
--      but the second term is not evaluated if the first is false
```

```
RESULT := FIRST_RESULT and then SECOND_RESULT;

NEW_LINE; PUT (" 3 >= 5 and then 'B' <= 'C' ? "); PUT (RESULT);

--      or else operation is the same as or as far as results
--      but the second term is not evaluated if the first is true

RESULT := FIRST_RESULT or else SECOND_RESULT;
NEW_LINE; PUT (" 3 >= 5 or else 'B' <= 'C' ? "); PUT (RESULT);

end BOOLEAN_OPERATIONS;
```

The BOOLEAN_OPERATIONS program begins with a generic instantiation of the package named ENUMERATION_IO in order to allow displaying the BOOLEAN values TRUE and FALSE. We met generic instantiation briefly in chapter 1 and will discuss it further in chapter 12.

The first test in the program checks if two integers are equal. The actual test is for the values 3 and 5, which have been stored in the variables named FIRST_NUMBER and SECOND_NUMBER. The result of this test will be FALSE since 3 does not equal 5, and as a result the display will show

```
3 = 5 ? FALSE
```

The test for equality can be made between two objects of any data type. It is one of the operations that is always available with one exception that you will learn about in chapter 15. The next test in the program tests if two character values are equal. The actual test is for the values 'B' and 'C', which are stored in the variables named FIRST_CHARACTER and SECOND_CHARACTER. The result of this test will also be FALSE since 'B' does not equal 'C'. The display will show

```
'B' = 'C' ? FALSE
```

The program uses the operator symbol ">=", which stands for greater than or equal to. This symbol is made up of two symbols on the keyboard that must be used in the order shown. The test checks if 3 is greater than or equal to 5, and since it is not true, the result will be FALSE. The display will show

```
3 >= 5 ? FALSE
```

The operator "<=" stands for less than or equal to. As with the previous comparison, this symbol is also made up of two symbols on the keyboard. The test is for whether 'B' <= 'C', which is a true statement, so the result is TRUE. The display will show

```
'B' <= 'C' ? TRUE
```

You may often wish to combine comparisons in one statement. This is done with the use of the Boolean operators shown in table 3.1, the truth tables for Boolean operations. Each line in the truth table represents the possible values of the six Boolean operators for one particular combination of inputs.

The simplest is the **not** operator, which merely takes the opposite of the value and is analogous to the minus operator in arithmetic. Taking the **not** of a TRUE value results in FALSE and vice versa. In the first line of the truth table, the first column gives a FALSE value to a, and the last column labeled **not a** states the result of the operation as TRUE. The example in the program also takes the **not** of a FALSE value stored in FIRST_RESULT so that the result is TRUE. Hence the display will show

```
the not of 3 >= 5 is TRUE
```

TABLE 3.1
TRUTH TABLES FOR BOOLEAN OPERATIONS

a	b	a or b a or else b	a and b a and then b	a xor b	not a
FALSE	FALSE	FALSE	FALSE	FALSE	TRUE
FALSE	TRUE	TRUE	FALSE	TRUE	TRUE
TRUE	FALSE	TRUE	FALSE	TRUE	FALSE
TRUE	TRUE	TRUE	TRUE	FALSE	FALSE

The second Boolean operation in the program is the **and** operation. For an **and** operation, consider that the result of an **and** operation is TRUE only if both parts are TRUE; otherwise, the result of an **and** is FALSE. In the example in the last program, FIRST_RESULT is FALSE, so the result will be FALSE. This example is represented in the truth table by the second line in which a is FALSE, b is TRUE, and the result is FALSE. In the program, the display will show

```
3 >= 5 and 'B' <= 'C' ? FALSE
```

The third operation in the program is the **or** operation. The result of an **or** is TRUE if either value is TRUE. Only if both parts are FALSE will the result of an **or** be FALSE. In the example program, SECOND_RESULT is TRUE, so the result will be TRUE. This is represented in the truth table by the second line, which shows that when a is FALSE and b is TRUE, a **or** b is TRUE. In the example program, the display will show

```
3 >= 5 or 'B' <= 'C' ? TRUE
```

The remaining operations are used more rarely. The first of these, **xor,** is called the *exclusive or* operation. The result of this operation is TRUE when both values are different. It is often used for comparing groups of bits called *bit strings*. Since our example has its two parts with different values, the result will be TRUE, and the display will show

```
3 >= 5 xor 'B' <= 'C' ? TRUE
```

The next operation, the **and then** operation is also called the *short circuit and*. If the program calculates that the first value is FALSE, it does not bother to evaluate the second value but immediately returns a FALSE result. The result is no different than if both parts of the expression were evaluated, but the time to compute the result will usually be shorter, and in some cases the first result protects the second from causing an error. In the statement:

```
RESULT := FIRST_NUMBER /= 0
          and then (SECOND_NUMBER/FIRST_NUMBER > 0) ;
```

the division after the **and then** will not be made if FIRST_NUMBER = 0. In our example, the first value, FIRST_RESULT, is FALSE so the short circuit will immediately evaluate to a FALSE. The display will show

```
3 >= 5 and then 'B' <= 'C' ? FALSE
```

The *short circuit or* is represented in Ada by an **or else.** In the short circuit **or**, the second operand is not evaluated if the first value is TRUE. Since the first operand in our example has a value of FALSE, the second will be examined, and the value will be set to be TRUE. The result will be displayed as

```
3 >= 5 or else 'B' <= 'C' ? TRUE
```

While the normal operations on values of the Boolean data type are the six logical operators, it is also possible to use the relational operators. The two values making up the Boolean data type are FALSE and TRUE where FALSE < TRUE.

FLOAT

The FLOAT data type is used to approximate real numbers. Computers cannot represent all the numbers possible in mathematics. Instead, computers represent real numbers to some degree of accuracy. In Ada, the FLOAT data type will represent real numbers to a specified number of decimal places. You can determine how many decimal places or significant digits are available on your computer by displaying the attribute FLOAT'DIGITS. The set of numbers belonging to the float data type will vary from machine to machine, but for most machines the set of numbers will range from at least -10.0^{63} to 10.0^{63}. Ada differentiates between approximate real numbers and integers by requiring that these numbers be typed with a decimal point in the number. Some examples of approximate numbers are:

```
3.14159
2.3
1.0
```

An approximate number cannot begin or end in a decimal point. Hence 1. and .5 are illegal numbers in Ada.

Because approximate numbers are used to represent such a wide range of values, a special notation is used to represent very large and very small numbers. The notation used to represent large numbers is called *exponential* or *scientific notation*. The letter E is used to represent 10 to the power that follows the letter. For example,

1.0E6 represents 1000000.0 or $1.0*10^6$
1.0e3 represents 1000.0 or $1.0*10^3$
1.0E−3 represents 0.001 or $1.0*10^{-3}$
1.0e−1 represents 0.1 or $1.0*10^{-1}$

To make numbers with many places more readable, it is also possible to use an underscore in any number including integers. The underscore takes the place of where a comma might be used in a normal notation. Some examples are

2.147_159
3.141_160
123_456_789.0e−5

When the number following the E is positive, move the decimal point that many times to the right, adding in zeros if necessary. When the number following the E is negative, move the decimal point that many times to the left, adding in zeros if necessary.

The approximation of the Ada floating-point numbers to actual real numbers is defined in terms of model numbers. The specification of the type FLOAT contains a specification of the number of significant digits in the type. You can define your own floating-point type by a declaration such as

```
type REAL is digits 6;
```

Your compiler may complain that it is unable to handle a very accurate type specification such as

```
type REAL is digits 100;
```

You can generally expect at least six significant digits for your floating-point data types.

The next program demonstrates many operations for the FLOAT data type. We have declared three objects of the FLOAT data type with the declarations

```
FIRST_REAL, SECOND_REAL, RESULT :   FLOAT;
```

in the declaration part of the program.

Declarations for objects of the float data type have the general form:

list of data names : FLOAT;

The program sets FIRST_REAL to be 3.5 and SECOND_REAL to be 2.6.

Next, each of the float operations is used. For addition, the plus sign is used so the program will display

```
3.5 + 2.6 = 6.10000E+00
```

The number of zeros following 6.1 will be compiler-dependent.

For subtraction, Ada uses the minus sign, so the program will display

```
3.5 - 2.6 = 9.00000E-01
```

For multiplication, Ada uses the asterisk, so the program will display

```
3.5 * 2.6 = 9.10000E+00
```

For division, Ada uses the slash, so the program will display

```
3.5 / 2.6 = 1.34615E+00
```

Note that this is a different result than integer division as it presents the approximation to the true result.

For negation, Ada uses the minus sign. Hence the result for negation will be displayed as

```
- 3.5 = -3.50000E+00
```

For exponentiation, Ada uses the double asterisk (**), so the program will display

```
3.5 ** 2 = 1.22500E+01

with TEXT_IO;
package FLOAT_IO is new TEXT_IO.FLOAT_IO (FLOAT);

with TEXT_IO, FLOAT_IO;
use  TEXT_IO, FLOAT_IO;

procedure FLOAT_OPERATIONS is
    FIRST_NUMBER, SECOND_NUMBER, RESULT : FLOAT;

--  A program to demonstrate float operations
--  float operations include +, -, *, and /
--  as well as **

begin

  PUT_LINE (" The float operation program has started to execute. ");

  FIRST_NUMBER  := 3.5; -- assign 3.5 to first_number
  SECOND_NUMBER := 2.6; -- assign 2.6 to second_number

  RESULT := FIRST_NUMBER + SECOND_NUMBER; -- float addition
  NEW_LINE; PUT (" 3.5 + 2.6 = "); PUT (RESULT);

  RESULT := FIRST_NUMBER - SECOND_NUMBER; -- float subtraction
  NEW_LINE; PUT (" 3.5 - 2.6 = "); PUT (RESULT);
```

```
    RESULT := FIRST_NUMBER * SECOND_NUMBER; -- float multiplication
    NEW_LINE; PUT (" 3.5 * 2.6 = "); PUT (RESULT);

    RESULT := FIRST_NUMBER / SECOND_NUMBER; -- float division
    NEW_LINE; PUT (" 3.5 / 2.6 = "); PUT (RESULT);

    RESULT := - FIRST_NUMBER; -- float negation
    NEW_LINE; PUT (" -3.5 = "); PUT (RESULT);

    RESULT := FIRST_NUMBER ** 2; -- float exponentiation
    NEW_LINE; PUT (" -3.5 ** 2 = "); PUT (RESULT);
end FLOAT_OPERATIONS;
```

FLOAT data values may be compared with the operators for equality, inequality, less than, greater than, less than or equal to, and greater than or equal to. As with the case of integers, characters, or Booleans used in comparisons, the result of the comparison will always be a Boolean value.

Because the FLOAT type is an approximation to arithmetic as we usually know it, there is a small error in every arithmetic operation on a FLOAT type value. For this reason, although Ada allows the equality operation on FLOAT values, it is important *never* to have a program depend on equality between two FLOAT type values. Instead, the program should set up a region of error. For example, instead of testing that an expression has reached exactly 0.0, the program should test that the expression is less than some small value. For example, the expression can be

```
HEIGHT < SMALL_VALUE
```

but should never be

```
HEIGHT = 0.0
```

The SUCC and PRED operations are not available for the FLOAT data type.

FIXED

There are two types of approximate data types in Ada, floating-point types and fixed-point types. The fixed-point types have an accuracy specification that is absolute. That is, you can specify that the fixed point numbers are to be accurate to 0.1 or 0.001. There is no predefined fixed-point data type. This class of data types will be covered in a later chapter.

WHAT HAVE YOU LEARNED?

The four predefined data types

INTEGER	for whole numbers
CHARACTER	for single ASCII characters
BOOLEAN	for TRUE and FALSE
FLOAT	for approximate numbers

How to declare objects of the four predefined data types:

> general forms:
> *list of data names* : INTEGER ;
> *list of data names* : CHARACTER ;
> *list of data names* : BOOLEAN ;
> *list of data names* : FLOAT ;
> examples:
> SMALL, MEDIUM, LARGE : INTEGER;
> FIRST_INITIAL, MIDDLE_INITIAL, LAST_INITIAL : CHARACTER;
> ABSOLUTE_TRUTH, LADY_AND_THE_TIGER : BOOLEAN;
> HEIGHT_OF_EVEREST, POPULATION_OF_SANTA_BARBARA : FLOAT;

How to operate on objects of the four predefined data types:

Arithmetic operators for the INTEGER and FLOAT data types:

+	for addition
−	for subtraction
*	for multiplication
/	for division
**	for exponentiation
−	for negation

Additional arithmetic operators for the INTEGER data type:

mod	for modulo arithmetic
rem	for remainder

Operations on the CHARACTER data type:

CHARACTER'SUCC	for successor
CHARACTER'PRED	for predecessor
CHARACTER'POS	for INTEGER value of CHARACTER
CHARACTER'VAL	for CHARACTER value of INTEGER

Note these same operations apply to integers:

> INTEGER'SUCC   INTEGER'PRED

Operations on the BOOLEAN data type:

and	
or	
not	
xor	for exclusive or
and then	for short circuit and
or else	for short circuit or

Relational operators for the INTEGER, CHARACTER, BOOLEAN and FLOAT data type:

=	for equality
<	for less than
>	for greater than
<=	for less than or equal to
>=	for greater than or equal to

Never use = for FLOAT data type. The inaccuracies in the operations for the FLOAT data type cannot guarantee exact equality in expressions.

PROBLEMS

1. Define the meaning of *type* in Ada and state why the type concept is important.

2. Evaluate the following INTEGER expressions.
   a. 6 + 5
   b. 23 − 7
   c. 4 * 8
   d. 6 / 3
   e. 3 ** 2
   f. 5 / 4
   g. 5 **mod** 3
   h. 7 **rem** 4
   i. − 3 **rem** 2
   j. INTEGER'SUCC (10)

3. Evaluate the following CHARACTER expressions.
   a. CHARACTER'SUCC ('F')
   b. CHARACTER'PRED ('M')
   c. CHARACTER'POS ('P')
   d. CHARACTER'VAL (73)
   e. CHARACTER'SUCC (';')
   f. CHARACTER'PRED ('''')

4. Evaluate the following BOOLEAN expressions.
   a. TRUE **or** FALSE
   b. FALSE **and** TRUE
   c. FALSE **xor** FALSE

d. TRUE **or else** FALSE

e. FALSE **and then** TRUE

5. Evaluate the following relational expressions.

    a. 7 > 6

    b. 50 < 40

    c. 6 >= 6

    d. 2 = 3

    e. 9 <= 17

6. Evaluate the following FLOAT expressions.

    a. 2.0 + 6.0

    b. 7.0 − 3.0

    c. 5.0 * 4.0

    d. 6.0 / 4.0

    e. 3.0 ** 2.0

7. What is the type of each of the following expressions.

    a. 5 > 3

    b. CHARACTER'PRED ('E')

    c. TRUE **and** TRUE

    d. 7.0 − 2.0

    e. CHARACTER'POS ('D')

8. What is wrong with each expression. Rewrite each expression to be a correct Ada expression.

    a. 2 > 6.0

    b. 1. < 2.

    c. CHARACTER'SUCC (DEL)

    d. CHARACTER'PRED ("g")

    e. 2 *** 3

CHAPTER
❖ 4 ❖

CONSTANTS AND EXPRESSIONS

❖ In the last chapter we learned simple expressions and the four predefined data types, which can be constants and can be used in expressions. We also learned the set of values and the set of operators that make up each of these predefined data types. In this chapter we will see how you can use the data types with expressions and assignment statements to make complete programs.

CONSTANTS

Often there are values in a program that remain constant throughout the program; a program is easier to understand and will contain fewer errors if these values are declared to be constant. Examples of numeric constants that are often used in programs are the speed of light, the radius of the earth, the number of centimeters per inch, and the number of pennies in a dollar.

The general form of a numeric constant declaration is

data name : **constant** := *value* ;

Some examples are:

```
SPEED_OF_LIGHT : constant := 3.0E10 ;    -- speed in cm/sec
RADIUS_OF_EARTH : constant := 6.37E6;     -- radius in meters
CENTIMETERS_PER_INCH : constant := 2.54;
PENNIES_PER_DOLLAR : constant := 100;
```

43

It is even possible to write simple expressions with the operators we used in the last chapter to define constants such as

```
TWO_PI : constant := 2 * 3.14159;   -- two pi
```

or to write expressions in terms of constants we have already defined in previous lines such as

```
DIAMETER_OF_EARTH : constant := 2 * RADIUS_OF_EARTH;
```

Ada has only two types of numeric constant: the integer constants, or the *universal integers*, and the float constants, or *universal reals*. Universal integers and universal reals have special properties that allow them to be used much more freely than the integers or floats. In the examples above, SPEED_OF_LIGHT, RADIUS_OF_EARTH, and CENTIMETERS_PER_INCH are universal real constants of type UNIVERSAL_REAL. Universal reals can be multiplied by universal integers as was done in the statement defining TWO_PI. Such an operation is not legal between an INTEGER and a FLOAT data type.

An expression containing only universal integers results in a value of type UNIVERSAL_INTEGER. Likewise, an expression containing only universal reals results in a value of type UNIVERSAL_REAL. It is also possible to use universal integers and universal reals in mixed expressions if the following rules are observed:

> multiplication between universal integers and universal reals is allowed, and a universal real may be divided by a universal integer

In both cases the result is of the type UNIVERSAL_REAL. In the example for the DIAMETER_OF_EARTH, the universal integer 2 multiplies the universal real 6.37E6 to result in the universal real constant.

Constants can also be nonnumeric. In fact, any data type may have constants. The general form of such a declaration is

data name : **constant** *data type* := *value* ;

Some examples of such declarations are

```
ABSOLUTE_TRUTH : constant BOOLEAN := TRUE;
CARRIAGE_RETURN : constant CHARACTER := ASCII.CR;
```

These constant declarations may be placed anywhere that a declaration is allowed, usually in the declaration part of a program. Once declared, a constant cannot be changed anywhere in the program.

Universal real constants are represented exactly in the computer and may be specified to an unlimited number of places. For example, we may represent the value for pi to be

```
PI : constant := 3.141592654;
```

In a universal real expression such as 2 * PI, the number for PI will be represented exactly as written. Universal real expressions are not approximations such as expressions of the FLOAT data type. It is not until a float value is used that the expression will be limited to the number of significant digits that are available on the computer being used.

EXPRESSIONS

In chapter 3, we learned about expressions that used one operator. In this chapter we will learn how to use expressions that have many operators. In fact, there is no limit to how complicated an expression you may write. In any of the places where a *data_name* is used in an expression, an expression may be used instead. In order to make a program more readable, it is a good idea to break up any expression that requires more than two lines into smaller expressions.

Care must be taken that expressions preserve the data type. That is, an INTEGER expression must be made up of operands of the INTEGER data type. In an assignment statement such as

```
GROSS_WEIGHT := WEIGHT_OF_CLOTHES + WEIGHT_OF_BOX +
                WEIGHT_OF_PACKING_MATERIALS;
```

all four data names must be declared to be of type INTEGER. This example shows three items are added together and the result is placed in GROSS_WEIGHT. This restriction against mixing data types across assignments and in expressions is called *strong* typing. The type on the left side of an assignment statement and the type on the right side of an assignment statement must be the same. Likewise, the type on the left side of a binary operator and the type on the right side of a binary operator must be the same. Ada will check that this is always true and as a result will find many errors that other languages do not find.

When you use just one kind of operation in an expression, you need not usually worry about the order of evaluation. When you use combinations of operators, you must learn something about the order of operations. In an Ada program, you must not depend on the evaluation of an expression being done from right to left or from left to right. The Ada compiler you use will chose the order of operations, which can be different from compiler to compiler. You should control the order of evaluation by using parentheses when it is important. For example, if you have an Ada expression such as

$$3 + 2 + 1$$

you will not know if the computer added 3 to 2 and then added 1 to 5 to form the result of 6 or if the computer added 1 to 2 and then added 3 to 3 to form the result. If you wanted to make sure that the 3 was added to 2 before adding the 1 to the partial sum, you need to write

$$(3 + 2) + 1$$

Whatever is enclosed in parentheses will always be evaluated first.

Similarly, in the expression

$$3 - 2 - 1$$

you do not know if the computer computes

$$(3 - 2) - 1 \quad \text{or} \quad 3 + (-2 - 1)$$

In the expression

$$4 ** 3 ** 2$$

the order of evaluation is defined from left to right.

It is usually not important to use parentheses when the same operation is used more than once in a statement. Instead, parentheses specify the order of operation when more than one kind of operator is used. Ada follows the order of operations used in normal mathematics:

**	exponentiation
* / **mod rem**	multiplication, division, modulo, remainder
− **abs**	negation, absolute value
+ −	addition, subtraction

That is, exponentiation will be done before multiplication, and multiplication will be done before negation. Similarly, negation will be done before addition. Hence the expression

$$-3 + 2 * 3 ** 2$$

would be evaluated as $(-3) + (2 * (3**2))$. That is, exponentiation of 3 by 2 would result in a value of 9, which would be multiplied by 2 to form 18. Then 3 would be negated before being added to 18 with a final result of 15.

Another name for the order of operations is the *precedence of operations*; exponentiation has a higher precedence than addition. In case you forget the precedence of operations, you can use parentheses to determine the precedence yourself.

Parentheses are commonly used when a formula to be evaluated uses a combination of multiplication and addition or subtraction. For example, to convert a temperature from Fahrenheit to Celsius, we need to subtract 32 from the Fahrenheit temperature and multiply the result by 5/9. In many books this formula is written as

$$t_{celsius} = \frac{5}{9} (t_{Fahrenheit} - 32)$$

If we want to work this problem in whole numbers, we could write a short program:

```
with TEXT_IO;
package INTEGER_IO is new TEXT_IO. INTEGER_IO(INTEGER);

with TEXT_IO, INTEGER_IO;
use TEXT_IO, INTEGER_IO;

procedure TEMPERATURE is

-- program to convert Fahrenheit to Celsius

    TEMPERATURE_IN_FAHRENHEIT, TEMPERATURE_IN_CELSIUS :
                            INTEGER;
begin
    PUT_LINE ("Type a temperature in degrees Fahrenheit ";
    GET (TEMPERATURE_IN_FAHRENHEIT);
    NEW_LINE; PUT (TEMPERATURE_IN_FAHRENHEIT);
    TEMPERATURE_IN_CELSIUS : =
        ((TEMPERATURE_IN_FAHRENHEIT −32) * 5)/9;
    NEW_LINE;
    PUT_LINE ("The equivalent temperature in degrees Celsius is");
    PUT (TEMPERATURE_IN_CELSIUS);
end TEMPERATURE;
```

The expression that computes the temperature uses parentheses to alter the normal order of operations. The innermost set of parentheses guarantees that 32 will be subtracted from TEMPERATURE_IN_FAHRENHEIT before the multiplication by 5 takes place. The second parentheses guarantees that the multiplication will take place before the division. This is necessary to preserve some semblance of accuracy since the integer division will cause truncation.

When this program was executed with an input temperature of 99, it produced the following output:

```
Type a temperature in degrees Fahrenheit
>99

        99
The equivalent temperature in degrees Celsius is
        37
```

Any expression can be enclosed in parentheses and then acted on as a value. The character operations can be applied more than once by enclosing the result in parentheses and applying the operation again. Thus the expression

```
CHARACTER'SUCC (CHARACTER'SUCC ('C'))
```

will result in a value 'E'; the expression

```
CHARACTER'PRED (CHARACTER'PRED ('C'))
```

will result in a value 'A'; and the expression

```
CHARACTER'PRED  (CHARACTER'SUCC  ('C'))
```

will result in a value 'C'.

Although you are unlikely to use them, you should be able to understand that the expression

```
CHARACTER'VAL  (CHARACTER'POS  ('C'))
```

will result in a value of 'C', and the expression

```
CHARACTER'POS  (CHARACTER'VAL  (67))
```

will result in an integer value of 67.

The combination of the Boolean operations, **and, or,** and **xor** are treated with equal precedence. Hence the expression

```
FALSE and TRUE or TRUE
```

is ambiguous since it is not specified which is to be done first, the **and** or the **or.** If the **and** were done first, the expression would be TRUE. If the **or** were done first, the expression would be FALSE. This statement is illegal in Ada because of the ambiguity. Anytime you mix Boolean operations of the same precedence, you must use parentheses:

```
(FALSE and TRUE) or TRUE
```

in which case the value of the expression will be TRUE.

The Boolean operation, **not,** is treated with the same precedence as the negation operation, but all the other Boolean operations, including the short circuit forms, have a lower precedence than the other arithmetic and relational operations. For clarity and so as not to be confused by the different precedence of the **not** operation, it is recommended that *all* Boolean operations be enclosed in parentheses whenever more than one of them is used in the same expression. For example, although it is legal to write

```
not FALSE or TRUE
```

it is recommended that one write

```
(not FALSE) or TRUE
```

The relational operators fall between the arithmetic operations and the Boolean operations so the precedence hierarchy of operations is

```
arithmetic operations
relational operations
Boolean operations
```

This allows most tests to be written without parentheses. For example, a test such as

```
SPILL_CONDITION := WATER_HEIGHT + TEN_FEET >= DAM_GATE_HEIGHT;
```

can be written without the need for parentheses since the addition is performed before the comparison. Even more complex expressions can be used in assignment statements such as

```
DANGER_CONDITION := AGE < 10 and TEMPERATURE > 104
                    and WEIGHT < 50;
```

This statement can be written without parentheses since **and** is the only Boolean operation used in the expression.

When multiple operations are combined with objects of the FLOAT data type, the order of operations can be controlled by parentheses as was the case with the INTEGER data type. Also, as in integer arithmetic, exponentiation will be done before multiplication, multiplication will be done before negation, and negation will be done before addition.

The following program calculates the interest on a credit card loan over a period of a month and calculates the new value of the loan. It assumes a constant interest rate of 21%. The interest is computed with the formula:

```
INTEREST = LOAN_VALUE * RATE * TIME
```

Since the time is one month and the rate is in terms of one year, the time must be calculated as one-twelfth of a year.

```
with TEXT_IO;
package FLOAT_IO is new TEXT_IO.FLOAT_IO(FLOAT);

with TEXT_IO, FLOAT_IO;
use  TEXT_IO, FLOAT_IO;

procedure LOAN is

   INTEREST, LOAN_VALUE : FLOAT;
   NEW_LOAN_VALUE       : FLOAT;

   RATE : constant := 0.21;      -- 21% per year
   TIME : constant := 1.0/12.0;  -- one month

begin

-- A program to calculate credit card loan interest
--   and new loan value after one month

   PUT_LINE (" The loan program has started to execute. ");

   PUT_LINE (" Type in loan value ");
   GET (LOAN_VALUE);
   NEW_LINE; PUT (LOAN_VALUE);
```

```
INTEREST := LOAN_VALUE * RATE * TIME;

NEW_LINE; PUT (" Interest for one month is ");
PUT (INTEREST);

NEW_LOAN_VALUE := LOAN_VALUE + INTEREST;

NEW_LINE; PUT (" Loan is now ");
PUT (NEW_LOAN_VALUE);
```

    end LOAN;

When the credit card loan program was executed to calculate the interest on a $500 loan, the program gave the following output:

```
The loan program has started to execute.
Type in loan value
>500.00

5.00000E+02
Interest for one month is  8.75000E+00
Loan is now  5.08750E+02
```

The next program demonstrates a calculation that requires a number of operations. It calculates the distance between two points on a map where the map coordinates are given in meters, as is done in maps for the Army. It is partially through the mechanism of combining operations that powerful programs can be written.

The program calculates the square of the distance between two points in a map, given the coordinates of the points in meters.

$$\text{distance}^2 = (x_2 - x_1)^2 + (y_2 - y_1)^2$$

First the value of x_1 is obtained, and its name given as FIRST_X. Then y_1 is assigned a value as FIRST_Y. Subsequently the value x_2 is stored in SECOND_X and the value for y_2 is stored in SECOND_Y. The calculation for the distance squared uses the combination of subtraction and exponentiation operators. In Ada, exponentiation can be done only to integer powers so the constant 2 is used to obtain the square of the expression in parentheses.

```
with TEXT_IO;
package FLOAT_IO is new TEXT_IO.FLOAT_IO(FLOAT);

with TEXT_IO; FLOAT_IO;
use  TEXT_IO, FLOAT_IO;

procedure DISTANCE_SQUARED is

-- A program to calculate square of distance
-- between two map coordinates
```

```
   FIRST_X, FIRST_Y : FLOAT;
   SECOND_X, SECOND_Y : FLOAT;
   DISTANCE : FLOAT;

begin

   PUT_LINE (" The distance squared program has started to execute. ");

   PUT_LINE (" Type first x coordinate ");
   GET (FIRST_X);
   NEW_LINE; PUT (FIRST_X); NEW_LINE;

   PUT_LINE (" Type first y coordinate ");
   GET (FIRST_Y);
   NEW_LINE; PUT (FIRST_Y); NEW_LINE;

   PUT_LINE (" Type second x coordinate ");
   GET (SECOND_X);
   NEW_LINE; PUT (SECOND_X); NEW_LINE;

   PUT_LINE (" Type second y coordinate ");
   GET (SECOND_Y);
   NEW_LINE; PUT (SECOND_Y); NEW_LINE;

   DISTANCE := (SECOND_X - FIRST_X) ** 2 +
               (SECOND_Y - FIRST_Y) ** 2;

   PUT (" Square of distance is "); PUT (DISTANCE);

end DISTANCE_SQUARED:
```

When this program was executed with some sample data, it produced the following output:

```
The distance squared program has started to execute.
Type first x coordinate
>4.5

 4.50000E+00
Type first y coordinate
>3.2

 3.20000E+00
Type second x coordinate
>7.6

 7.60000E+00
Type second y coordinate
>25.4

 2.54000E+01
Square of distance is   5.02450E+02
```

What Have You Learned?

How to declare constants

The general forms for constant declarations are:

data name : **constant** := *value* ;
data name : **constant** *data type* := *value* ;

Some examples are:

```
SPEED_OF_LIGHT : constant := 3.0E10 ;    -- speed in cm/sec
CENTIMETERS_PER_INCH : constant := 2.54;
PENNIES_PER_DOLLAR : constant := 100;
MY_MIDDLE_INITIAL : constant CHARACTER := 'H';
AXIOM : constant BOOLEAN := TRUE ;
```

Order of arithmetic operations:

exponentiation
multiplication or division
negation
addition or subtraction

Use of parentheses to control order of evaluation.

(5 − 3) * 2
to give a value of 4

Order of operations among different classes of operations

arithmetic operations
relational operations
Boolean operations

Exponentiation can be done to an integer power.

Constants can be universal integers or universal reals. An expression containing only universal integers results in a value of type UNIVERSAL_INTEGER. Likewise, an expression containing only universal reals results in a value of type UNIVERSAL_REAL. It is also possible to use universal integers and universal reals in mixed expressions if the following rules are observed:

multiplication between universal integers and universal reals is allowed
a universal real may be divided by a universal integer

In both cases the result is of the type UNIVERSAL_REAL.

PROBLEMS

1. Evaluate the following integer expressions
   a. 3 + 7 − 3
   b. 3/2 + 1
   c. 4 + 5*6 − 2
   d. 7**3 − 2

2. Evaluate the following float expressions
   a. 6.5 + 1.5 − 2.0
   b. 4.0/2.0 − 1.0
   c. 2.5 * 2.0 + 1.0
   d. 3.5 − 2.0 / 4.0 − 1.5

3. Evaluate the following character expressions
   a. CHARACTER'SUCC (CHARACTER'SUCC ('d'))
   b. CHARACTER'PRED (CHARACTER'PRED (CR))
   c. CHARACTER'SUCC (CHARACTER'PRED ('A'))
   d. CHARACTER'VAL (CHARACTER'POS ('D'))

4. Write a program to input the value of five stocks on the New York Stock Exchange. Add up the total value of the stocks and divide by five to obtain what is called a *stock average*.

5. Write a program to convert temperatures from degrees Celsius to degrees Fahrenheit. To convert from Celsius to Fahrenheit, multiply the temperature by 9/5 and then add 32 degrees. Use the FLOAT data type.

6. Substitute the character for the question mark so that the expression is TRUE.
   a. CHARACTER'POS (?) = 0
   b. CHARACTER'SUCC (CHARACTER'PRED (?)) = 'A'
   c. CHARACTER'POS (CHARACTER'VAL (?)) = 2
   d. CHARACTER'SUCC (CHARACTER'VAL (?)) = 'Z'
   e. CHARACTER'POS ('9') − CHARACTER'POS (?) = 9

CHAPTER
❖ 5 ❖
CONTROL STRUCTURES

❖ Thus far we have studied simple programs in which each statement executes just once. However, most statements in Ada programs execute many times. Also, the programs we have seen have only one *path* through the program as shown in figure 5.1. A path in a program represents which statements execute in the program. *Control structures* are a way of causing some statements to be executed while other statements are not executed—they cause programs to have more than one path. Most Ada programs will have a few paths through the program depending on the data provided to the program or special events such as the time of day.

There are three kinds of control structures in Ada:

the conditional control structure
the loop control structure
the unconditional control structure

The conditional control structure tests a condition and executes one group of statements instead of another depending on the result of the test. The loop control structure repeats a group of statements. The unconditional control structure transfers control to another part of the program. It is best to avoid the unconditional control structure and use the other control structures instead;

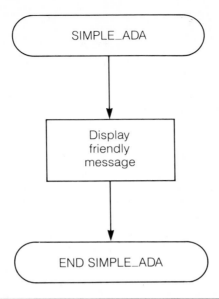

Figure 5.1 One Path Program

the other control structures, if properly used, will allow you to write programs that are well structured and easily understood by others. The unconditional control structure can lead to poorly structured programs.

CONDITIONAL CONTROL

Two statements in Ada perform conditional control:

> the **if** statement
> the **case** statement

The **if** statement performs a test on a Boolean expression. A Boolean expression, as discussed in chapter 4, is an expression that yields a TRUE or a FALSE value. If the result of the expression is TRUE, the program executes one set of statements. If the result of the expression is FALSE, it executes another set of statements. The **if** statement is often portrayed as shown in figure 5.2, where the test is written in the diamond-shaped box, and the two paths are represented by the lines coming out of the box. When the test is TRUE, the program follows the path labeled *true,* and when the test is FALSE, the other path is followed.

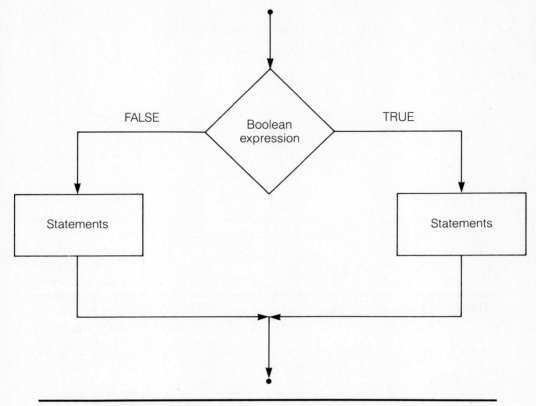

Figure 5.2   If Statement

One useful application for the **if** statement tests that values typed into a computer fall into a legal range. The following program tests that the input value falls between 5 and 100. If the test is TRUE, the program squares the number and outputs the result. Otherwise, it prints an error message and exits. The program could be diagrammed as shown in figure 5.3.

```
with TEXT_IO;
package INTEGER_IO is new TEXT_IO. INTEGER_IO(INTEGER);

with TEXT_IO,  INTEGER_IO;
use   TEXT_IO,  INTEGER_IO;

procedure TEST_INPUT is

  INPUT_DATA :  INTEGER;
  RESULT     :  INTEGER;
```

```
begin
    -- Square the input for values between 5 and 100
    -- Print an error message otherwise
    PUT_LINE (" Type a number between 5 and 100 ");
    GET (INPUT_DATA);
    if INPUT_DATA >= 5 and INPUT_DATA <= 100 then
    -- TRUE side
        RESULT := INPUT_DATA ** 2;
        NEW_LINE; PUT (" Number squared is "); PUT (RESULT);
    else
    -- FALSE side
        NEW_LINE; PUT (" Number typed is outside range of 5 to 100 ");
    end if;
end TEST_INPUT;
```

When the test in the **if** statement is TRUE, the statements following the **then** will be executed. When the test is FALSE, the statements following the **else** will be executed. There is no semicolon after the **then** or the **else**. The **if** statement ends with an **end if**, which is followed by a semicolon. Each of the statements between the **then** and the **else** is considered a separate statement and is thus terminated by a semicolon. The same is true for the statements between the **else** and the **end if**—note the space between the **end** and the **if**. It is customary to indent the statements in the two parts of the **if** statement to portray the alteration in the control flow at this point in the program.

This program was run two times in order to execute each path in the program. When executed the output was

```
Type a number between 5 and 100
>10


Number squared is          100


Type a number between 5 and 100
>101


Number typed is outside range of 5 to 100
```

A simpler form of the **if** statement omits the **else** part of the statement if there are no statements to be performed when the test is FALSE. The test is often portrayed as in figure 5.4. It is sometimes called an **if** statement with an empty **else** part. The next program demonstrates the use of such a statement to calculate the sine of an angle using a linear term for angles less than 5 degrees and a cube term for angles greater than 5 degrees. This program is reasonably accurate for angles between 0 and 45 degrees.

Using the **if** statement with the null **else** is not encouraged because there is almost always something that should be done on both sides of an **if** state-

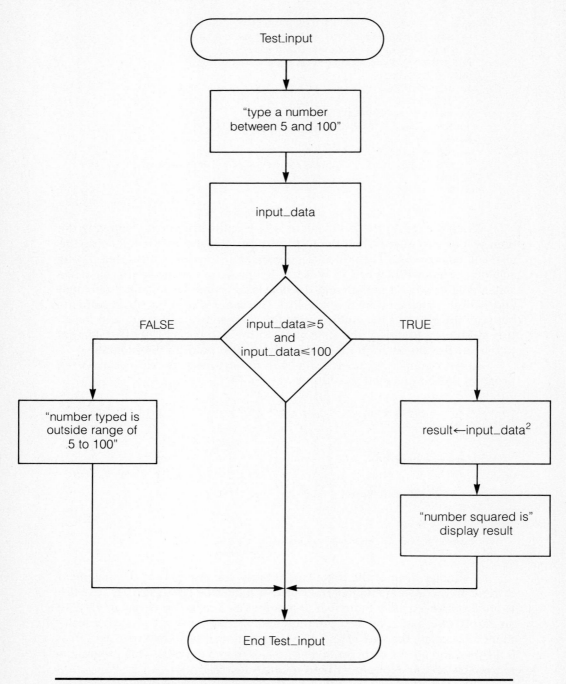

Figure 5.3   TEST_INPUT Diagram

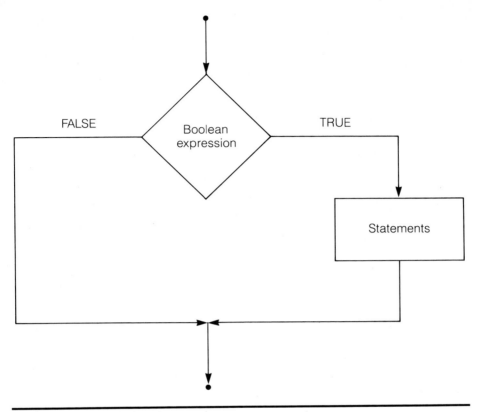

Figure 5.4   If Statement with Empty Else

ment. An empty **else** often indicates missing logic in a program, and it is one error situation that is difficult to detect.

The general form of the **if** statement is

if *Boolean expression* **then**
        statements
else
        statements
end if;

```
with TEXT_IO;
package FLOAT_IO is new TEXT_IO.FLOAT_IO(FLOAT);
with TEXT_IO, FLOAT_IO;
use  TEXT_IO, FLOAT_IO;
```

```
procedure SINE is

-- A program to compute the sine of an angle
-- using a linear term for small angles
-- and a cubic term for angles greater than 5 degrees.
-- The angle is input in degrees.

   INPUT_ANGLE : FLOAT;
   OUTPUT_SINE : FLOAT;

   PI : constant := 3.14159;
   DEGREES_TO_RADIANS : constant := PI/180.0;

begin

   PUT_LINE (" Type an angle in degrees ");
   GET (INPUT_ANGLE);

   OUTPUT_SINE := INPUT_ANGLE * DEGREES_TO_RADIANS;

   if INPUT_ANGLE > 5.0 then
      OUTPUT_SINE := OUTPUT_SINE - OUTPUT_SINE ** 3 / 6.0;
   end if;

   NEW_LINE; PUT (" Sine of angle is "); PUT (OUTPUT_SINE);

end SINE;
```

The program computing the sine of an angle was executed twice with two different angles. The record of execution follows:

```
Type an angle in degrees
>45.0

Sine of angle is  7.04652E-01

Type an angle in degrees
>2.0

Sine of angle is 3.49065E-02
```

You can compare these answers with the more exact values in a trigonometry table.

Another form of the **if** statement is the multiway decision form, which eliminates the need to put **if** statements inside **if** statements. While it is possible to nest **if** statements one inside the other, it is considered poor style. For example, if you feel the need to write another **if** after a **then**, you should rewrite the test to combine the two **if**s. If you need to write another **if** after an **else**, you should use the multiway decision form—often called the *else if* form—instead. It is written with the keyword **elsif**.

The **elsif** form of the **if** statement may also be written with or without an **else** part. Just as with the two-way form, an empty **else** is possible but not encouraged. The multiway **if** statement is useful when there are many conditions to test, only one of which is expected to be TRUE. In the next program a multiway **if** statement is used to select a message based on the time, which is input as a FLOAT number in terms of a twenty-four-hour clock.

The first **if** statement in the program tests if the TIME_OF_DAY falls between 0.0 and 6.0. If the test is TRUE, the display will show

```
It's too early!
```

If the test is FALSE, the test in the next **elsif** part of the statement is evaluated. This test checks if TIME_OF_DAY is between 6.0 and 12.0. If the test is true, the display will show

```
Good morning
```

If this test is also FALSE, the program tests whether the TIME_OF_DAY falls between 12.0 and 18.0. A TRUE result will cause the display to show

```
Good afternoon
```

The last test will be evaluated if all the previous tests have been FALSE. The last test tests if TIME_OF_DAY is between 18.0 and 24.0. If the test is TRUE, the display will read

```
Good evening
```

Finally, if none of the tests is true, the display will show

```
Invalid time typed in.

with TEXT_IO;
package FLOAT_IO is new TEXT_IO.FLOAT_IO(FLOAT);

with TEXT_IO, FLOAT_IO;
use  TEXT_IO, FLOAT_IO;

procedure GREETING is

   -- Present a greeting depending on the time of day

   TIME_OF_DAY : FLOAT;

begin

   PUT_LINE (" The greeting program has started to execute. ");
   PUT     ("Enter the time of day in terms of a 24 hour clock. ");
   NEW_LINE;

   GET (TIME_OF_DAY);
   NEW_LINE; PUT (TIME_OF_DAY); NEW_LINE;
```

```
    if TIME_OF_DAY >= 0.0 and TIME_OF_DAY <= 6.0 then
        PUT_LINE (" It's too early! ");
    elsif TIME_OF_DAY >= 6.0 and TIME_OF_DAY <= 12.0 then
        PUT_LINE (" Good morning ");
    elsif TIME_OF_DAY >= 12.0 and TIME_OF_DAY <= 18.0 then
        PUT_LINE (" Good afternoon ");
    elsif TIME_OF_DAY >= 18.0 and TIME_OF_DAY <= 24.0 then
        PUT_LINE (" Good evening ");
    else
        PUT_LINE (" Invalid time typed in. ");
    end if;

end GREETING;
```

This program was executed with several values of time.

```
The greeting program has started to execute.
Enter the time of day in terms of a 24 hour clock.
>3.0

 3.00000E+00
It's too early!
```

```
The greeting program has started to execute.
Enter the time of day in terms of a 24 hour clock.
>9.0

 9.00000E+00
Good morning
```

```
The greeting program has started to execute.
Enter the time of day in terms of a 24 hour clock.
>15.0

 1.50000E+01
Good afternoon
```

```
The greeting program has started to execute.
Enter the time of day in terms of a 24 hour clock.

>24.0

 2.40000E+01
Good evening
```

```
The greeting program has started to execute.
Enter the time of day in terms of a 24 hour clock.
>26.0

2.60000E+01
Invalid time typed in.
```

Although the example shows only one statement in each part of the **if** statement, it is possible to put many statements in each part. The multiway **if** statement can be graphically portrayed as shown in figure 5.5

The general form of the if statement in its multiway form is

if *Boolean expression* **then**
    statements
elsif *Boolean expression* **then**
    statements
elsif *Boolean expression* **then**
    statements
        .
        .
        .

else
    statements
end if;

The **case** statement is another multiway test statement somewhat like the multiway **if** statement, but in the **case** statement, there is no Boolean test. Instead, the program must decide whether the test expression takes on one of the possible values for the variable. For each possible value, there is some case to be executed. The **case** statement cannot be used on FLOAT variables. It is valid only for the discrete types such as the INTEGER, CHARACTER, and BOOLEAN variables. In chapter 6 we will learn to define our own discrete types, which can be used in a **case** statement.

The general form of the **case** statement is

case *discrete data name* **is**
    when *discrete data values* => *statements*
    when *discrete data values* => *statements*
        .
        .
        .
    when *discrete data values* => *statements*
end case;

Embedded in the **case** statement are other statements just as in the **if** statement. To keep things straight it is recommended that the statements in

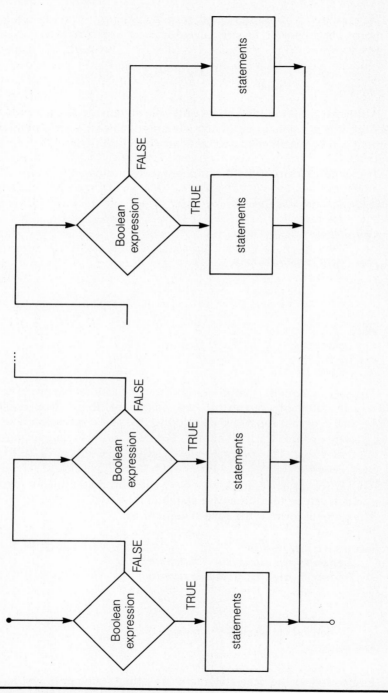

Figure 5.5   Multiway If Statement

the **case** statement should not be other **case** statements or other **if** statements. The use of other control structures in a control structure makes the program logically complex. Very often by rethinking the problem, a simpler control structure can perform the same logic. An example of the use of the **case** statement is shown in the next program, which asks the question "Do you like Ada?" The response is to be a single character *Y* for yes or *N* for no.

The example program displays the message, "Do you like Ada?" It also displays the instruction, "Type Y for yes or N for no." The program then waits for a single character to be typed and placed in the data object RESPONSE. Since RESPONSE is a character variable, it can take on one of 128 ASCII values as listed in Appendix B.

When we use the **case** statement, we must tell the program what to do for each of those values. In the first **when** clause, we test for whether the value is *Y* or *y*. The bar between the two characters stands for the *selector operation*, which lists several values for a particular case. In the example, just two possibilities are listed so that the response can be either a lower- or uppercase *y*. If the response fits either possibility, the program will execute the statements following the $=>$ symbol. Hence if a *y* is typed, the display will show

```
Good, I like it too! Have a nice day.
```

If the response had been a lower- or uppercase *n*, the display will show

```
Too bad, it is very powerful.

with TEXT_IO; use TEXT_IO;

procedure QUESTION is

-- Program to respond to question " Do you like Ada? "

  RESPONSE : CHARACTER;

begin
  PUT_LINE (" Do you like Ada? ");
  PUT_LINE (" Type Y for yes or N for no ");
  GET (RESPONSE);
  NEW_LINE; PUT (RESPONSE); NEW_LINE;

  case RESPONSE is
    when 'Y'|'y' =>
      PUT (" Good, I like it too! ");
      PUT_LINE (" Have a nice day. ");
    when 'N'|'n' =>
      PUT (" Too bad, ");
      PUT_LINE (" it is very powerful. ");
    when others =>
      PUT (" Invalid response. ");
      PUT_LINE (" Y or N are valid. ");
  end case;

end QUESTION;
```

In the last **when** clause in our example, the **when others** clause handles what to do when the response is a character but not one of the previously specified cases. Note that **others** is a keyword. In a **case** statement the **when others** part is like an **else** clause in an **if** statement. However, you can omit the **others** part only when you have specified all possible values in the other **when** clauses. Thus, if we did not use a **when others** clause, we would have to specify all the 128 possible values that the data object, RESPONSE, could take on.

When this program was executed, the display showed:

```
Do you like Ada?
 Type Y for yes or N for no
>y

y
 Good, I like it too! Have a nice day.
```

The second execution case was also executed:

```
Do you like Ada?
 Type Y for yes or N for no
>N

N
 Too bad, it is very powerful.
```

To demonstrate the **others** case, a third execution produced:

```
Do you like Ada?
 Type Y for yes or N for no
>z

z
 Invalid response. Y or N are valid.
```

In addition to the notation for alternative choices in the **when** part of a **case** statement, there is also a way to specify a range of values. For example,

```
case RESPONSE is
   when 'a'..'z' => PUT_LINE (" little letter ");
   when 'A'..'Z' => PUT_LINE (" big letter ");
   when '0'..'9' => PUT_LINE (" digit ");
   when  others  => PUT_LINE (" special or control character ");
   end case;
```

If RESPONSE is of the CHARACTER data type, then the first **when** clause tests if RESPONSE is in the range of characters from *a* to *z* and displays an appropriate message. The second test is for when the range is *A* to *Z* and the third test is whether the response is in the range 0 to 9.

The two notations for choice and for range may be combined such as in

```
case RESPONSE is
    when 'a'..'z' | 'A'..'Z'  => PUT_LINE (" letter ");
    when '0'..'9'             => PUT_LINE (" digit ");
    when  NUL .. US | DEL      => PUT_LINE (" control character ");
    when others               => PUT_LINE (" special character ");
end case;
```

In this example, if RESPONSE is of the CHARACTER data type, the first **when** clause tests if the response is *a* to *z* or *A* to *Z*. Hence the usual way to think of FIRST_VALUE . . SECOND_VALUE in Ada is to read it as FIRST_ VALUE to SECOND_VALUE. It is also called a *range of values*. The way to think of FIRST_VALUE|SECOND_VALUE is to read it as FIRST_VALUE or SECOND VALUE. It is also called a *choice*.

The **case** statement can also be used for the data type BOOLEAN where there are only two values to test, TRUE and FALSE. It probably makes sense to use the **if** statement instead of the **case** statement for the BOOLEAN data type.

The **case** statement can be used for the INTEGER data type in which each possible value of the INTEGER data type is specified. In most situations where there are cases on integers you should define a *user* data type (as is covered in chapter 6) or use an **if** statement. This is because the INTEGER data type has a very large range of values, all of which must be enumerated in the **case** statement. It is also because it is likely that you are using only a small range of the values when your application calls for a **case** statement. If you need the large range of values that the INTEGER data type provides, do not use the **case** statement because you must specify all the values in the **case** statement.

LOOP CONTROL

The other major control structure is the **loop** statement. All the forms of the **loop** statement are designed to introduce repetition into a program. There are three basic forms of the **loop** statement:

the plain **loop** statement for infinite loops
the **for loop** statement for finite loops
the **while loop** statement for logically controlled loops

The first form of the **loop** statement is very useful. It says to repeat the statements contained in the **loop** statement forever. Forever does not really mean forever since the program will stop under some action such as control-Y, break, or escape depending on the kind of computer you are using. You should learn the way to stop infinite loops before trying **loop** statements on your computer. The program will also usually stop if power is turned off or the computer breaks or Ada detects an error in the program.

A more normal way of exiting an infinite loop is to use an **exit** statement. There are two forms of the exit statement:

   exit;

and

   exit when *Boolean expression;*

The first form usually appears in an **if** statement to cause an exit from the loop under some condition. The second form is intended to eliminate the need for the **if** statement.

```
with TEXT_IO; use TEXT_IO;

procedure FOREVER is
begin
  loop
    PUT_LINE (" Help! I can't stop! ");
  end loop;
end FOREVER;
```

This program will execute the statement contained in the loop until the program is stopped by external means. It will repeat displaying the message, "Help! I can't stop!" until the program is stopped. The actual output follows. It was stopped by a control-Y, which shows as Ŷ.

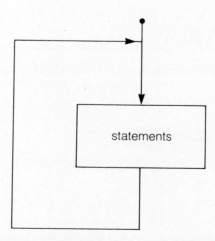

Figure 5.6   Loop Statement

```
Help! I can't stop!
Help! I can't stop!
Help! I can't stop!
Help! I can't stop!
Help! I can't stop!
^Y
```

Infinite loops are good for displaying schedules in airports, for automatic bank tellers, for games, for controlling aircraft, and many other applications. The general form of an infinite loop is

loop
    statements
end loop;

The graphical form of a **loop** statement is shown in figure 5.6.

The safest form of a loop to use is the **for loop** statement. In a **for loop** statement, you specify how many times to execute the loop. For example you may specify the loop is to be executed ten times by writing

```
for i in 1..10 loop
```

at the start of the loop. In the **for** statement, the data name after the **for** is called the *loop parameter*. It is not declared in the declaration part of the program. The **for** statement is considered to declare the loop parameter. After the loop parameter is given a name, the range of the loop parameter is specified by giving it its first and last value. The loop parameter may be used in the loop for calculations or tests, but it cannot be altered by assignment statements. The loop parameter may not be used outside the **loop** statement.

In the following example, we use a **for loop** to read in the prices of ten stocks on the New York Stock Exchange, add up the prices as we read them into the computer, and then divide the result by ten to calculate the average price.

The statements in the **for loop** will be repeated ten times. Hence the message, "Type a stock price," will be seen ten times and the computer will read in ten FLOAT numbers, each time keeping a running sum in the data object SUM. Very often a running sum is kept in a loop, which must be initialized before the loop starts. In this example, the initialization was done with an assignment statement. There is one more way to initialize data objects and that is with an assignment during declaration. For example, we could have initialized SUM by the declaration

```
SUM : FLOAT := 0.0;
```

which assigns the value 0.0 to SUM as it is declared in the declaration part of the program. Note that the only difference between this statement and a constant assignment is the lack of the **constant** keyword.

The program when executed produced the following output for some simple sample data:

```
Stock program has started to execute.
Type in price of stock
>1.0

 1.00000E+00
Type in price of stock
>2.0

 2.00000E+00
Type in price of stock
>3.0

 3.00000E+00
Type in price of stock
>4.0

 4.00000E+00
Type in price of stock
>5.0

 5.00000E+00
Type in price of stock
>6.0

 6.00000E+00
Type in price of stock
>7.0

 7.00000E+00
Type in price of stock
>8.0

 8.00000E+00
Type in price of stock
>9.0

 9.00000E+00
Type in price of stock
>10.0

 1.00000E+01
Average price of ten stocks is
 5.50000E+00
```

```ada
with TEXT_IO;
package FLOAT_IO is new TEXT_IO.FLOAT_IO(FLOAT);

with TEXT_IO, FLOAT_IO;
use  TEXT_IO, FLOAT_IO;
```

```
procedure STOCK is

-- Program to calculate average price of stocks

   SUM, PRICE, AVERAGE : FLOAT;

begin

   PUT_LINE (" Stock program has started to execute. ");
   SUM := 0.0;   -- initialize running sum

   for I in 1..10 loop
     PUT_LINE (" Type in price of stock ");
     GET (PRICE);
     NEW_LINE; PUT (PRICE); NEW_LINE;
     SUM := SUM + PRICE;
   end loop;

   AVERAGE := SUM / 10.0;

   PUT_LINE (" Average price of ten stocks is ");
   PUT (AVERAGE);

end STOCK;
```

The general form of the **for** statement is

> **for** *loop parameter name* **in** *first value . . last value* **loop**
>   *statements*
> **end loop;**

in which the range *first value . . last value* can be any discrete type such as 'A'
. . 'Z'. The graph of this control structure is shown in figure 5.7. Note that the
test for whether the loop parameter is in the range is at the beginning of the
loop.

The second form of the **for** statement is used to allow the loop parameter
to be decremented in value instead of incremented. The general form of this
second version of the **for** statement is

> **for** *loop parameter name* **in reverse** *first value . . last value* **loop**
>   *statements*
> **end loop;**

The keyword **reverse** causes the loop parameter to start at the *first value* and
to end up at the *last value*. In both forms of the **for** statement, the *first value*
must be less than the *last value*.

The last version of the **loop** statement is the **while loop** statement. The
while statement is useful for staying in a loop until some unpredictable condition occurs, for example, in performing a search on some input data or in
testing the result of a complex calculation or just for testing the time of day.

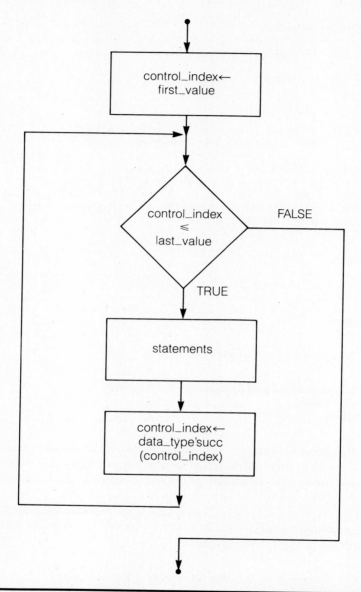

Figure 5.7 For Loop Statement

The general form of the **while** statement is

> **while** *Boolean_expression* **loop**
>   *statements*
> **end loop**;

The next program uses a **while** statement to decide when to stop purchasing from a catalog of Christmas toys. The program reads in a budget in dollars and individual purchases are made until the budget is exceeded. The program displays how much remains in the budget after each purchase and how much has been spent after each purchase.

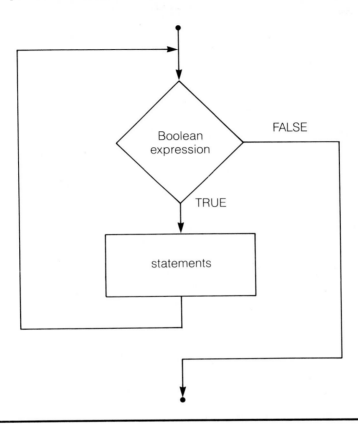

Figure 5.8   While Loop Statement

```
with TEXT_IO;
package FLOAT_IO is new TEXT_IO.FLOAT_IO(FLOAT);

with TEXT_IO, FLOAT_IO;
use  TEXT_IO, FLOAT_IO;

procedure BUDGET is

-- A budget program to keep track of the remaining amount
-- in a budget and the total amount of purchases

  AMOUNT_TO_SPEND, AMOUNT_LEFT : FLOAT;
  TOTAL_SPENT, PURCHASE : FLOAT;
```

```
begin

    PUT_LINE (" The budget program has started to execute. ");
    PUT_LINE (" Type the amount to spend in the budget ");
    GET (AMOUNT_TO_SPEND);
    NEW_LINE; PUT (AMOUNT_TO_SPEND); NEW_LINE;

    AMOUNT_LEFT := AMOUNT_TO_SPEND;

    TOTAL_SPENT := 0.0;

    while AMOUNT_LEFT > 0.0 loop
      PUT_LINE (" Type the cost of the next purchase ");
      GET (PURCHASE);
      NEW_LINE; PUT (PURCHASE); NEW_LINE;

      AMOUNT_LEFT := AMOUNT_LEFT - PURCHASE;
      TOTAL_SPENT := TOTAL_SPENT + PURCHASE;

      NEW_LINE; PUT (" Amount left in budget is ");
      PUT (AMOUNT_LEFT); NEW_LINE;
      NEW_LINE; PUT (" Amount of purchases is ");
      PUT (TOTAL_SPENT); NEW_LINE;

    end loop;

end BUDGET;
```

The budget program produced the following results:

```
 The budget program has started to execute.
 Type the amount to spend in the budget
>4000.0

 4.00000E+03
 Type the cost of the next purchase
>2500.00

 2.50000E+03

 Amount left in budget is 1.50000E+03

 Amount of purchases is  2.50000E+03
 Type the cost of the next purchase
>1500.00

 1.50000E+03

 Amount left in budget is  0.00000E+00

 Amount of purchases is 4.00000E+03
```

UNCONDITIONAL TRANSFER

There are two forms of unconditional transfer of control in Ada. One is called the **goto** statement and the other is called the **exit** statement. The **goto** statement should be avoided. Its use results in unstructured programs which are difficult to understand. The **exit** statement is sometimes useful in loops, especially for exiting infinite loops.

The **goto** statement immediately transfers control to another part of the program, which has been labeled with a name. You can set up any of the control structures that we have seen in this chapter with the use of the **goto** statement. For example, an infinite loop can be set up with the statement sequence:

```
<<INFINITE>> PUT_LINE (" I will not use goto statements. ");
             goto INFINITE;
```

This statement sequence will cause the display of "I will not use goto statements." until the program is stopped. The label used in the program is the name within << and >>.

The **exit** also should be used with care. The **exit** statement allows transfer out of a loop in the middle of the loop instead of at the top of the loop. With it, the budget program used in the last example could be rewritten to exit before AMOUNT_LEFT became negative, by using the **exit** statement to disallow the last purchase. We could add the following **if** statement in the loop after the purchase amount has been entered into the program. The **if** statement will test whether to allow the purchase. If the purchase would cause the budget to be exceeded, the purchase will be disallowed, and, after displaying the amounts, the loop will exit. Since the next statement is the **end** for the program, the program will stop.

The budget program was altered to include the **exit** statement in an **if** statement to cause an early exit.

```
while AMOUNT_LEFT > 0.0 loop
   PUT_LINE (" Type the cost of the next purchase ");
   GET (PURCHASE);
   NEW_LINE; PUT (PURCHASE); NEW_LINE;

   if AMOUNT_LEFT - PURCHASE < 0.0 then
     PUT_LINE (" Budget has been exceeded. ");
     PUT_LINE (" This purchase is not allowed. ");
     NEW_LINE; PUT (" Amount left is ");
     PUT (AMOUNT_LEFT); NEW_LINE;
     NEW_LINE; PUT_LINE (" The total amount purchased is ");
     PUT (TOTAL_SPENT); NEW_LINE;
     exit;
   end if;

   AMOUNT_LEFT := AMOUNT_LEFT - PURCHASE;
   TOTAL_SPENT := TOTAL_SPENT + PURCHASE;
```

```
    NEW_LINE; PUT (" Amount left in budget is ");
    PUT (AMOUNT_LEFT); NEW_LINE;
    NEW_LINE; PUT (" Amount of purchases is ");
    PUT (TOTAL_SPENT); NEW_LINE;
end loop;
```

The new version of the program produced the following output.

```
The budget program has started to execute.
Type the amount to spend in the budget
>4000.00


4.00000E+03
Type the cost of the next purchase
>5000.00


5.00000E+03
Budget has been exceeded.
This purchase is not allowed.


Amount left is  4.00000E+03


The total amount purchased is
0.00000E+00
```

What Have You Learned?

Conditional Control Structures

The general form of the **if** statement is

> **if** *Boolean expression* **then**
>   *statements*
> **else**
>   *statements*
> **end if;**

The general form of the **if** statement in its multiway form is

> **if** *Boolean expression* **then**
> > *statements*
>
> **elsif** *Boolean expression* **then**
> > *statements*
>
> **elsif** *Boolean expression* **then**
> > *statements*
>
> > .
> > .
> > .
>
> **else**
> > *statements*
>
> **end if**;

Both these forms of the **if** statement may omit the **else** part. The general form of the **case** statement is

> **case** *discrete data name* **is**
> > **when** *discrete data values* => *statements*
> > **when** *discrete data values* => *statements*
> >
> > > .
> > > .
> > > .
> >
> > **when** *discrete data values* => *statements*
>
> **end case**;

Discrete value range

> *first value . . last value*

Choice of values

> *first value | another value*

LOOP STRUCTURES

The general form of an infinite loop is

> **loop**
> > *statements*
>
> **end loop**;

Infinite loops can be exited with the **exit** statements:

> **exit**;

or

exit when *Boolean expression;*

The general form of the **for** statement is

for *loop parameter* in *first value . . last value* **loop**
    statements
end loop;

The general form of the **while** statement is

while *Boolean_expression* **loop**
    statements
end loop;

Unconditional Control

The **goto** statement.

goto *label;*

<<INFINITE>> PUT_LINE (" I will not use goto statements. ");
    goto INFINITE;

The **exit** statement.

exit;

Problems

1. Write a program that asks a question that requires a yes or no answer. Use the character *Y* for a yes and *N* for a no. Display appropriate responses for the answers.

2. Rewrite the program in problem 1 with a **case** statement.

3. Rewrite the program in problem 2 in an infinite loop with a **loop** statement.

4. Rewrite the program in problem 2 with a **for loop** that executes five times.

5. Write a program that will calculate the yearly interest on a loan. Type a message so that the user inputs the loan amount. If the loan amount is less than or equal to $2000.00, compute the yearly interest using a rate of 21%. If the loan amount is greater than $2000.00, compute the yearly interest using a rate of 18%.

6. Write a program to compute the sine of an angle using the following formulas:

   If the angle, theta, is between 0 and 5 degrees, compute the sine of the angle to be theta' where theta' is the angle converted to radians.

   If the angle, theta, is between 5 and 45 degrees, compute the sine of the angle to be theta' − theta' **3/6.

   If the angle, theta, is between 45 and 85 degrees, compute the sine of the angle to be theta" − theta"**3/6 where theta" is the angle 90 − theta converted to radians.

   If the angle, theta, is between 85 and 90 degrees, compute the sine of the angle to be 1.0 − theta".

7. Input a number into N and use it to compute the sum of the first N integers. That is $1 + 2 + 3 + \ldots + N$.

8. Modify the program in problem 7 to compute the average value of the sum of N integers.

$$\text{AVERAGE\_VALUE} = \frac{\text{SUM}}{N}$$

9. Modify the program in problem 7 to compute the sum of only the odd integers. Use the **rem** operation with a divisor of 2 to decide if a number is even or odd.

10. Compute two stock averages of the first ten stocks on the New York Stock Exchange. The first average is for stocks that are less than $30 a share. The second average is for stocks that are at least $30 a share.

11. Compute N! as long as N! is less than 32000. Display the result for each value of N starting at 1!.

    1! = 1
    2! = 1 * 2
    3! = 1 * 2 * 3
    N! = 1 * 2 * 3 * . . . * N

C H A P T E R
❖ 6 ❖

USER-DEFINED
TYPES

❖ You know how to use the four predefined data types in assignment statements, in expressions, and in control structures. Now you are ready to learn how to define your own data types, which can be used in assignment statements, in expressions, and in control structures much like those in which predefined data types are used.

User-defined data types provide you with much protection from common programming errors that other languages leave undetected. Ada provides some additional error-detection when the program executes using type information.

In Ada, every data type needs to be defined—you should define all your data types at a single point in the program. When a program is used for a long time, changes are inevitable; since the type definition occurs in only one place, the use of type definitions makes these changes simpler and gives you fewer chances for error.

You should be careful about the names you give data types. Unlike variables, which are generally given abstract names such as x, y, and z, data types should have names that contain some meaning to those who will be reading the program. This is particularly useful in large programs.

In chapter 3 we learned some of the operators that are available for the predefined data types. Three of these operators are available for almost all data types. Later, when we learn how to give other meanings to operators, we will learn that these three operators cannot be redefined. The three operators are the most important operators in Ada:

The comparison operators for equality and inequality
> = and /=

The assignment operator
> :=

A data type has a name, a set of values, and a set of operations.

ENUMERATED DATA TYPE

The first user-defined data type we will look at is the *enumerated data type*, which contains a detailed list of the values or identifiers that make up the data type. These can be numeric, character, or identifier values. In a list of values, the first values in the list have lower values than the latter values in the list.

Some examples of the definition of the enumerated data type are:

```
type  WEEK_DAY is  (MONDAY,   TUESDAY,   WEDNESDAY,
                     THURSDAY, FRIDAY);
type  LIGHT_STATE is (ON,  OFF);
type AUTOPILOT_STATE is (IDLE, TAKE_OFF, CRUISE, LAND);
```

In the first example, the type named WEEK_DAY has the values MONDAY, TUESDAY, WEDNESDAY, THURSDAY, and FRIDAY. A program that calculates a payroll or makes airline reservations might need to define such a data type.

The next example shows a data type named LIGHT_STATE, which has only the two values ON and OFF. A program that turns status lights on or off can use such a data type. It is better to use such a data type which has meaningful values than to use a data type such as

```
type LIGHT_STATE is  (FALSE. . TRUE);
```

The last example shows a data type named AUTOPILOT_STATE. It contains four values: IDLE, TAKE_OFF, CRUISE, and LAND. A program often has different states in which various functions are performed. In this example, a simple autopilot that flies a plane, the program has been given four states corresponding to different activities the autopilot needs to do.

The general form for the enumerated data type definition is

type *data type name* **is** (*list of values*);

To introduce the data items that store these values, we define them in the same way that we defined variables for the predefined data types. We name the variable, and then, following a colon, we name the data type. This is called a *data declaration*. Here are some examples:

```
DAY : WEEK_DAY;
POWER_LIGHT : LIGHT_STATE;
AUTOPILOT : AUTOPILOT_STATE;
```

Data declarations can come anywhere after the type declaration for the data type used in the data declaration. It is probably a good idea to place all your type declarations before your data declarations, but if another organization seems easier to read, feel free to do it that way.

We can even declare initial values and constants for data in the same manner that we did for data of the predefined data types. For example,

```
GOLF_DAY : constant WEEK_DAY := WEDNESDAY;
HALL_LIGHT : LIGHT_STATE := OFF;
```

The first example shows a constant named GOLF_DAY with the value of WEDNESDAY. The second example shows the definition of a data item named HALL_LIGHT with the initial value of OFF.

By judicious use of user-defined data types, a program can become more readable and hence informative about its functions. With the definitions that we have made, we can write statements in the executable part of the program such as

```
AUTOPILOT := CRUISE;
POWER_LIGHT := ON;
DAY := MONDAY;
```

Note that the assignment operator is available for *all* enumerated data types. We cannot state

```
AUTOPILOT := CRUISE + 1;      -- no mixing of data types
POWER_LIGHT := IDLE;          -- no mixing of data types
DAY := MONDAY + TUESDAY;      -- no arithmetic operators for
                              -- enumerations
GOLF_DAY := FRIDAY;           -- assignment to a constant
```

The Ada compiler will detect all these errors.

In addition to the assignment operator and the comparison operator for equality and inequality, all the other relational operators are available for the enumerated data types. We can test the value of expressions using $>$, $<$, $<=$, and $>=$ as well as $=$ and $/=$. We can make statements such as

```
if DAY = FRIDAY then
    PUT_LINE ("Have a nice weekend");
end if;
```

There are also two other operators that are useful for the enumerated data types, the SUCC and PRED operators we saw in chapter 3. The SUCC operator is also called the *successor operator*. It takes the next value in an enumerated list. It will *not* wrap around at the end of the list to take the first value in the list; if you try this, Ada will give you an error message. The PRED operator, also called the *predecessor operator*, takes the previous value in the enumerated list. The PRED operator is not defined for first value in the list.

Some examples of the use of these operators are

```
DAY := WEEK_DAY'SUCC (MONDAY);      -- sets day to Tuesday
DAY := WEEK_DAY'PRED (THURSDAY);   -- sets day to Wednesday
POWER_LIGHT   := LIGHT_STATE'SUCC (ON);   -- turns light off
```

The POS and VAL operators are also available for any enumerated data type. The POS operator yields the position of a value in an enumeration list. The VAL operator yields the value for a specified position in an enumeration list. Some examples of their use are

```
WEEK_DAY'POS (MONDAY)      -- expression has value of 0
WEEK_DAY'VAL (1)           -- expression has value of TUESDAY
WEEK_DAY'VAL (WEEK DAY'POS (WEDNESDAY))   -- expression has
                             -- value of WEDNESDAY
```

Our example program uses the enumerated data type to display information on aircraft flights. The program starts out defining four enumerated data types: DAY_TYPE, PLANE_TYPE, MEAL_TYPE, and TIME_TYPE. Then, four variables are defined, one for each data type. The program inputs the name of the day into the variable named DAY. Next, a test is made using a **case** statement on the value in DAY, and, as a result, a Boeing 747 is chosen to leave at 5 P.M. or a Douglas DC8 is chosen to leave at 3 P.M. The 5 P.M. flight has a dinner, and the 3 P.M. flight has a snack.

Just as with the other uses of GET and PUT in previous examples, we instantiate the TEXT_IO package for each data type. In the example, the instantiation is made inside the program after the types are defined. This is necessary because the names of the types are known only after the type definition. ENUMERATION_IO is the name of the package to be instantiated for any enumeration type. For example, the line

```
package WEEK_DAY_IO is new ENUMERATION_IO (WEEKDAY);
```

causes GET and PUT to be available for data of type WEEKDAY. If there is a data type for which you do not need to input or output information, you need not instantiate the package for the type.

```
with TEXT_IO;
use  TEXT_IO;

procedure FLIGHT_INFORMATION is
-- A program to provide flight information on the type of
-- plane, the kind of meal, and the time of flight
   type DAY_TYPE  is (SUN, MON, TUE, WED, THU, FRI, SAT);
   type PLANE_TYPE is (BOEING_747, DOUGLAS_DC_8, LOCKHEED_1011);
   type MEAL_TYPE  is (BREAKFAST, LUNCH, SNACKS, DINNER);
   type TIME_TYPE  is (FIVE_PM, THREE_PM);
```

```
      package DAY_IO    is new ENUMERATION_IO (DAY_TYPE);
      package PLANE_IO  is new ENUMERATION_IO (PLANE_TYPE);
      package MEAL_IO   is new ENUMERATION_IO (MEAL_TYPE);
      package TIME_IO   is new ENUMERATION_IO (TIME_TYPE);

      use     DAY_IO, PLANE_IO, MEAL_IO, TIME_IO;

      DAY   : DAY_TYPE;
      PLANE : PLANE_TYPE;
      MEAL  : MEAL_TYPE;
      TIME  : TIME_TYPE;

   begin

      PUT_LINE (" Flight information program has started. ");
      PUT_LINE (" Type the three letter initial for the day. ");

      GET (DAY);  NEW_LINE;

      PUT (" Flight information for "); PUT (DAY); NEW_LINE;

      case DAY is

         when MON..FRI =>
            PLANE : = BOEING_747;
            TIME  : = FIVE_PM;
            MEAL  : = DINNER;

         when others    =>
            PLANE : = DOUGLAS_DC_8;
            TIME  : = THREE_PM;
            MEAL  : = SNACKS;

      end case;

      NEW_LINE;
      PUT (" Today's plane is a "); PUT (PLANE); NEW_LINE;
      PUT (" It will leave at ");   PUT (TIME);  NEW_LINE;
      PUT (" We will serve ");      PUT (MEAL);  NEW_LINE;

   end FLIGHT_INFORMATION;
```

Two samples of the program output are shown below:

```
 Flight information program has started.
 Type the three letter initial for the day.
>MON

 Flight information for MON

 Today's plane is a BOEING_747
 It will leave at FIVE_PM
 We will serve DINNER
```

```
Flight information program has started.
Type the three letter initial for the day.
>SUN

Flight information for SUN

Today's plane is a DOUGLAS_DC_8
It will leave at THREE_PM
We will serve SNACKS
```

The two executions show the result of executing the two parts of the **case** statement. The enumeration output is normally shown in uppercase.

ATTRIBUTES

Attributes are special and often useful operations on values of a data type, and every enumerated data type has two attributes that are often used in a computer program. These attributes are FIRST and LAST. An attribute of a data type is always written with a single quote or apostrophe between the data type name and the attribute name. The 'FIRST attribute is the first value in the enumeration and the 'LAST attribute is the last value in the enumeration.

Some examples of attributes for the two enumerations are

```
WEEKDAY'FIRST     which has a value of MONDAY
WEEKDAY'LAST      which has a value of FRIDAY


AUTOPILOT_STATE'FIRST     which has a value of IDLE
AUTOPILOT_STATE'LAST      which has a value of LAND


LIGHT_STATE'FIRST     which has a value of ON
LIGHT_STATE'LAST      which has a value of OFF
```

Where possible, it is better to use attributes in a program instead of the constant values in the list. One place in particular where an enumerated type name should be used instead of values is in **for** statements. For example, a loop over the weekdays could be written as

```
for I in MONDAY..FRIDAY loop
    -- statements
end loop;
```

is better written as

```
for I in WEEK_DAY'RANGE loop
    -- statements
end loop;
```

The reference to the data type in the loop instead of a constant value means that if the definition of WEEKDAY was ever changed to be MONDAY to THURSDAY, only the one place where WEEKDAY was defined would need to be changed.

The next program uses attributes to loop through a list of cities. Each instance of the loop asks for the population of the city. After all the cities have had their population specified, the program displays the value for the largest city.

The program demonstrates a common technique in finding the largest value in a group of data. The maximum value, LARGEST_NUMBER, is initially set to 1; as the next values are input to the computer, the trial maximum is tested against the new values. When the test establishes that the new value is larger than the old maximum, the maximum is reset to the new value. The output from the program when run follows.

```
POPULATION PROGRAM HAS BEGUN.
 Type in population for city LOS_ANGELES
>7000000

    7000000
 Type in population for city SAN_FRANCISCO
>2000000

    2000000
 Type in population for city SAN_DIEGO
>1000000

    1000000
 Type in population for city SANTA_BARBARA
>80000

      80000

 Largest population is      7000000

with TEXT_IO;
use  TEXT_IO;
procedure POPULATION is

-- Program to input city populations and to select the
-- largest population

   type CITY_TYPE is (LOS_ANGELES, SAN_FRANCISCO, SAN_DIEGO,
                      SANTA_BARBARA);

   package CITY_IO is new TEXT_IO.ENUMERATION_IO (CITY_TYPE);
   package INTEGER_IO is new TEXT_IO.INTEGER_IO (INTEGER);
```

```
   use CITY_IO, INTEGER_IO;

   POPULATION : INTEGER;
   LARGEST_POPULATION : INTEGER := 1;

begin

   PUT_LINE (" POPULATION PROGRAM HAS BEGUN. ");
   for I in CITY_TYPE loop
      PUT (" Type in population for city "); PUT (I);
      NEW_LINE;
      GET (POPULATION);
      NEW_LINE;
      PUT (POPULATION);
      NEW_LINE;
      if POPULATION > LARGEST_POPULATION then
         LARGEST_POPULATION := POPULATION;
      end if;
   end loop;
   NEW_LINE;
   PUT (" Largest population is "); PUT (LARGEST_POPULATION);
end POPULATION;
```

Attributes are also useful in other statements, such as in the next example, which uses a successor operation. Attributes protect against the erroneous use of the operator with an **if** statement testing the last value in the list. In the case of the last value in the list, the **if** statement selects the first value in the list.

```
   if AUTOPILOT /= AUTOPILOT_STATE'LAST then
       AUTOPILOT := AUTOPILOT_STATE'SUCC (AUTOPILOT);
   else
       AUTOPILOT := AUTOPILOT_STATE'FIRST;
   end if;
```

If at some later time one more state is added to the list of autopilot states, these lines of code would not need to be changed. Whereas if the test were

```
   if AUTOPILOT /= LAND then
       AUTOPILOT := AUTOPILOT_STATE'SUCC (AUTOPILOT);
   else
       AUTOPILOT := IDLE;
   end if;
```

the test as well as the data type definition would need to be changed.

Two of the predefined data types are really enumerated data types. For example, the type BOOLEAN is defined in Ada to be

```
   type BOOLEAN is (FALSE, TRUE);
```

The type CHARACTER is defined in Appendix B to be the list of all characters in the 128 ASCII character set. The attribute CHARACTER'FIRST is NUL and CHARACTER'LAST is DEL.

The type INTEGER is defined to be the list of integers from the most negative integer implemented in the computer, which is INTEGER'FIRST, to INTEGER'LAST, the largest possible integer implemented in the computer. The INTEGER data type shares many of the attributes of enumeration types.

Subtype

Once you have defined an enumeration type it is often useful to pick out a subrange of the enumeration. This is done with the use of subtypes. A *subtype* in Ada has all the operations of the base type but with only a subrange of the values of the base type. A useful subtype, for instance, is the definition of capital letters from the base type CHARACTER, which contains all the character values. Such a definition is accomplished with

```
subtype CAPITAL_LETTERS is CHARACTER range 'A'..'Z';
```

Two subtypes are so useful that they have been predefined for you. These are the NATURAL subtype and the POSITIVE subtype, which both have the INTEGER data type as a base. They are defined as

```
subtype NATURAL is INTEGER range 0 .. INTEGER'LAST;
subtype POSITIVE is INTEGER range 1 .. INTEGER'LAST;
```

The NATURAL subtype has the values from 0 to the largest integer available, and the POSITIVE subtype has the values from 1 to the largest integer available. Both these subtypes have all the numeric operations defined for the INTEGER data type.

In most programs, extensive use of subranges should be used for the numeric types. By placing constraints on numeric data with subtypes, Ada will detect many more errors than if we just use the predefined data types. It is unlikely that the full range of values for any object is from the largest possible number on the computer to the smallest possible number on the computer. For example, the temperature-conversion program we examined in chapter 3 can be improved if a subtype is used for the temperature, which could go from −273 to 10000 degrees or perhaps from only −50 to 212 degrees depending on the application.

The subtype may also be used for the fourth predefined data type, FLOAT, which is not an enumerated data type. The FLOAT data type is an approximation to the real numbers and there are far too many real numbers to list. Some examples of subtypes for FLOAT are:

```
subtype ALTITUDE is FLOAT range 0.0 .. 100_000.0;
subtype SPEED is FLOAT range 0.0 .. 3.0e10;
subtype HEADING is FLOAT range 0.0 .. 360.0;
```

The first example defines a new subtype named ALTITUDE that has all the numeric operations of the FLOAT data type but is constrained in range to be between 0.0 and 100_000.0. This could represent the possible altitudes for an airplane that is never expected to land in Death Valley. The second example names a subtype called SPEED that can take on values between 0.0 and 3.0e10, or a maximum speed of the speed of light if the units are in centimeters per second. The third subtype represents types that might be used for heading angles between 0.0 and 360.0 degrees.

The general form for subtype declarations is

subtype *data type name* **is** *base data type name* **range** *first value .. last value;*

A subtype does not introduce a new type. It merely sets up a more restrictive range. You can use all the operations of the base type with data of the subtype. Also, data of different subtypes can be assigned to each other when they are in the correct range. For example, the following small procedure contains legal assignment statements between subtypes.

```
procedure ASSIGN is
--   Program demonstrates legal assignments between
--   data of different subtypes but same base type

   subtype LOW_HEIGHT_TYPE  is FLOAT range 0.0..100.0;
   subtype HIGH_HEIGHT_TYPE is FLOAT range 100.0..10000.0;

   LOW  : LOW_HEIGHT_TYPE;
   HIGH : HIGH_HEIGHT_TYPE;
   BOUNDARY : FLOAT := 100.0;

begin

   LOW   := BOUNDARY;
   HIGH  := BOUNDARY;
   LOW   := HIGH;

end ASSIGN;
```

CONVERSION BETWEEN TYPES

You can convert between data types using a *conversion operation*. For example, to convert between FLOAT and INTEGER in the case where these data declarations have been made:

```
TEMPERATURE : FLOAT := 32.0;
BOILING : constant INTEGER := 212;
HEIGHT : INTEGER;
MT_WHITNEY : constant FLOAT := 14496.1;
```

we can state,

```
TEMPERATURE := FLOAT (BOILING);
HEIGHT := INTEGER (MT_WHITNEY);
```

Conversion is possible between all the numeric data types and between related subtypes. Conversion is possible between all types that share the same values.

The general form for type conversion is

data type name (*data object name*)

The type conversion is an expression that may be used in an assignment statement or a control statement.

The next program uses subtypes and expressions that include several subtypes. It computes the speed of a runner in miles per hour given the distance traveled in feet and the time in seconds. A sample execution of the program follows.

```
The runner's speed program has started

Type in a distance in feet
>1320.0

1.32000E+03
Type in a time in seconds
>122.0

1.22000E+02
The runner's speed is   7.37704E+00 miles per hour
```

```
with TEXT_IO;
package FLOAT_IO is new TEXT_IO.FLOAT_IO (FLOAT);

with TEXT_IO, FLOAT_IO;
use  TEXT_IO, FLOAT_IO;
procedure RUNNER_SPEED is
-- Program to calculate a runner's speed in miles per hour
-- given the distance traveled in feet
-- and the time in seconds

-- speed type is good for 0 to 25 miles per hour
  subtype SPEED_TYPE is FLOAT range 0.0..25.0;

-- distance type good for 0 to 100 miles in feet
  subtype DISTANCE_TYPE is FLOAT range 0.0..528_000.0;

-- time type good for 0 to one day in seconds
  subtype TIME_TYPE is FLOAT range 0.0..60.0*60.0*24.0;

-- data items
  FEET_PER_MILE    : constant := 5280.0;
  SECONDS_PER_HOUR : constant := 60.0*60.0;

  SPEED    : SPEED_TYPE;
  DISTANCE : DISTANCE_TYPE;
  TIME     : TIME_TYPE;
```

```
begin

    PUT_LINE (" The runner's speed program has started ");
    NEW_LINE;
    PUT (" Type in a distance in feet ");   NEW_LINE;
    GET (DISTANCE);   NEW_LINE;
    PUT (DISTANCE);   NEW_LINE;
    PUT (" Type in a time in seconds ");   NEW_LINE;
    GET (TIME);   NEW_LINE;
    PUT (TIME);   NEW_LINE;

    SPEED := (DISTANCE/FEET_PER_MILE)/(TIME/SECONDS_PER_HOUR);

    PUT (" The runner's speed is "); PUT (SPEED);
    PUT (" miles per hour "); NEW_LINE;

end RUNNER_SPEED;
```

WHAT HAVE YOU LEARNED?

The three most important operators available for almost all data types are

The comparison operators for equality and inequality
    = and /=
The assignment operator
    :=

The general form for the enumerated data type definition is

type data type name **is** (list of values);

Attributes for enumerated data types include

'FIRST
'LAST

Examples are INTEGER'FIRST, CHARACTER'LAST
    The general form for subtype declarations is

subtype data type name **is** base data type name   **range** first value .. last value;

The general form for type conversion is

data type name (data object name)

The type conversion is an expression that may be used in a statement such as an assignment statement or a control statement.

Problems

1. Determine which statements are in error. Correct them.

   a. type MONEY = PENNY, NICKEL, DIME, QUARTER

   b. CHANGE : type MONEY,

   c. QUARTER : = 25

   d. CHANGE : = SUCC DIME;

   e. CHANGE: = PRED (PENNY);

2. Define a data type that can take on values of FINE, SLEEPY, ILL, and AWAKE.

3. Define a data type that can take on the values SQUARE, TRIANGLE, and RECTANGLE. Write a program to ask a person to answer yes or no to questions indicating which shape the person is thinking of.

4. Define a data type that can take on the values HOT, COLD, and TEMPERATE. Write a program to read in a temperature and display if it is hot, cold, or temperate. Let hot temperatures be between 40 and 100 degrees centigrade. Let cold temperatures be between 0 and −50 degrees centigrade, and let temperate temperatures be between 1 and 39 degrees centigrade. All other temperatures will not be included in the legal definition for temperatures.

5. Write a program to display the attributes covered in this chapter for the four predefined data types: CHARACTER, BOOLEAN, INTEGER, and FLOAT.

6. Write a program to input a character. If it is a letter, display, " It is a letter". If it is a digit, display, " It is a digit". If it is a punctuation mark, display, " It is a punctuation mark". If it is some other character, display, " It is a control or special character".

7. Write a program to input the name of a day of the week. Display the name of the previous day in the week. If the input is "Sunday," the program should output "Saturday."

8. List the values for

   a. BOOLEAN'FIRST

   b. CITY_TYPE'LAST -- from the population program

   c. NATURAL'FIRST

   d. POSITIVE'FIRST

   e. CHARACTER'LAST

9. Alter the RUNNER_SPEED program to input the time and the distance in whole numbers (INTEGER) representing the distance in yards and to output the speed in miles per hour in FLOAT.

10. Alter the population program to output the name of the city with the largest population along with the size of the population.

11. Write a program to input the name of a month and to output the number of days in that month. Use the assumption that in years divisible by 4, but not divisible by 100, the number of days in February is 29. In other years, the number of days in February is 28.

CHAPTER
❖ 7 ❖

DATA STRUCTURES

❖ Up to now, we have used single data items. In many computer applications, however, we will want to group many data items together under the same name. This chapter covers three useful groupings: arrays, strings, and records.

ARRAYS

Arrays are ordered collections of data items, each of which has the same data type. Examples of arrays include the number of products a company sells each day of the month, the temperature in each area of a plant, or the number of seats in each kind of wide-body jet.

The best way to define an array is first to declare the array data type and then declare the array using the array data type. This is much like the definition of an enumerated type variable where we first defined the enumerated type and then used it to declare the variable.

To define an array data type, we first define the name of the array data type, the data type for each data item in the array, and the indices, or the way in which each item in the array is identified, for the array. We define the type of the index and the range of the index. Each item in the array is often called an *element* of the array or a *component* of the array.

For example, to define an array of the number of products a company sells each day of the month, we can use an array that defines a group of 31 integers.

```
type PRODUCTS_ARRAY is array (INTEGER range 1..31)  of INTEGER;
NUMBER_OF_PRODUCTS_SOLD :  PRODUCTS_ARRAY;
```

The type definition is named PRODUCTS_ARRAY. Each element in the array is of the type specified after the keyword **of;** in this example each element is an INTEGER. The part of the definition enclosed within parentheses defines the array indices. This example has a single index of the type INTEGER, and the index can have values between 1 and 31 as specified by the range expression **range** 1..31. You can use any of the discrete types (enumeration type or integer type) as indices, but you cannot use a floating-point type as an index. A floating-point type is an approximation to the real numbers and can theoretically take on an infinite number of values.

To use such an array in an assignment statement, we state the name of the array and specify which component we want to use within parentheses:

```
NUMBER_OF_PRODUCTS_SOLD (1) := 5_000;
```

This statement assigns the value 5,000 to the first element in the array. (Remember from chapter 3 that we use an underscore in numbers.) In our example, 5,000 products were sold on the first day of the month. We might portray the array as shown in figure 7.1, which has 31 slots, one for each possible value of the index. The first element has been set to 5,000 as a result of the assignment statement. The rest of the array does not show any value to demonstrate that it has not been set.

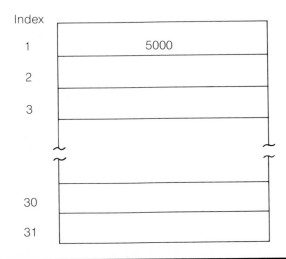

Figure 7.1   NUMBER_OF PRODUCTS_SOLD array

We can also use array elements in tests:

```
if NUMBER_OF_PRODUCTS_SOLD (10) >= 1000 then
    PUT_LINE (" Congratulations. It looks like a great month");
else
    PUT_LINE (" Increase the advertising budget ");
end if;
```

In our second example, an array of temperatures is specified for five different locations in a plant: the inlet, pump, radiator, room, and outlet.

Although we could specify an array where the index lies between 1 and 5, it is better to name a small number of values in an enumerated type.

```
type PLACES is (INLET, PUMP, RADIATOR, ROOM, OUTLET);
type TEMPERATURE_TYPE is array (PLACES range INLET..OUTLET)
                                of FLOAT;
TEMPERATURES : TEMPERATURE_TYPE;
```

When the entire enumeration range is used in the array definition, as in this example, the index definition may be simplified to just

```
array (PLACES)
```

This is preferable to using the **range** notation to define the possible index values. If you need to change the number of places that the program must handle, it will only be necessary to change the type definition. Now, instead of indexing by integers, we use the values of the enumeration:

```
TEMPERATURES (ROOM) := 68.5;
```

After this assignment, the TEMPERATURES array would appear as in figure 7.2.

It is usually a good idea not only to define the array index separately from the array definition, but also to define a type or subtype definition for

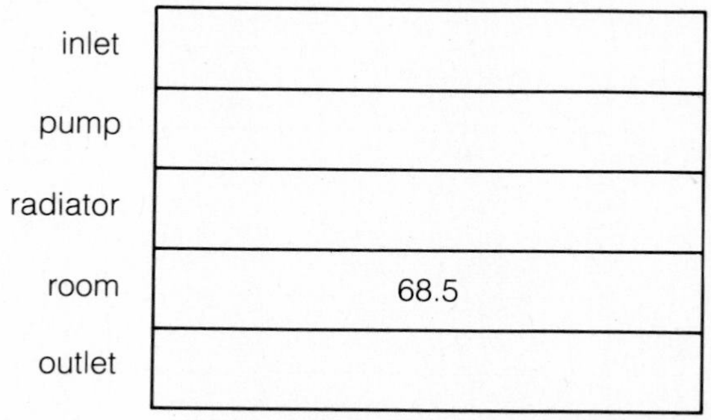

inlet	
pump	
radiator	
room	68.5
outlet	

Figure 7.2 TEMPERATURES array

each array element. This keeps each definition shorter, more readable, and, most important, assigns a type name to each element that can be used in expressions. In our third example, which specifies the number of seats on wide-body aircraft, we follow this guideline.

```
type WIDE_BODY_AIRCRAFT is ( B_747, DC_10, L_1011 );
subtype SEAT_TYPE is INTEGER range 150 ..550;
type NUMBER_OF_SEATS_ARRAY is array (WIDE_BODY_AIRCRAFT)
                        of SEAT_TYPE;
NUMBER_OF_SEATS : NUMBER_OF_SEATS_ARRAY;
```

The general form of a type definition for an array is

type *array type name* **is array** (*index definition*) **of** *component type definition*;

To refer to an element in an array, the general form of a reference is

array object name (*array index value*)

We can give an initial value to an array in a declaration or even have a constant array. In either case, an assignment to each array element is specified using one of two possible notations, *positional* or *named order* notation, for the group assignment. Either notation is also known as an *aggregate*.

In positional notation, each element is assigned a value from a list of values, with the first value going to the first element and so forth. For example, to give an initial value to our TEMPERATURES array,

```
TEMPERATURES : TEMPERATURE_TYPE := (50.0, 60.0, 70.0, 65.0, 63.0);
```

sets TEMPERATURES (INLET) to 50.0, TEMPERATURES (PUMP) to 60.0, and so forth, as figure 7.3 shows.

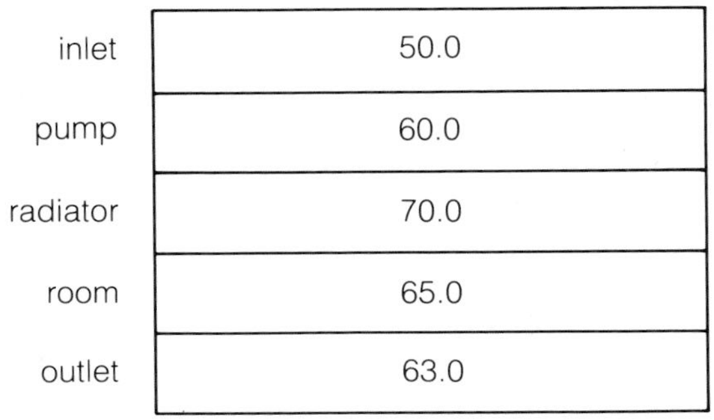

inlet	50.0
pump	60.0
radiator	70.0
room	65.0
outlet	63.0

Figure 7.3 Initial value of TEMPERATURES array

In named order notation, the indices are named in any position order:

```
TEMPERATURES : TEMPERATURE_TYPE := (INLET => 50.0,
                                     PUMP  => 60.0,
                                     RADIATOR => 70.0,
                                     ROOM =>  65.0,
                                     OUTLET => 63.0);
```

To set several elements to the same value, such as might be done to set the initial value to zero, there are two possible notations.

```
TEMPERATURES : TEMPERATURE_TYPE := (INLET..OUTLET  => 0.0);
```

or

```
TEMPERATURES : TEMPERATURE_TYPE := ( others => 0.0);
```

Both these notations will set all the array elements to zero. The keyword **others** can also be used to set the remaining elements in an array using positional notation.

A constant array containing constant temperatures can be defined as

```
EXPECTED_TEMPERATURES : constant TEMPERATURE_TYPE :=
                         (INLET => 50.0,
                          OUTLET => 60.0,
                          others => 65.0);
```

This sets EXPECTED_TEMPERATURES (INLET) to 50.0, EXPECTED_TEMPERATURES (OUTLET) to 60.0, and the other three elements to 65.0.

The assignment operator and the tests for equality and inequality are available for all array data types, so we can use them in such statements as

```
TEMPERATURES := EXPECTED_TEMPERATURES;
```

ARRAY ATTRIBUTES

The next program inputs the temperature for each place into the list of places and stores the temperature in the array to use for later processing. In this program, a loop over the places sums up the temperatures; note that the loop uses the type name PLACES—this keeps the loop count independent of the number of places. If another place was to be considered in the average, the only line of the program that would need changing would be the **type** declaration for PLACES. Where possible, it is recommended that loops use the type name or range attributes instead of specific counts.

The program also uses an array attribute, 'LENGTH, which gives the length of the array, which in this example is five elements long. The 'LENGTH attribute keeps track of the number of places in the array. The type of the 'LENGTH attribute is UNIVERSAL_INTEGER. The average temperature is calculated by dividing the sum by the value of the 'LENGTH attribute.

Two other useful array attributes are the 'FIRST and the 'LAST attribute. We saw these attributes for the predefined data types. For those types, 'FIRST and 'LAST give the values for the smallest and largest values of the type. For arrays, the attributes 'FIRST and 'LAST give the values of the first and last indices of the array. TEMPERATURE'FIRST is INLET and TEMPERATURE'LAST is OUTLET.

LOOPS AND ARRAYS

Loops are commonly used with arrays

to test each element of the array against some value, such as,
to test which places in the array have temperatures greater than 65 degrees;
to sum up all the values in the array, such as, to calculate the average temperature;
to search for some value in the array, as when a search is made for temperatures equal to 70 degrees.

```
with TEXT_IO;
use  TEXT_IO;
procedure TEMPERATURE_AVERAGE is

-- Program to calculate the average temperature over
-- a number of different places

   type PLACES is (INLET, PUMP, RADIATOR, ROOM, OUTLET);
   subtype TEMPERATURE_TYPE is FLOAT range 0.0..212.0;
   type TEMPERATURE_ARRAY is array (PLACES) of TEMPERATURE_TYPE;

   package PLACE_IO is new ENUMERATION_IO (PLACES);
   package TEMPERATURE_IO is new FLOAT_IO (TEMPERATURE_TYPE);

   use PLACE_IO, TEMPERATURE_IO;

   TEMPERATURES : TEMPERATURE_ARRAY;
   SUM : FLOAT   := 0.0;
   AVERAGE : TEMPERATURE_TYPE;
   LENGTH  : INTEGER;

begin
   PUT_LINE (" Temperature average program has started. ");
   for I in PLACES loop
     PUT (" Type temperature for "); PUT (I); NEW_LINE;
     GET (TEMPERATURES (I)); NEW_LINE;
     PUT (TEMPERATURES (I)); NEW_LINE;

     SUM := SUM + TEMPERATURES (I);

   end loop;
```

```
LENGTH   := TEMPERATURES'LENGTH;
AVERAGE := SUM / FLOAT (LENGTH);
PUT (" Average temperature is "); PUT (AVERAGE);
NEW_LINE;

  end TEMPERATURE_AVERAGE;
```

The program produced this output when executed with some sample data.

```
Temperature average program has started.
Type temperature for INLET
>50.0

 5.00000E+01
 Type temperature for PUMP
>60.0

 6.00000E+01
 Type temperature for RADIATOR
>70.0

 7.00000E+01
 Type temperature for ROOM
>65.0

 6.50000E+01
 Type temperature for OUTLET
>63.0

 6.30000E+01
 Average temperature is 6.16000E+01
```

TWO-DIMENSIONAL ARRAYS

In some applications it is desirable to keep two pieces of information together in one array, for example, the x and y coordinates of a graph to be plotted or the time at which a measurement is taken. This is done with two-dimensional arrays. Ada allows you to use any number of dimensions in arrays, it is just necessary to specify the indices for each dimension.

In the following example a two-dimensional array that uses four places for the first index and five different times for the second index is defined.

```
type PLACES is (INLET, RADIATOR, ROOM, OUTLET);
type TIMES is (MORNING, NOON, AFTERNOON, EVENING, NIGHT);
type TEMPERATURE_ARRAY is array (PLACES, TIMES) of FLOAT;
TEMPERATURES : TEMPERATURE_ARRAY;
```

We can then refer to an element of the array:

```
TEMPERATURES (PUMP, NOON) := 50.0;
```

Two-dimensional arrays are also commonly found in mathematics—matrices are best represented with two-dimensional arrays.

The following program defines three arrays named A, B, and C. These matrices may be portrayed as figure 7.4 shows. Each array has two rows and three columns. In the definition of the type for the array, the first index range specification defines the indices for the rows and the second index range specification defines the indices for the columns. The two specifications are separated by a comma. To select an element in the array named A, we need to specify the row number and the column number. For example, A(1,2) names the element in the first row, second column. Using the figure, this element is set to the value 7. Just as with the one-dimensional arrays, it is possible to set the array element by element using positional or named notation.

$$
\begin{array}{ccc}
A & B & C
\end{array}
$$

$$
\begin{bmatrix} 2 & 7 & 5 \\ 6 & 3 & 2 \end{bmatrix} + \begin{bmatrix} 6 & 7 & 6 \\ 1 & 2 & 8 \end{bmatrix} = \begin{bmatrix} 8 & 14 & 11 \\ 7 & 5 & 10 \end{bmatrix}
$$

Figure 7.4   Two Dimensional Arrays

Some examples of setting the array named A to the values shown in the figure 7.4 are

A := ((2, 7, 5), (6, 3, 2)); -- positional notation

or

A := (1 => (2, 7, 5), 2 => (6, 3, 2)); -- combined named
                                       -- and positional notation

or

A := (1 => (1 => 2, 2 => 7, 3 => 5), 2 => (1 => 6, 2 => 3, 3 => 2));

Multidimensional arrays also have the attributes of 'FIRST, 'LAST, 'RANGE, and 'LENGTH. However, for multidimensional arrays, we need to specify which dimension the attribute is for. This is done by writing the dimension number in parentheses after the name of the attribute. For example, A'LAST(1) refers to the last index value for the first dimension of A. In our example, A'LAST(1) is 2 and A'LAST(2) is 3.

In the following program the elements are set one by one in a loop within a loop, this is called a *nested loop*. Nested loops commonly appear in programs that use two-dimensional arrays. The outermost loop indexes the rows, and the innermost loop indexes the columns in the matrix. The sequence of events is that the loop control variable, I, is set to 1 and then the loop control variable, J, is set to 1 , 2, and 3 before the value for I is changed. Next I is set to 2 and J is set to 1, 2, and 3. At each combination, a value of the matrix is set.

```
with TEXT_IO;
package INTEGER_IO is new TEXT_IO.INTEGER_IO (INTEGER);

with TEXT_IO, INTEGER_IO;
use  TEXT_IO, INTEGER_IO;
procedure ADD_MATRICES is
   type SMALL_MATRIX is array (INTEGER range 1..2,
                               INTEGER range 1..3) of INTEGER;
   A,B,C : SMALL_MATRIX;
begin
  PUT (" The add matrices program is beginning.");
  NEW_LINE;
  PUT (" Type in the six values for the matrix A in row order ");
  NEW_LINE;
  for I in  SMALL_MATRIX'RANGE(1) loop
    for J in SMALL_MATRIX'RANGE(2) loop
      GET (A(I,J));
    end loop;
  end loop;
  NEW_LINE;
  PUT (" Type in the six values for the matrix B in row order ");
  NEW_LINE;
  for I in SMALL_MATRIX'RANGE(1) loop
    for J in SMALL_MATRIX'RANGE(2) loop
      GET (B(I,J));
    end loop;
  end loop;
  NEW_LINE;
  PUT (" The result of adding the two matrices is ");
  NEW_LINE;
  for I in SMALL_MATRIX'RANGE(1) loop
    for J in SMALL_MATRIX'RANGE(2) loop
      C(I,J) := A(I,J) + B(I,J);
      PUT (C(I,J));
    end loop;
  NEW_LINE;
  end loop;
end ADD_MATRICES;
```

This is output from the ADD_MATRICES program using the data from figure 7.4.

```
The add matrices program is beginning.
Type in the six values for the matrix A in row order
>2 7 5
>6 3 2

Type in the six values for the matrix B in row order
>6 7 6
>1 2 8

The result of adding the two matrices is
        8              14             11
        7               5             10
```

First, the values of the matrix A are set, and the same is done for the matrix B. Last, the matrix C is set to the sum of matrix A and B by adding together the individual elements of the two matrices. As each element in the matrix C is calculated, the result is displayed. The loops are controlled with the 'RANGE attribute. For example, SMALL_MATRIX'RANGE(2) yields range expression 1..3, which is the second dimension of the array type.

ARRAY OF ARRAY

Occasionally it is also useful to define each component of an array as an array. For example, in using displays that can display one of several pages of information, each page can be a two-dimensional array. The definition for such an array can take the form:

```
type DISPLAY_PAGE is array (INTEGER  range  1..24,
                     INTEGER  range 1..80) of CHARACTER;
type PAGES_TYPE is array (INTEGER  range   1..4) of
                     DISPLAY_PAGE;
PAGES : PAGES_TYPE;
```

To reference an element in the third page, second row, fourth column, we write

```
PAGES (3) (2,4)
```

STRINGS

The STRING data type is a predefined data type that uses a special case of an array data type called an *unconstrained array*. In an unconstrained array, the array elements are specified and the type of the index is specified, but the size of the array is not specified.

The definition for the STRING data type is based on the POSITIVE subtype, which is also predefined. You can use these definitions in your program without restating them.

```
subtype POSITIVE is INTEGER range 1 .. INTEGER'LAST;
type STRING is array (POSITIVE range <>) of CHARACTER;
```

The definition of the STRING data type states that it is an array of characters. The "<>" symbol in the index definition for STRING is called a *box;* it means that the specification of the indices is to come later, and that the indices will be POSITIVE.

The data declaration of a STRING gives the type of the STRING and the index values of the STRING, such as

```
NAME : STRING (1..10);   -- 10 character string
TOWN : STRING (1..15);   -- 15 character string
ZIP_CODE : STRING (1..6);  -- 6 character string
HOME : constant STRING := "Santa Barbara";
```

The notation for strings is to place them within double quotes, as was done in the constant assignment HOME. Ada differentiates between strings and characters. Characters are placed within single quotes. Although the string named HOME is thirteen characters long, you do not need to specify the number of characters when you have defined it as a constant string.

Some examples of assignments to strings using various notations are

```
NAME := "Judy Smith";
NAME := ('J', 'u', 'd', 'y', ' ', 'S', 'm', 'i', 't', 'h');
```

These both set NAME to the value "Judy Smith".

In the first assignment example, the normal notation for a character string is used. In the second assignment, the positional notation for assigning to each element of the array is used. Since each element of a STRING is a CHARACTER, the individual characters are used.

A slice of an array is a cut through an array. Since strings are arrays, a slice of a string has the same notation as a slice of an array. In the following line, we see an example of a slice from a string being set to another string.

```
TOWN (1..13) := HOME;
```

This assignment sets the first thirteen characters of TOWN to the string named HOME, which is set to "Santa Barbara". The range expression 1..13 is called a *slice*.

A useful operator for strings is the *concatenation* operator, "&", which puts two strings together. For example, if we wrote

```
TOWN := HOME & "  ";
```

the object named TOWN would be set to the fifteen-character string defined by the concatenation of HOME and two blanks.

Similarly, the assignment

```
NAME := "Judy " & "Smith";
```

would set NAME to be the ten-character string "Judy Smith".

Strings in Ada are fixed in length; for instance, you may not put "George Washington" in NAME because "George Washington" is too long. It contains sixteen characters and there is room for only ten characters in NAME. You also cannot put in NAME a string less than ten characters long such as "Joe" unless you pad the name with blanks or refer to a slice of the string. You must always put ten characters in an assignment to NAME because Ada checks that the number of characters on the left side of an assignment statement is equal to the number on the right side of an assignment statement.

```
NAME := "Joe";   -- illegal, too short
NAME := "Sammy Davis Junior";  -- illegal, too long
NAME (1..3) := "Joe"; -- ok, but be careful
NAME := "Joe       "; -- ok
```

Although a slice is acceptable, there is a danger that what was left in positions 4 to 10 of the string will not be consistent with the new value. Hence it is recommended that the full string be set where possible.

```
with TEXT_IO;
package INTEGER_IO is new TEXT_IO.INTEGER_IO (INTEGER);
```

```
with TEXT_IO, INTEGER_IO;
use  TEXT_IO, INTEGER_IO;
procedure TELEPHONE_LIST is
-- Program to look up telephone numbers
   type NAME_ARRAY is array  (INTEGER range 1..4)
                             of STRING(1..4);
   type TELEPHONE_ARRAY is array (INTEGER range 1..4)
                             of INTEGER;
   NAMES : NAME_ARRAY := ( "Jane", "John", "Mary", "Dave");
   NUMBERS : TELEPHONE_ARRAY  := (964_0074, 968_1254,
                                  967_2837, 987_2176);
   NAME   : STRING (1..4);
   NUMBER : INTEGER;
begin
   PUT_LINE (" Telephone number program has started ");
   PUT (" Type a name ");   NEW_LINE;
   GET (NAME); NEW_LINE;
   for I in NAME_ARRAY'RANGE loop
     if NAME = NAMES (I) then
       PUT ( " Telephone number is "); PUT (NUMBERS(I));
     end if;
   end loop;
end TELEPHONE_LIST;
```

In the preceding program, an array of four names and an array of four telephone numbers are given initial values. The array of four names is meant to correspond to the array of four telephone numbers. When a name is typed in while the program is running, the program will test each element of the names array for equality with the name typed in. If found, the value of the telephone number for that name will be displayed.

The program executed four times to produce this output:

```
Telephone number program has started
Type a name
>Mary

Telephone number is     9672837




Telephone number program has started
Type a name
>John

Telephone number is     9681254




Telephone number program has started
Type a name
>Jane

Telephone number is     9640074
```

```
Telephone number program has started
Type a name
>Dave

Telephone number is     9872176
```

BIT STRINGS

In many programs that receive data from special devices such as radio equipment and telephone equipment, the data comes into the computer in what are commonly called *bit strings*. There is no predefined data type for the bit string in Ada, but it is easy to define a BIT_STRING data type as an array of Booleans just as the STRING type was defined.

```
type BIT_STRING is array (POSITIVE range<> )
                       of BOOLEAN;
```

Now each element of an array of the type BIT_STRING can take on values of TRUE or FALSE. We can declare BIT_STRING objects such as

```
STATUS_REGISTER : BIT_STRING (1..8) := ( 1..8 => FALSE );
INPUT_REGISTER  : BIT_STRING (1..8) := ( others => TRUE);
RESULT_REGISTER : BIT_STRING (1..8);
```

and perform logical operations such as

```
RESULT_REGISTER := STATUS_REGISTER and INPUT_REGISTER;
RESULT_REGISTER := STATUS_REGISTER or INPUT_REGISTER;
```

In the first assignment RESULT_REGISTER is set to (1..8 => FALSE) because all eight bits in STATUS_REGISTER are FALSE. In the second assignment statement, RESULT_REGISTER is set to (1..8 => TRUE) because all eight bits in INPUT_REGISTER are TRUE. This manipulation of bits in a single statement allows Ada to perform logical operations on groups of bits very quickly. In many implementations of Ada, TRUE will be represented as a "1" and FALSE will be represented as a "0" as figure 7.5 shows.

	1	2	3	4	5	6	7	8
STATUS_REGISTER	FALSE 0	FALSE 0	FALSE 0	FALSE 0	FALSE 0	FALSE 0	FALSE 0	FALSE 0

	1	2	3	4	5	6	7	8
INPUT_REGISTER	TRUE 1	TRUE 1	TRUE 1	TRUE 1	TRUE 1	TRUE 1	TRUE 1	TRUE 1

Figure 7.5   Bit Strings

ARRAY SUBTYPES

We have seen two useful type definitions for unconstrained arrays, STRING and BIT_STRING. In many programs the unconstrained array is extremely useful to define a general type of array that is later given dimensions. Two useful examples are

```
type TABLE is array (INTEGER range <>) of INTEGER;
type MATRIX is array (INTEGER range <>, INTEGER range <>)
                    of FLOAT;
```

Although we could define arrays such as

```
WEIGHT_TABLE : TABLE (1..10);
A : MATRIX (1..2, 1..3);
```

it is better to define a subtype that constrains the array such as

```
subtype WEIGHT_TABLE_TYPE is TABLE (1..10);
subtype SMALL_MATRIX is MATRIX (1..2, 1..3);
```

Then, if more than one matrix of the same size is used in the program, such as A, B, and C, their definitions will all refer to one place.

```
A, B, C : SMALL_MATRIX;
```

If you decide to change the size of the SMALL_MATRIX or the WEIGHT_TABLE, you can do it at one place in the program.

RECORDS

Records are a powerful composite data type. Like arrays, records are a collection of objects that are given the same general name. Unlike arrays, the objects in a record may be of different data types.

The classical example for a record is a collection of information on an employee consisting of the employee's first name, the employee's last name, the employee's social security number, and the employee's employee number.

The following type definition defines the names to be strings of twenty-five characters in length and the numbers to be positive numbers.

```
type EMPLOYEE_LIST is
   record
         FIRST_NAME : STRING (1..25);
         LAST_NAME : STRING (1..25);
         SOCIAL_SECURITY_NUMBER : POSITIVE;
         EMPLOYEE_NUMBER : POSITIVE;
   end record;
```

To define an object with this record type, we define it just as we have defined all other objects:

```
EMPLOYEE : EMPLOYEE_LIST;
```

The individual parts of the record are called the record's *components*. In our example, the record has four components. We can refer to each individual component or to the collection of all four components. The names we can use in referring to the record or its parts are

```
EMPLOYEE  -- for the entire record
EMPLOYEE.FIRST_NAME -- for the FIRST_NAME component
EMPLOYEE.LAST_NAME  -- for the LAST_NAME component
EMPLOYEE.SOCIAL_SECURITY_NUMBER  -- for the
                       --  SOCIAL_SECURITY_NUMBER component
EMPLOYEE.EMPLOYEE NUMBER   -- for  the  EMPLOYEE_NUMBER
                       --  component
```

The names with the period in them are called *qualified names*.

The general form of a record type definition is

type *record type name* **is record** *record component definitions* **end record**;

Each record component is defined in the same manner as an object declaration.

To assign values to the record we have the choice of assigning values to the individual components:

```
EMPLOYEE.LAST_NAME := ('S','m','i','t','h', others => ' ');
EMPLOYEE.EMPLOYEE_NUMBER := 1611;
```

or to assign to the entire record with a positional or named notation. In the positional notation, the components are set in order.

```
EMPLOYEE := (('M','a','r','y', others => ' '),
             ('S','m','i','t','h', others => ' '),
             560_54_1650,
             1611);
```

will set the FIRST_NAME component to "Mary", the LAST_NAME component to "Smith", the SOCIAL_SECURITY_NUMBER component to 560_54_1650, and the EMPLOYEE_NUMBER component to 1611. We can portray the definition as figure 7.6 shows.

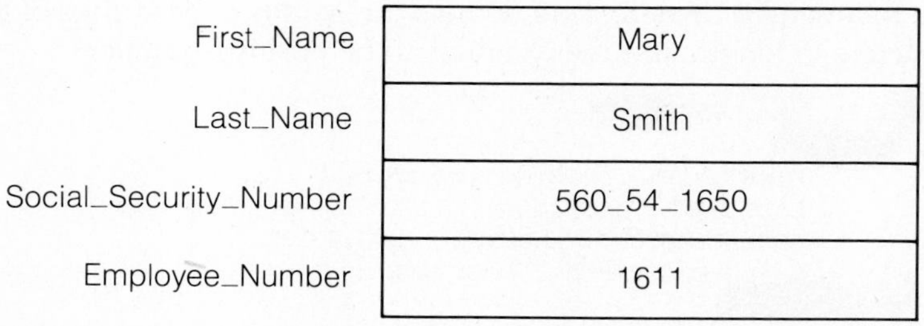

First_Name	Mary
Last_Name	Smith
Social_Security_Number	560_54_1650
Employee_Number	1611

Figure 7.6   EMPLOYEE record

In the named setting of components, each component defines the setting.

```
EMPLOYEE := (EMPLOYEE_NUMBER => 1611,
             SOCIAL_SECURITY_NUMBER => 560_54_1650,
             FIRST_NAME => ('M','a','r','y', others => ' '),
             LAST_NAME  => ('S';'m','i','t','h', others => ' '));
```

This manner of setting the components is identical to the last method, but you do not have to remember the order of names in the record.

In many applications, there is a need to group records together. This is often done with an array of records. For example, a business usually has several items of information on each employee. This information can be defined in a record definition such as we have seen for employee list. Then the collection of records can be defined in another type definition that uses the previously defined record definition.

```
MAX_EMPLOYEES : constant := 2000;
type EMPLOYEE_LIST  is
     record
          FIRST_NAME : STRING (1..25);
          LAST_NAME : STRING (1..25);
          SOCIAL_SECURITY_NUMBER : POSITIVE;
          EMPLOYEE_NUMBER : POSITIVE;
     end record;
type EMPLOYEES_TYPE is array (NATURAL range <>)
                of EMPLOYEE_LIST;
subtype EMPLOYEES_SUBTYPE is EMPLOYEES_TYPE (1..MAX_ EMPLOYEES);
EMPLOYEES : EMPLOYEES_SUBTYPE;
```

Now EMPLOYEES is an array of records.
To refer to the tenth employee's record, we write

```
EMPLOYEES (10)
```

To refer to the tenth employee's first name, we write

```
EMPLOYEES (10).FIRST_NAME
```

In the next program we specify a record with only two components; one component has an employee name, and one has an employee salary. The program calculates the average salary for all employees.

```
with TEXT_IO;
package FLOAT_IO is new TEXT_IO.FLOAT_IO (FLOAT);

with TEXT_IO, FLOAT_IO;
use  TEXT_IO, FLOAT_IO;
procedure AVERAGE_SALARY is
  type EMPLOYEE_RECORD is
    record
      NAME : STRING (1..4);
      SALARY : FLOAT range 0.0..1000.0;
    end record;
```

```
   type EMPLOYEE_ARRAY is
        array (NATURAL range <>) of EMPLOYEE_RECORD;
   NUMBER_EMPLOYEES : constant := 4;
   subtype EMPLOYEE_DATA_TYPE is
            EMPLOYEE_ARRAY (1..NUMBER_EMPLOYEES);
   EMPLOYEE_DATA : EMPLOYEE_DATA_TYPE;
   LENGTH : INTEGER;
   SUM : FLOAT := 0.0;
   AVERAGE_SALARY : FLOAT;
begin
   for I in EMPLOYEE_DATA'RANGE loop
     PUT ( " Type in four character name and salary rate per hour ");
     NEW_LINE;
     GET (EMPLOYEE_DATA(I).NAME); GET (EMPLOYEE_DATA(I).SALARY);
     SUM := SUM + EMPLOYEE_DATA(I).SALARY;
   end loop;
   LENGTH := EMPLOYEE_DATA'LENGTH;
   AVERAGE_SALARY := SUM/FLOAT(LENGTH);
   NEW_LINE;
   PUT (" Average salary per hour is "); PUT (AVERAGE_SALARY);
   NEW_LINE;
end AVERAGE_SALARY;
```

When the program executed, it produced this output.

```
 Type in four character name and salary rate per hour
>Jane 35.00

 Type in four character name and salary rate per hour
>John 27.50

 Type in four character name and salary rate per hour
>Mary 42.50

 Type in four character name and salary rate per hour
>Dave 57.50

 Average salary per hour is  4.06250E+01
```

WHAT HAVE YOU LEARNED?

ARRAYS

Arrays are an ordered collection of data items each of which has the same data type. To define an array data type, we define the name of the array data type, the data type for each data item in the array, and the indices for the array. Each data item in the array is often called an *element* of the array or a *component* of the array.

The general form of a type definition for an array is

> **type** *array type name* **is array** (*index definition*) **of** *component type definition;*

To refer to an element in an array, the general form of a reference is

> *array object name* (*array index value*)

Operations on arrays

> := -- for assignment
> = -- for test on equality
> /= -- for test on inequality

In positional notation, each element is assigned a value from a list of values, with the first value going to the first element, and so forth.

In named notation, the indices are named in any position order

```
TEMPERATURES : TEMPERATURE_TYPE := (INLET => 50.0,
                                    PUMP => 60.0,
                                    RADIATOR => 70.0,
                                    ROOM => 65.0,
                                    OUTLET => 63.0);
```

To set all the elements of an array to the same value, such as might be done for setting the initial value to zero, there are two possible notations.

```
TEMPERATURES : TEMPERATURE_TYPE := (INLET..OUTLET => 0.0);
```

or

```
TEMPERATURES : TEMPERATURE_TYPE := ( others => 0.0);
```

Both these notations will set all the array elements to zero. The keyword **others** can also be used to set the remaining elements in an array in the positional notation.

Constant arrays can be defined by using the keyword **constant** ahead of the array type name in an object definition.

```
EXPECTED_TEMPERATURES : constant TEMPERATURE_TYPE :=
                        (INLET => 50.0,
                         OUTLET => 60.0,
                         others => 65.0);
```

Useful array attributes:

```
ARRAY_NAME'RANGE    -- range  of index values for the  array
ARRAY_NAME'LENGTH   -- length of the array
ARRAY_NAME'FIRST    -- first index value for the array
ARRAY_NAME'LAST     -- last  index value for the array
```

```
ARRAY_NAME'RANGE(n)     -- range of index values for  dimension n
ARRAY_NAME'LENGTH(n)    -- length of the nth dimension
ARRAY_NAME'FIRST(n)     -- first index value of the nth dimension
ARRAY_NAME'LAST(n)      -- last index value of the nth dimension
```

LOOPS AND ARRAYS

Loops are commonly used with arrays

to test each element of the array against some value,
to sum up all the values in the array,
to search for some value in the array.

Two-dimensional arrays use nested loops.

STRINGS

The string data type is a predefined data type.

```
NAME : STRING (1..10);     -- 10 character string
TOWN : STRING (1..15);     -- 15 character string
ZIP_CODE : STRING (1..6);  -- 6 character string
HOME : constant STRING := "Santa Barbara";
```

Operations on strings

```
:= -- for assignment
 = -- test for equality
/= -- test for inequality
&  -- for concatenation
```

BIT STRINGS

A suggested definition for bit strings is

```
type BIT_STRING is array(POSITIVE range <>)
                   of BOOLEAN;
```

We can declare BIT_STRING objects:

```
STATUS_REGISTER : BIT_STRING (1..8) := (1..8 => FALSE );
INPUT_REGISTER  : BIT_STRING (1..8) := (others => TRUE);
RESULT_REGISTER : BIT_STRING (1..8);
```

and perform logical operations:

```
RESULT_REGISTER := STATUS_REGISTER and INPUT_REGISTER;
RESULT_REGISTER := STATUS_REGISTER or INPUT_REGISTER;
```

Operations on bit strings

:=	-- for assignment
=	-- for equality
/=	-- for inequality
&	-- for concatenation
and	-- for element by element and
or	-- for element by element or
not	-- for element by element not
xor	-- or element be element xor
and then	-- for element by element and then
else or	-- for element by element else or

ARRAY SUBTYPES

The general form of an array subtype is

subtype *array subtype name* **is** *array type name* (*index range specification*);

Examples are

subtype WEIGHT_TABLE_TYPE **is** TABLE (1..10);
subtype SMALL_MATRIX **is** MATRIX (1..2, 1..3);
subtype SHORT_NAME **is** STRING (1..5);

RECORDS

Records are a collection of data items that may be of different data types.

The general form of a record type definition is

type *record type name* **is record** *record component definitions* **end record**;

Each record component is defined in the same manner as an object declaration.

We can refer to a record or its parts. Some examples are

```
EMPLOYEE                  -- for the entire record
EMPLOYEE.FIRST_NAME  -- for the FIRST_NAME component
EMPLOYEE.LAST_NAME   -- for the LAST_NAME component
EMPLOYEE.SOCIAL_SECURITY_NUMBER     -- for the
                     -- SOCIAL_SECURITY_NUMBER component
EMPLOYEE.EMPLOYEE_NUMBER   -- for   the   EMPLOYEE_NUMBER
                     -- component
```

We can use positional or named notation to set the components in a record. Some examples are setting just one component in the record:

```
EMPLOYEE.LAST_NAME   := ('S','m','i','t','h',  others =>  ' ');
EMPLOYEE.EMPLOYEE_NUMBER := 1611;
```

Setting the entire record with positional notation:

```
EMPLOYEE := (('M','a','r','y', others => ' '),
             ('S','m','i','t','h', others => ' '),
             560_54_1650,
             1611);
```

Setting an entire record with named notation.

```
EMPLOYEE := (EMPLOYEE_NUMBER => 1611,
             SOCIAL_SECURITY_NUMBER => 560_54_1650,
             FIRST_NAME => ('M','a','r','y', others => ' '),
             LAST_NAME => ('S','m','i','t','h', others => ' '));
```

PROBLEMS

1. Write a program that reads ten voltage values into an array. Calculate the average of the ten values and display the result.

2. Write an array that stores the days of the month for each of the twelve months in the year. Use this array in a program that inputs the name of a month and then displays how many days in the month there are.

3. Write an array that computes the average selling value of ten stocks on the New York Stock Exchange. Use an array and a loop to set the array from input.

4. Change the program written in problem 3 to use an array of records where the name of the stock and the price of the stock form two components in the array.

5. Define a record to be used for a car inventory. The record should have the name of a car manufacturer, the number of cars on hand, and the price per car. Write a program that uses an array of five records. Set the data in the program using assignment statements and named notation. Compute the total value of the inventory.

6. Rewrite program 5 to input the data from a terminal using a loop. Display the total value of the inventory.

7. Write a program that uses a two-dimensional array to compute a multiplication table for the numbers 1 to 10.

8. Change the EMPLOYEE_LIST record definition used in the text to include a salary component. Define an array of employees which is of length 4.

Input data to set the information in the component. Then use the program to give everyone a 20% raise. Display the result as the name of the employee and their salary on the terminal.

9. Rewrite program 8 to use assignment statements to set the components. Compute the average salary before and after the raise.

10. Write a program that translates English to Spanish. Define an array of ten English words and an array of ten corresponding Spanish words. When you type in an English word, the display should show the corresponding Spanish word.

CHAPTER
❖ 8 ❖
SUBPROGRAMS

 So far, we have looked at complete programs. For several reasons, we will divide any sizeable program into subprograms. We will do this to

♦ make the program more understandable;
♦ make it easier to divide work among members of a group;
♦ allow the use of subprograms in future projects;
♦ allow the use of previously written subprograms;
♦ isolate problems more easily; and
♦ ease making future changes.

Ada has two types of subprograms: the *procedure* and the *function*. The procedure subprogram divides a program into smaller, more easily understood and more easily tested parts. You use a function subprogram where a new operation is needed. A function yields a value and is treated like an expression.

The packages mentioned in chapter 1 are often collections of subprograms that work together; included in the packages are data types on which the subprograms operate. Libraries contain packages of subprograms. These predefined packages contain subprograms for many applications and are being planned and implemented today. We have seen the use of a few of these predefined procedures such as GET and PUT, which are in the package TEXT_IO.

PROCEDURES

We have seen the basic form of a procedure in chapter 1. All the programs that you have written contained a single procedure, called a *main procedure*. Normally, a program will contain several procedures as well as the main procedure. The main procedure starts executing and causes other procedures to execute, which is done with a statement that names the procedure to be executed. We say the statement *invokes* or *calls* the other procedure.

To see the organization of procedures included with a main procedure, let's look at a program that performs census calculations. The body of the main program might appear as:

```
procedure CENSUS is
   procedure INPUT_CENSUS_DATA is separate;
   procedure ADD_BY_CENSUS_AREA is separate;
   procedure PRESENT_RESULTS is separate;
begin
   INPUT_CENSUS_DATA;
   ADD_BY_CENSUS_AREA;
   PRESENT_RESULTS;
end CENSUS;
```

In the declaration part of this program, the names INPUT_CENSUS_DATA, ADD_BY CENSUS_AREA, and PRESENT_RESULTS are all declared to be procedures that are separately compiled. This declaration is called a *procedure specification*. In the body of the program, the three procedures are executed in turn in the order named in the individual statements. The effect is the same as if the main program contained all the statements in the three subprograms, but the division of the problem into three parts will let different people work on each of the three problem areas. They can compile and test each subprogram individually and then bring the subprograms together for testing as an entire program.

A general form for a procedure specification is

procedure *procedure name;*

This informs the program's reader that there is a procedure with the given name; it is much like the declaration for an data item. Such a declaration is also called a *forward reference* because it allows us to use the name of the procedure before it is completely specified what the procedure is to do.

Another general form for a procedure specification is the one that gives the name of the procedure and information that the procedure is compiled separately. This form is

procedure *procedure name* **is separate;**

The main program will often be an infinite loop to show that the program never stops. For example, in this main program, the three subprograms are repeated forever.

```
procedure AIRLINE_RESERVATION is
   procedure INPUT_RESERVATION_REQUEST is separate;
   procedure HANDLE_RESERVATION is separate;
   procedure DISPLAY_RESERVATION is separate;
begin
   loop
      INPUT_RESERVATION_REQUEST;
      HANDLE_RESERVATION;
      DISPLAY_RESERVATION;
   end loop;
end AIRLINE_RESERVATION;
```

This example shows a program that will continually execute the three subprograms in turn. Similar programs can be outlined for automatic elevators, automatic bank tellers, or telephone switchboards. A statement that names another procedure is a *procedure invocation* or a *procedure call*. A declaration statement defining a procedure is a *procedure specification*.

In both examples, we defined the new procedures so we could divide the program into smaller parts. Each of the subprograms will have a structure just like the main procedure; the only difference is that each subprogram will have a special clause, called a *separate compilation clause*, which names the program to which it belongs ahead of the procedure. The separate clause starts with the keyword **separate**. The name of the program to which the procedure belongs is contained within parentheses following the keyword. There is no semicolon after the parentheses as the separate clause is not considered to be a statement. For example,

```
separate (AIRLINE_RESERVATION)
procedure INPUT_RESERVATION_REQUEST is
begin
   null;
end INPUT_RESERVATION_REQUEST;

separate (AIRLINE_RESERVATION)
procedure HANDLE_RESERVATION is
--    declarations
begin
--    statements
   null;
end HANDLE_RESERVATION;

separate (AIRLINE_RESERVATION)
procedure DISPLAY_RESERVATION is
begin
   null;
end DISPLAY_RESERVATION;'
```

states that the subprograms INPUT_RESERVATION_REQUEST, HANDLE_ RESERVATION, and DISPLAY_RESERVATION are part of the AIRLINE_RES- ERVATION procedure. They will be written just as we have written other programs. They can be further subdivided into subprograms until a small procedure can be written.

The previous examples show the most common organization of a pro- gram into procedures—a main procedure and other, separately compiled pro- cedures. These subprograms are also known as *external procedures* because the statements which are executed are external to the main procedure. Information communicated between these procedures will be done via data declared in packages. Ada also allows *parameter passing,* a method of communication between procedures. We have used parameter passing in our use of the input and output procedures GET and PUT.

Procedures that use or set values for other programs have *parameters.* For example, when we state

```
GET (TIME);
```

we invoke the procedure GET with the actual parameter named TIME. The actual parameter is the data item in our program that we want the GET pro- cedure to put data into. The procedure GET then sets this parameter for our use.

When we write a procedure with a parameter, we define a *formal param- eter.* We name the formal parameter and write the subprogram using the name of the formal parameter in statements just as though it were a declared data item. In writing a procedure that sets a value, we give a name to the parameter; we define the type of the parameter; and we define whether the procedure sets the parameter, uses the parameter, or sets and uses the parameter. All these definitions are done in the formal part of the procedure specification.

For example, if we wished to write a procedure to set a single integer value and named the procedure SET_INTEGER, the specification could appear as

```
procedure SET_INTEGER (X : out INTEGER) is separate;
```

The formal part of the procedure specification is in parentheses. The keyword **out** defines the single parameter, X, to be an output from the procedure. The type of parameter is the INTEGER data type. Also, if we wish to write a procedure to use a single integer value and name the procedure TAKE_INTE- GER, the specification can appear as

```
procedure TAKE_INTEGER (Y: in INTEGER) is separate;
```

In both instances, when we go to write the body of the procedures SET INTEGER and TAKE_INTEGER, we use the names defined in the parameter list just as though they had been declared in the declaration part of the pro- cedure. However, the parameters can be given different names by the pro- grams that invoke the procedures.

For example, if a main program contains the two procedure specifications, then the main program can state

```
TAKE_INTEGER (HEIGHT);
SET_INTEGER (ALTITUDE);
```

when HEIGHT and ALTITUDE are integers. The one program treats HEIGHT as an input to the procedure, and the other treats ALTITUDE as an output from the procedure. It is also possible to both use and set a parameter by combining the two keywords, **in** and **out** as in the following specification:

```
procedure BOTH (Z in out: INTEGER) is separate;
```

In this example, the single parameter, Z, can be both used and set. The keywords **in** and **out** must be separated by a space.

When a formal parameter is an **in** parameter, it can be used on the right-hand side of assignment statements in the subprogram. It is not allowed to be set by the subprogram. If you try to set it, Ada will declare an error during the compilation of the program. The subprogram can treat an **in** parameter only as a value to be used in the subprogram. If you leave out the keyword **in** and the keyword **out** in the formal definition of the subprogram parameter, the Ada compiler assumes that you mean **in** by default.

When a formal parameter is specified to be an output parameter with the keyword **out**, the subprogram cannot use the value in the parameter, it can only set the parameter. The formal parameter cannot appear on the right-hand side of an assignment statement; it must appear on the left-hand side of an assignment statement. For a parameter that is to be both used and set as a variable, the keywords **in out** are used together.

Procedures are also used to remove redundant code from a program. When you find yourself writing code over again to perform the same functions with just a change in the names of the variables, you should think about placing that code in a procedure. In the last chapter, a program that added matrices together had redundant code—the code to input the values of the matrices was similar except for the names of the matrices. In the next program we rewrite the program as a main program with a procedure. Later we will see how to collect such useful procedures as the matrix input program into a package, a collection of programs.

This example shows the use of procedures contained inside a main procedure. Such a procedure is called an *internal procedure* to differentiate it from the external procedures, which are compiled separately. The original program's redundant code has been collected in the GET procedure.

The GET procedure has a single output parameter of the type SMALL_MATRIX. The first time the procedure is used in the program, the actual parameter is the matrix A. The procedure acts as though it were written for matrix A instead of the formal parameter M. The second time the procedure is used in the program, the actual parameter is the matrix B. The GET procedure acts as though it were written for matrix B instead of the formal parameter M.

The procedure uses the predefined procedure, which is also named GET, to read one value of the matrix into the computer. It is perfectly acceptable to name both procedures GET. Ada uses the type of the parameter to differentiate between the procedures. In this example, it will know if the parameter is SMALL MATRIX instead of INTEGER and use the procedure we have written. When we give the same name to two different procedures, we say that we are *overloading* the name. It is best to restrict overloading to procedures having similar functions.

```ada
with TEXT_IO;
package INTEGER_IO is new TEXT_IO.INTEGER_IO (INTEGER);

with TEXT_IO, INTEGER_IO;
use  TEXT_IO, INTEGER_IO;
procedure ADD_MATRICES is
   type SMALL_MATRIX is array (INTEGER range 1..2,
                               INTEGER range 1..3) of INTEGER;

   A,B,C : SMALL_MATRIX;

   procedure GET (M : out SMALL_MATRIX) is
   begin
      for I in SMALL_MATRIX'RANGE(1) loop
         for J in SMALL_MATRIX'RANGE(2) loop
            GET (M(I,J));
         end loop;
      end loop;
      NEW_LINE;
   end GET;

begin
   PUT_LINE (" The add matrices program is beginning.");
   PUT_LINE (" Type in the six values for the matrix A in row order ");
   GET (A);
   PUT_LINE (" Type in the six values for the matrix B in row order ");
   GET (B);
   PUT_LINE (" The result of adding the two matrices is ");
   for I in SMALL_MATRIX'RANGE(1) loop
      for J in SMALL_MATRIX'RANGE(2) loop
         C(I,J) := A(I,J)  + B(I,J);
         PUT (C(I,J));
      end loop;
      NEW_LINE;
   end loop;
end ADD_MATRICES;
```

The ADD_MATRICES program can also be written with GET as a separate procedure. In the second version, we say GET is a separately compiled external procedure. The two organizations of subprograms, external and internal, result in the same program when everything is brought together, but the organization into separately compiled procedures allows for a better separation of the problem. The separation also allows the compiler to operate on smaller units of code and as a result often speeds up the compilation process.

```
with TEXT_IO;
package INTEGER_IO is new TEXT_IO.INTEGER_IO (INTEGER);

with TEXT_IO, INTEGER_IO;
use  TEXT_IO, INTEGER_IO;
procedure ADD_MATRICES is
   type SMALL_MATRIX is array (INTEGER range 1..2,
                               INTEGER range 1..3) of INTEGER;

   A,B,C : SMALL_MATRIX;

   procedure GET (M : out SMALL_MATRIX) is separate;

begin
   PUT_LINE (" The add matrices program is beginning.");
   PUT_LINE (" Type in the six values for the matrix A in row order ");
   GET (A);
   PUT_LINE (" Type in the six values for the matrix B in row order ");
   GET (B);
   PUT_LINE (" The result of adding the two matrices is ");
   for I in SMALL_MATRIX'RANGE(1) loop
     for J in SMALL_MATRIX'RANGE(2) loop
       C(I,J) := A(I,J)  + B(I,J);
       PUT (C(I,J));
     end loop;
     NEW_LINE;
   end loop;
end ADD_MATRICES;

separate (ADD_MATRICES)
procedure GET (M : out SMALL_MATRIX) is
begin
   for I in SMALL_MATRIX'RANGE(1) loop
     for J in SMALL_MATRIX'RANGE(2) loop
       GET (M(I,J));
     end loop;
   end loop;
   NEW_LINE;
end GET;
```

Procedures may also have many parameters, and it is a good idea to try to limit the number of parameters. In the following procedure, we input a value in dollars and we output the value of sales tax and the resulting cost, which is the sum of the input and the sales tax.

```
with TEXT_IO;
package FLOAT_IO is new TEXT_IO.FLOAT_IO (FLOAT);

with TEXT_IO, FLOAT_IO;
use  TEXT_IO, FLOAT_IO;
procedure MAIN is
   COST : FLOAT;
   TAX  : FLOAT;
```

```
   procedure ADD_TAX (DOLLAR_VALUE :   in FLOAT;
                      SALES_TAX     :   out FLOAT;
                      TOTAL_COST    :   out FLOAT) is
   TAX_RATE : constant := 0.06; -- Sales tax rate
begin
   SALES_TAX := TAX_RATE * DOLLAR_VALUE;
   TOTAL_COST := DOLLAR_VALUE + SALES_TAX;
end ADD_TAX;

begin

   ADD_TAX (50.00, TAX, COST);
   PUT (" TAX ON $50.00 IS "); PUT (TAX);
   PUT (". FOR A TOTAL COST OF "); PUT (COST);

end MAIN;
```

Each of the three parameters is defined in the formal part of the procedure; the program may use these parameter names in the body of the procedure. The names normally have no meaning outside the procedure.

To use the procedure, it can be specified in another program. That program can invoke the procedure such as

```
ADD_TAX (50.00, TAX, COST);
```

if TAX and COST are declared to be of the FLOAT type. This form of invoking a procedure is termed using *positional notation*. In positional notation, the parameters are listed in the same order as they appear in the procedure declaration.

It is also possible to use a named notation such as

```
ADD_TAX (DOLLAR_VALUE => 50.0, SALES_TAX => TAX,
    TOTAL_COST => COST);
```

where the name of each of the formal parameters sets the actual parameters in any order. In this example we kept the same order as in the procedure declaration; if we wish to alter the order of listing the parameters, we can state

```
ADD_TAX (TOTAL_COST => COST, DOLLAR_VALUE => 50.0,
    SALES_TAX => TAX);
```

This changes the order of the parameters but is also correct.

The ADD_TAX example can be rewritten to contain a default tax rate instead of a constant tax rate. A default is a value used unless otherwise changed. In the next program, TAX_RATE is given a default value of 6%. If the procedure is invoked as before, the fourth parameter remains as 0.06. But if the fourth parameter is set as in the statement

```
ADD_TAX ( 50.0, TAX, COST, 0.065);
```

the procedure uses the rate of 6.5% instead of 6%.

```
with TEXT_IO;
package FLOAT_IO is new TEXT_IO.FLOAT_IO (FLOAT);
```

```
with TEXT_IO, FLOAT_IO;
use  TEXT_IO, FLOAT_IO;
procedure MAIN is
   COST : FLOAT;
   TAX : FLOAT;

   procedure ADD_TAX (DOLLAR_VALUE :   in  FLOAT;
                      SALES_TAX    :   out FLOAT;
                      TOTAL_COST   :   out FLOAT;
                      TAX_RATE :  in  FLOAT := 0.06) is

   begin

      SALES_TAX := TAX_RATE * DOLLAR_VALUE;
      TOTAL_COST := DOLLAR_VALUE + SALES_TAX;
   end ADD_TAX;

begin

   ADD_TAX (50.00, TAX, COST, 0.065);
   PUT (" TAX ON $50.00 IS "); PUT (TAX);
   PUT (". FOR A TOTAL COST OF "); PUT (COST);

end MAIN;
```

When executed, this program output:

```
TAX ON $50.00 IS  3.25000E+00. FOR A TOTAL COST OF 5.32500E+01
```

FUNCTIONS

A *function* is a subprogram that yields a value and is treated as an expression. A function has a type, and, as with all other types in Ada, it has a set of legal values and a set of operators that can be used with the function. A function is normally used in an expression in combination with other functions or with variables and constants.

Like procedures, functions may be compiled separately or may be placed within other subprograms. If they are compiled separately and belong to a main program, functions are defined in the main program and then compiled with a separate clause just as is done with procedures. If they are internal to the main program, the text of the function is placed in the declaration part of the main program.

A function almost always has a parameter used to calculate the result of the function.

The general form for a function specification is similar to the specification for a procedure with parameters.

function *function name (parameter definitions)* **return** *type name;*

If the function is to be separately compiled the definition appears as

function *function name (parameter definitions)* **return** *type name* **is separate;**

In function subprograms, all the parameters are input to the function. There is one output from a function that is not associated with a parameter name but with the name of the function. This output is of the type declared in the part of the function specification following the keyword **return**. The output of a function is set not by an assignment statement but by a **return** statement, which has the general form

return expression;

An example of a simple function that returns a string by doubling the input string is

```
with TEXT_IO;
use  TEXT_IO;
procedure MAIN is

   NAME : STRING (1..3) := "JOE";
   DOUBLE_NAME : STRING (1..6);

   function DOUBLE (S : STRING) return STRING is
   begin
      return S & S;
   end DOUBLE;
begin

   DOUBLE_NAME := DOUBLE (NAME);
   PUT (DOUBLE_NAME);

end MAIN;
```

This program contains the internal function named DOUBLE. When the program executed, it displayed

```
JOEJOE
```

The function is invoked by naming the function and placing the name of the actual parameter in parentheses. Since the function has a value, it can be used in an assignment statement as the assignment to DOUBLE_NAME shows.

Note that in a function we do not need to give the length of the string, we only need to give the type name. Remember that STRING was predefined as an unconstrained array. In all subprograms the parameters may be unconstrained array types, so there is no need to specify a different subprogram for each length of the array. Instead, the subprogram uses the attributes of the array parameter. This is a powerful feature of Ada because one function can handle arrays of any length as long as the array's length is defined before the function is used.

The next program contains a function named ADD that replaces some of the code written in the previous version of ADD_MATRICES. In this version the inputs to the function and the output from the function are all of the type SMALL_MATRIX. The function is used in the main program to contain the result of adding the two matrices. The program has also been written to contain a procedure named PUT to display the result of the addition.

```ada
with TEXT_IO;
package INTEGER_IO is new TEXT_IO.INTEGER_IO (INTEGER);

with TEXT_IO, INTEGER_IO;
use  TEXT_IO, INTEGER_IO;
procedure ADD_MATRICES is
  type SMALL_MATRIX is array (INTEGER range 1..2,
                              INTEGER range 1..3) of INTEGER;

  A,B,C : SMALL_MATRIX;

  procedure GET (M : out SMALL_MATRIX) is
  begin
    for I in SMALL_MATRIX'RANGE(1) loop
      for J in SMALL_MATRIX'RANGE(2) loop
        GET (M(I,J));
      end loop;
    end loop;
    NEW_LINE;
  end GET;

  procedure PUT (M : in SMALL_MATRIX) is
  begin
    for I in SMALL_MATRIX'RANGE(1) loop
      for J in SMALL_MATRIX'RANGE(2) loop
        PUT (C(I,J));
      end loop;
      NEW_LINE;
    end loop;
  end PUT;

  function ADD (X, Y : SMALL_MATRIX) return SMALL_MATRIX is
    Z : SMALL_MATRIX;
  begin
    for I in SMALL_MATRIX'RANGE(1) loop
      for J in SMALL_MATRIX'RANGE(2) loop
        Z(I,J) := X(I,J)  + Y(I,J);
      end loop;
    end loop;
    return Z;
  end ADD;
```

```
begin
   PUT_LINE (" The add matrices program is beginning. ");
   PUT_LINE (" Type in the six values for the matrix A in row order ");
   GET (A);
   PUT_LINE (" Type in the six values for the matrix B in row order ");
   GET (B);
   PUT_LINE (" The result of adding the two matrices is ");
   C := ADD (A, B);
   PUT (C);
end ADD_MATRICES;
```

The program reads in the data for the matrices and then the function ADD adds the two matrices together. The value of the sum is returned to the name of the function that the assignment statement assigns to the matrix C.

For such common operations as adding matrices where the function is a true arithmetic operation on the type, it is possible to define the function as an operator. Instead of giving a name to the function such as ADD_MATRICES, we give it the name of the operator such as "+". When the name of the operator is used, we do not need to use parentheses to invoke the function. Instead, we just write the operator with its parameters on each side of the operator. Naturally, we must use two parameters with operators that take two parameters, and we use one parameter with operators that can take one parameter. This feature of giving a new meaning to an operator is called *overloading* the operator. Giving several meanings to a name of a subprogram is called *overloading* the subprogram.

In overloading the operators, common sense should prevail. Overloading the "+" operator should be for functions such as ADD_MATRICES. Overloading the "*" operator should be for functions that we associate with multiplication, and so forth.

This program is a rewrite of the ADD_MATRICES program, which uses the overloaded "+". The statement

```
C := A + B;
```

invokes the "+" function. Ada knows to use the "+" as defined by the function in contrast to the "+" defined for integers because A, B, and C are all of the SMALL_MATRIX type.

```
with TEXT_IO;
package INTEGER_IO is new TEXT_IO. INTEGER_IO (INTEGER);

with TEXT_IO, INTEGER_IO;
use  TEXT_IO, INTEGER_IO;
procedure ADD_MATRICES is
   type SMALL_MATRIX is array (INTEGER range 1..2,
                               INTEGER range 1..3) of INTEGER;

   A, B, C : SMALL_MATRIX;
```

```
procedure GET (M : out SMALL_MATRIX) is
begin
  for I in SMALL_MATRIX'RANGE(1) loop
    for J in SMALL_MATRIX'RANGE(2) loop
      GET (M(I,J));
    end loop;
  end loop;
  NEW_LINE;
end GET;

procedure PUT (M : in SMALL_MATRIX) is
begin
  for I in SMALL_MATRIX'RANGE(1) loop
    for J in SMALL_MATRIX'RANGE(2) loop
      PUT (C(I,J));
    end loop;
    NEW_LINE;
  end loop;
end PUT;

function "+" (X, Y : SMALL_MATRIX) return SMALL_MATRIX is
  Z : SMALL_MATRIX;
begin
  for I in SMALL_MATRIX'RANGE(1) loop
    for J in SMALL_MATRIX'RANGE(2) loop
      Z(I,J) := X(I,J)  + Y(I,J);
    end loop;
  end loop;
  return Z;
end "+";

begin
  PUT_LINE (" The add matrices program is beginning.");
  PUT_LINE (" Type in the six values for the matrix A in row order ");
  GET (A);
  PUT_LINE (" Type in the six values for the matrix B in row order ");
  GET (B);
  PUT_LINE (" The result of adding the two matrices is ");
  C := A + B;
  PUT (C);
end ADD_MATRICES;
```

The operators that can be overloaded are

abs	+	<
and	−	>
or	*	<=
xor	/	>=
not	**	&
mod	rem	

You normally cannot overload the assignment operator : = , the test for equality = , or the test for inequality /= as these have defined meanings for all types. There is one exception to this limitation that we will cover when we discuss limited private types.

Overloading operators is useful for defining arithmetic for types that are not built into Ada, for example, the operators used in complex arithmetic. In complex arithmetic, an object has two parts, a real part and an imaginary part. The real part is often denoted by RE and the imaginary part is denoted by IM. To define a complex type in Ada, the best way to do so is to define a record with two fields such as

```
type COMPLEX is
    record
            RE : FLOAT;
            IM : FLOAT;
    end record;
```

The specifications for some of the common operations on the COMPLEX type can be defined as

```
function "+"   (A, B: COMPLEX)  return COMPLEX;
function "−"   (A, B: COMPLEX)  return COMPLEX;
function "∗"   (A, B: COMPLEX)  return COMPLEX;
function "/"   (A, B: COMPLEX)  return COMPLEX;
function "abs" (A, B: COMPLEX)  return COMPLEX;
```

The function " + " can be written as

```
function "+" (A, B: COMPLEX)  return COMPLEX is
    C : COMPLEX;
begin
    C. RE := A. RE + B. RE;
    C. IM := A. IM + B. IM;
    return C;
end "+";
```

The new function is defined in terms of operations that have been defined on a lower level. The individual components of the record C.RE and C.IM are referenced using the notation we learned in chapter 7. This function can then be used in a main program such as

```
with TEXT_IO;
package FLOAT_IO is new TEXT_IO. FLOAT_IO (FLOAT) ;

with TEXT_IO, FLOAT_IO;
use  TEXT_IO, FLOAT_IO;
procedure MAIN is
    type COMPLEX is
      record
        RE : FLOAT;
        IM : FLOAT;
      end record;
```

```
    X, Y, Z : COMPLEX;

    function "+" (A, B : COMPLEX) return COMPLEX is
      C : COMPLEX;
    begin
      C.RE := A.RE + B.RE;
      C.IM := A.IM + B.IM;
      return C;
    end "+";

    procedure GET (X : out COMPLEX) is separate;
    procedure PUT (X : in COMPLEX) is separate;

  begin
    PUT (" Complex addition program. "); NEW_LINE;
    PUT (" Please enter a complex number. "); NEW_LINE;
    PUT (" Enter the number as two floating point numbers, ");
    PUT (" with the real part first. "); NEW_LINE;
    GET (X); -- Input a complex number
    PUT (" Enter another complex number. "); NEW_LINE;
    GET (Y); -- Input another complex number
    Z := X + Y;
    PUT_LINE (" Result of complex addition for the two numbers.");
    PUT (Z);              -- Result of complex addition
  end MAIN;

    separate (MAIN)
    procedure GET (X : out COMPLEX) is
    begin
      GET (X.RE);
      GET (X.IM);
    end GET;

    separate (MAIN)
    procedure PUT (X : in COMPLEX) is
    begin
      PUT (X.RE);
      PUT (X.IM);
    end PUT;
```

The normal notation for complex numbers follows the notation used for records. A value for Z in the program can be defined as

```
    Z := (1.0, 2.0);
```

in which case Z.RE will be 1.0 and Z.IM will be 2.0.

Operations such as "+" cannot be separately compiled.

WHAT HAVE YOU LEARNED?

Ada has two types of subprograms: the procedure and the function.

A procedure is a statement.
A function is an expression.

Some of the general forms for a procedure specification are

procedure *procedure name*;
procedure *procedure name* **is separate**;

procedure *procedure name* (*parameter definitions*);
procedure *procedure name* (*parameter definitions*) **is separate**;

Parameters for a procedure may be used as inputs to a procedure, as outputs from a procedure, or as both input and output. In the parameter definition list, the parameters are defined as to type and whether they are **in**, **out**, or **in out**. Each parameter definition is separated from other definitions by a semicolon.

The general form for a parameter definition is

parameter name list : *input output mode   type name*;

where the *parameter name list* is a list of parameters all of the same type. The *input output mode* is **in**, **out**, or **in out**. The *type name* is a type that has been defined previously in the program.

Parameters may have default values by placing an assignment to the parameter in the parameter definition.

Procedures may have the same name as another procedure when the number or types of the parameters differ. It is a good idea to avoid using the same name unless the functions are similar.

A procedure is invoked by naming the procedure in a statement. The procedure parameters, if any, follow the procedure name and are placed in parentheses. For example,

```
GET (MATRIX);   -- procedure invocation
```

The general forms for a function specification are

function *function name* (*parameter definitions*) **return** *type name*;
function *function name* (*parameter definitions*) **return** *type name* **is separate**;

A function can also be written without parameters, but this is rare. The form for a parameterless function is

function *function name* **return** *type name*;

Function parameters can only be input to the function. It is optional to use the keyword **in** with functions.

The output from a function is set by the **return** statement in the function.

return *expression*;

Functions are invoked by using the name of the parameter in an expression such as

```
C := ADD (A, B);   -- The add function is invoked
```

The operators that can be overloaded are

abs	+	<
and	−	>
or	*	<=
xor	/	>=
not	**	&
mod		
rem		

You cannot overload the assignment operator := , the test for equality = , or the test for inequality /= , as these have defined meanings for all types. The one exception to this limitation we will cover under limited private types.

A separately compiled subprogram will have a separate clause ahead of the subprogram definition naming the compilation unit that invokes it. A clause is an Ada construct that is not a statement.

separate (*higher unit name*)

PROBLEMS

1. Write a function to compute the average of an array of floating-point numbers. Make the function independent of the length of the array. Use the function in a main program that computes the average value of ten stocks on the New York Stock Exchange.

2. Write a function to locate the maximum number in an array of integers. Use the function in a main program that locates and prints the highest bowling score in an array of seven bowling games.

3. Write a function for complex subtraction. In complex subtraction, the real parts of the complex number are subtracted and the imaginary parts of the complex number are subtracted. For example, (4.0, 5.0) − (3.0, 1.0) would equal (1.0, 4.0). Test your function by writing a main program that inputs these values and displays the correct answer.

4. Write a function to compute the inner or dot product of two vectors, A and B. A vector can be represented as an unconstrained floating-point array. The dot product is computed by multiplying components of the

vector together and summing up the resulting product. It is often written as

$$A \cdot B = \text{sum } (A_i * B_i)$$

5. Write a function to compute the square root of a number using the formula

$$\text{next\_approximation} = \text{last\_approximation} -$$
$$0.5(\text{last\_approximation} - \text{number})$$

and where the first approximation is $0.5 *$ number. Use the recursion relation to compute a better approximation until the difference between the next_approximation and the last_approximation is 0.001. Test your function on a series of numbers such as 1, 2, 4, 5, 1000000.

6. Write three functions to determine if an input character is a letter, a digit, or a special character. Test the functions with a main program that uses the functions to input a character from the terminal and display a message that the character is a letter, digit, or a special character.

7. Write two functions to convert uppercase characters to lowercase characters and vice versa. Test the functions with a main program that uses the functions to transform the case of an input character.

8. Write a procedure to ring the bell on a terminal. Use the procedure in a main program to cause the bell to ring when the string "bell" is typed.

9. Write a procedure to normalize a matrix by calculating the average of all the elements in the matrix and then dividing each element in the matrix by the average value.

10. Write a checkbook balancing program where deposits, withdrawals, and fees are registered in an array of records. After each transaction, display the balance on the terminal.

CHAPTER
❖ *9* ❖

FORMATTED INPUT & OUTPUT

❖ We have been using the simplest forms of input and output, which call on the two predefined procedures GET and PUT. However, there are many other available predefined procedures to use for input and output, and in this chapter we will cover some that are useful for providing formatted input and output. Formatted output allows you to specify the placement of the output information, which you will find useful when you want to prepare an attractive report. You use formatted input when you want to input data from specific columns on a display. It is also used when you want to skip over previously prepared information.

FORMATTED OUTPUT

We know that the NEW_LINE procedure gives us a new line on the display. There is another form of the NEW_LINE procedure that will skip several lines on the display.

    NEW_LINE (2);

will skip two lines on the display.
The general form of NEW_LINE is

    NEW_LINE (*number of lines*);

where *number of lines* can be any positive integer or a variable of the POSITIVE_ COUNT data type.

There is a similar procedure that gives us a new page on the display. This procedure, NEW_PAGE, is invoked by

    NEW_PAGE;

Within a line, it is possible to skip over columns using the procedure SET_ COL, which has the general form

    SET_COL (*column number*);

For example,

    SET_COL (30);

will cause the display to start at column 30. This statement has several special cases. For example, if the display is already at column 30, it will stay at column 30. But if the display is at column 35, the display will not go backward. Instead, the display will go to column 30 on the next line.

This chapter's first program uses the SET_COL procedure to cause a pattern to be displayed across ten columns and down ten lines. The pattern consists of the letters *A* to *Z*.

The program when executed produced the following output:

```
ABCDEFGHIJ
 KLMNOPQRS
  TUVWXYZA
   BCDEFGH
    IJKLMN
     OPQRS
      TUVW
       XYZ
        AB
         C
```

```
with TEXT_IO;
use  TEXT_IO;
procedure ADA_PATTERN is
   C : CHARACTER;
begin
   C := CHARACTER'PRED('A');
   for I in 1..10 loop
     SET_COL (POSITIVE_COUNT(I));
     for J in I..10 loop
       if C /= 'Z' then
          C := CHARACTER'SUCC(C);
```

```
        else
            C := 'A';
        end if;
        PUT (C);
    end loop;
  end loop;
end ADA_PATTERN;
```

Within a page, it is possible to go to a specified line on the page by using the procedure SET_LINE. For example,

```
SET_LINE (25);
```

will cause the display to go to the page's twenty-fifth line. As with SET_COL, the procedure will not cause the display to reverse. If line 25 has already been displayed, a new page will be started and line 25 on the new page will be presented.

Three functions tell where you are on a display:

COL
LINE
PAGE

which all return a value of the type POSITIVE_COUNT, an integer subtype that takes on values greater or equal to one. COL returns the value of the present position of the display column. LINE returns the value of the line number, and PAGE gives the value of the current page number.

Ada recognizes that different terminals have different line widths and page lengths. Two procedures provide a means to set the line width and the page length. For example, to set a line width of 80 and a page length of 24, we write

```
SET_LINE_LENGTH (80);
SET_PAGE_LENGTH (24);
```

The general forms of these two procedures are

```
SET_LINE_LENGTH (number of columns in a line);
SET_PAGE_LENGTH (number of lines in a page);
```

where each procedure's parameter is of type COUNT. This means that for any integer variable to be passed as a parameter to the procedure, it must be converted to the type COUNT. You can use an expression such as

```
SET_LINE_LENGTH (COUNT(LINE_LENGTH));
```

if LINE_LENGTH is of type INTEGER. The procedures SET_COL, and SET_LINE have parameters of the subtype POSITIVE_COUNT. POSITIVE_COUNT is a subtype of the type COUNT, which is an integer type. The only difference between COUNT and POSITIVE_COUNT is that COUNT starts with the value 0 and POSITIVE_COUNT starts with the value 1.

We have also used formatting that the computer provides automatically. This is called the *default formatting*. For simple programs, this form of input and output is satisfactory, but it often provides too much space for a small amount of information. For example, the default size for an integer data type is often ten columns wide. To specify a different size we use another form of the familiar GET and PUT procedures.

FORMATTED STRINGS AND CHARACTERS

On inputting numbers or enumeration values, it is usually best to use the free format available with the normal GET operation. In the unformatted form of the GET procedure, the computer skips leading blanks until a value is located and then the number is read into the computer. On inputting characters or strings, there is no format specification possible. A useful procedure for inputting strings is the GET_LINE procedure, which reads in a line of text and provides a number indicating how long the line was. For example,

```
GET_LINE (NAME, LINE_LENGTH);
```

sets the variable NAME, which is of type STRING, to the data that was on a line and sets the variable LINE_LENGTH, which is of type NATURAL to the amount of information which was on the line. If the line of information is shorter than the length of the string, the remainder of the string is left in an undefined state.

The next program demonstrates the use of GET_LINE to input an arbitrary string and center it in a field of text. In this version of the compiler, a GET_LINE always asked for some additional input, so a second carriage return was required as the output demonstrates.

```
Type in a line of information, the computer will display
the line as a centered line of text in a field of 20.
Two carriage returns are sometimes needed.
>Test message
>

    Test message


with TEXT_IO;
use  TEXT_IO;
procedure LINE_DEMO is
-- Program to show use of GET_LINE
  LINE : STRING (1..20);
  CENTERED_LINE : STRING (1..20);
  CENTER : NATURAL;
  LENGTH : NATURAL;
```

```
begin
    PUT (" Type in a line of information, the computer will display ");
    NEW_LINE;
    PUT (" the line as a centered line of text in a field of 20.");
    NEW_LINE;
    PUT (" Two carriage returns are sometimes needed. ");
    NEW_LINE;
    GET_LINE (LINE, LENGTH);   -- Input information in one line
    NEW_LINE;
    CENTER := (20 - LENGTH)/2;   -- Calculate position to center text
    CENTERED_LINE := (others => ' ');
    PUT_LINE (CENTERED_LINE);
    CENTERED_LINE (CENTER + 1 .. CENTER + LENGTH) := LINE (1..LENGTH);
    PUT (CENTERED_LINE);
end LINE_DEMO;
```

The program also demonstrates the use of slices to manipulate strings. First the new string CENTERED_LINE is set to all blanks. Then the slice from CENTER + 1 to CENTER + LENGTH is set to the input string using the value in LENGTH to pick out the correct number of characters.

Most of the useful formatting is done on output to a printer or terminal instead of on input. On outputting characters or strings, Ada does not provide formatting. Instead, you must make the string the length that you desire to be displayed or printed.

To specify the format on output, the width of the field is an additional parameter to the PUT procedure. For example,

```
SET_COL (5);
PUT (32, 2);
```

will result in the number 32 being displayed in columns 5 and 6. If instead we write

```
SET_COL (5);
PUT (32, 3);
```

the number 32 will be displayed in columns 6 and 7 and column 5 will be blank. If there is a greater width specified for an integer data type than is necessary for the display, then blanks are placed in front of the number.

For enumerations, the normal situation is to have the output be in upper-case and to provide trailing blanks if the width of the specified field is wider than that necessary to display the value. For example, if we write

```
SET_COL (10);
PUT (TRUE, 5);
```

The display will show

```
TRUE
```

in columns 10 to 14 and leave column 15 blank.

We can change the enumeration value to be lower case by setting a third parameter with the CASE type. If we write,

```
SET_COL (10);
PUT (TRUE, 5, LOWER_CASE);
```

The display will show as a result

```
true
```

in columns 10 through 14 and leave column 15 blank.

There are two useful attributes that are used for input and output of enumeration types. These are 'IMAGE and 'VALUE. The first attribute, 'IMAGE, produces a string for any discrete type. For an enumeration type, the attribute generates an uppercase string for the value of the enumeration type. When we need to output an enumeration type, we do not need to instantiate ENUMER-ATION_IO; instead, we can invoke the PUT procedure with the 'IMAGE attribute of the data item we wish to display. For example, if Monday is a value of the enumeration type DAY_TYPE, we can write

```
PUT (DAY_TYPE'IMAGE (Monday);
```

and the display will show

```
MONDAY
```

The attribute 'VALUE has similar uses on input of data. The data can be input as a string and then converted to a discrete type with the use of the attribute 'VALUE, which converts a string to a discrete type. Using our previous example for types, we can have the normal GET procedure input a string value into the variable day of type DAY_TYPE with the statement

```
GET (DAY_TYPE'VALUE(DAY));
```

The next program shows the use of protecting against typing errors in the input of an integer to a simple program. Instead of using the normal INTE-GER_IO procedures, the program inputs the number as a string, tests the string for legitimate values in the string, and then converts the string to an integer with the 'VALUE attribute. The number is then displayed with the 'IMAGE attribute. Any errors detected on input allow you to enter another number. If, instead, INTEGER_IO procedures had been used, an error would cause the program to abort.

```
with TEXT_IO; use TEXT_IO;
procedure PROTECT_IO is
  DATA   : STRING (1..20);
  LENGTH : NATURAL;

  NUMBER : INTEGER;
  DONE   : BOOLEAN := FALSE;
begin
  PUT_LINE (" The protect io program has begun. ");
  PUT_LINE (" Type an integer ");
  NEW_LINE;
```

```
while not DONE loop
  DATA := (others => ' ');
  GET_LINE (DATA, LENGTH);
  NEW_LINE;
    DONE := LENGTH > 0; -- No string entered test
  for I in 1..LENGTH loop
  -- Skip over blanks
  -- Check rest are digits
    if DATA (I) not in '0'..'9' and
    DATA (I) /= ' ' then
    SET_COL (POSITIVE_COUNT(I));
    PUT (" ^ is not a digit. Input again.");
    NEW_LINE;
    DONE := FALSE;
    SKIP_LINE;
    exit;
    end if;
  end loop;
end loop;
-- Integer OK
NUMBER := INTEGER'VALUE (DATA);
-- Display Integer
PUT (INTEGER'IMAGE(NUMBER));
end PROTECT_IO;
```

The sample output from the PROTECT_IO program shows how the program responded to a series of two erroneous inputs. In the first case, the input was all letters. In the second case the letter *O* was used instead of a zero. In the third case, the number was entered correctly. The use of **in** in the if statement is called the *membership* operation. It tests whether DATA(I) is in the range '0' to '9'.

```
The protect io program has begun.
Type an integer

>ABC
>

 ^ is not a digit.   Input again.
>507
>

  ^ is not a digit.   Input again.
>507
>

  507
```

In the next program we use formatted output to print a month for a calendar that has thirty-one days and starts on Sunday. The output appeared as

To print a report involving money or many physical quantities, two or three decimal places are all that are desired. In the checkbook balancing program, formatted output displays results to two decimal points. The program sets a balance with an initial input value. It then goes into an infinite loop, asking whether the program should accept a deposit or subtract a check. After each transaction, the program displays the new balance.

```
with TEXT_IO;
package FLOAT_IO is new TEXT_IO.FLOAT_IO (FLOAT);

with TEXT_IO, FLOAT_IO;
use  TEXT_IO, FLOAT_IO;
procedure CHECK_BALANCE is
  subtype MONEY is FLOAT range 0.0..9999.99;
  BALANCE : MONEY;
  AMOUNT  : MONEY;
  DEPOSIT : MONEY;
  REPLY   : CHARACTER;
begin
  PUT (" Check balance program. "); NEW_LINE;
  PUT (" What is your current balance ?"); NEW_LINE;
  GET (BALANCE);  -- Get current balance
  loop  -- loop forever program
    NEW_LINE;
    PUT_LINE (" Enter D if you want to make a deposit. ");
    PUT_LINE (" or enter C if you want to subtract a check. ");
    PUT_LINE (" Enter E if you want to exit the program. ");
    NEW_LINE;
    GET (REPLY);
    case REPLY is
      when 'D' =>
        PUT_LINE (" Enter amount of deposit ");
        GET (DEPOSIT); NEW_LINE;
        BALANCE := BALANCE + DEPOSIT;
        PUT (" New balance is "); PUT (BALANCE, 4, 2, 0);
        NEW_LINE;
      when 'C' =>
        PUT_LINE (" Enter amount of check ");
        GET (AMOUNT); NEW_LINE;
        BALANCE := BALANCE - AMOUNT;
        PUT (" New balance is "); PUT (BALANCE, 4, 2, 0);
        NEW_LINE;
      when 'E' =>
        PUT_LINE (" Have a nice day. ");
        exit;  -- leave infinite loop
      when others =>
        PUT_LINE (" Only C, D, or E are legal values ");
    end case;
  end loop;
end CHECK_BALANCE;
```

The checkbook program's output for a sample set of transactions looked like this:

```
Check balance program.
What is your current balance ?
>4000.00

Enter D if you want to make a deposit.
or enter C if you want to subtract a check.
Enter E if you want to exit the program.

>D

Enter amount of deposit
>1500.00

New balance is 5500.00

Enter D if you want to make a deposit.
or enter C if you want to subtract a check.
Enter E if you want to exit the program.

>C

Enter amount of check
>3000.00

New balance is 2500.00

Enter D if you want to make a deposit.
or enter C if you want to subtract a check.
Enter E if you want to exit the program.

>E

Have a nice day.
```

FORMATTED INPUT OF NUMBERS

It is possible to specify exactly how many columns are to be input using a form of the GET procedure that has a width parameter. For example, the statement

```
GET ( YEAR, 4);
```

will examine the next four columns for the value to be used for YEAR. A problem can arise if the GET attempts to read an end of line character. If this happens, a value of 0 may be assigned to the variable. The SET_COL, SET_LINE, SKIP_LINE, and NEW_LINE procedures can be used to control input as well as output.

WHAT HAVE YOU LEARNED?

How to skip lines and columns:

NEW_LINE (*number of lines*); NEW_LINE (2); -- skip two lines
SET_COL (*column number*);   SET_COL (30); -- go to column 30
SET_LINE (*line number*);   SET_LINE (25); -- go to line 25

How to go to the next page:

NEW_PAGE;

How to determine where the next output will be placed:

COL -- a function which returns the current column
LINE -- a function which returns the current line
PAGE -- a function which returns the current page

How to specify the width and length of a page of output.

SET_LINE_LENGTH (*number of columns*);
SET_PAGE_LENGTH (*number of lines*);
SET_LINE_LENGTH (80); -- for an 80-column display or page
SET_PAGE_LENGTH (24); -- for a 24-line display or page

How to specify an input format:

GET (*name, field length*);   — input numeric data to variable
                                           — *name* from next *field length*
                                           — columns

How to specify variable string input:
GET_LINE (*name, line length*);   — input string data to variable
                                           — *name* from next *line length*
                                           — columns

How to specify an output format:

-- for integers and enumerations

PUT (*expression, number of columns*);
PUT (32, 2); — display the number 32 in two columns
PUT (TRUE, 5); — display the value TRUE in 5 columns

-- for floating point

> PUT (*expression, number of columns before the decimal,*
> *number of columns after the decimal);*
> PUT (3.14159, 3, 3); -- *display the result 3.142 in 7*
> -- *columns*

PROBLEMS

1. Change the Ada PATTERN program to be independent of the length and width of a display. Use some of the predefined functions to do this.

2. Change the CALENDAR_MONTH program to have input parameters provide the name of the first day of the month and the number of days in the month.

3. Write a program to print this year's calendar.

4. Change the Ada PATTERN program to display a sequence of special characters such as %* − +&$. Let the pattern be repeated across every other line and every other column.

5. Write a program to fill a page with the name "Ada". Surround the name with a blank in front of and behind the name to make it stand out. Offset each line by one character so the name in the second line starts in column two.

6. Change the checkbook program to exit when a reply of 'R' is given.

7. Change the checkbook program to provide an automatic deposit in increments of $100 every time the balance is going to go negative.

8. Write a program to read in check values one by one and store them in an array. Print out the values in a column. Each check should be listed to two decimal points.

9. Write a better GET_LINE procedure that sets the rest of a string on input to blanks when the information on a line does not fill the string variable.

10. Write a better PUT_STRING procedure that specifies a width of an output field for a string. If the width is too small the information will be truncated. If the width is larger than the string, the width will be filled up with blanks.

CHAPTER
❖ 10 ❖
PACKAGES

❖ Ada's most important feature is the *package*, which is a group of related subprograms, data, and data types. Packages can be used to define software components, which can then be treated as *black boxes*. A black box is a piece of electronic equipment such as a radio—you know how to use a radio's inputs, the volume control and the station control, but you probably do not know or care what is inside a radio. Similarly, if carefully designed, you should be able to use what is inside a package without knowing the details of its contents. After you learn how to use packages, you should try to put all your future programs in packages. This chapter examines the structure of packages and the use of packages in design. Chapter 11 shows some examples of complete packages.

PACKAGE SPECIFICATIONS

Ada is a very symmetrical language. Almost every construct in Ada has two parts, and packages are no exception—they have a *specification part* and a *body*. Unlike the two parts of a procedure, the two parts of a package can be compiled separately, a valuable feature. It means that the package specifications for a program can be written and when the specifications are shown to be consistent with one another, the package bodies can be written.

When people say they are using Ada as a design language, it usually means that they are using the package specifications to describe the design. The Ada package specification contains information that could be considered the specification sheet for the package just as we have a specification sheet for a piece of stereo equipment or an automobile. The package specification is always available to any user of the package. It can also be used by the designer of the package to check that the high-level design is correct and that the later development of the package body is consistent with the specification.

The normal user of an Ada package is concerned primarily with the package specification. It is the specification that allows the package to be treated as a black box containing related subprograms, data, and data types. These subprograms are named in the package specification, and the description of the inputs and outputs for each subprogram is given. In any use of the package, the Ada compiler will check that the interface to the package matches the package specification. It is also a good idea to add comments to the package specification listing the programmer responsible for the package, a brief statement of the function of each subprogram and data item in the package, and a change history for the package.

DATA PACKAGES

An example of an Ada package specification containing only data and data types is

```
package STATUS_PANEL is
-- Package for types and data
-- Describes data used for X-27 automobile dash instrumentation
-- Programmed by Chuck Glenn
   type TEMPERATURE_TYPE is (HOT, NORMAL, COLD);
   type PRESSURE_TYPE  is (HIGH, NORMAL, LOW);
   type ELECTRICAL_TYPE is (CHARGING, NORMAL, DISCHARGING);
   type FUEL_TYPE is (EMPTY, LOW, NORMAL, FULL);

   TEMPERATURE : TEMPERATURE_TYPE;
   PRESSURE    : PRESSURE_TYPE;
   ELECTRICAL  : ELECTRICAL_TYPE;
   FUEL        : FUEL_TYPE;

end STATUS_PANEL;
```

This example shows a collection of data objects and data types placed in a package specification named STATUS_PANEL. Any other Ada program can use these four objects or declare other objects with the four data types if the package specification is compiled by an Ada compiler and stored in a program library. The four objects are of the enumeration types placed in the package. Packages containing only data and data types do not have a package body.

We can define another package specification for some other data objects such as:

```
package SENSORS is
-- Package for describing types and data
-- Used in Diablo power plant
-- Programmed by David Young
   subtype TEMPERATURE_TYPE is FLOAT range 0.0..100.0;
   subtype PRESSURE_TYPE is FLOAT range 0.0..1000.0;
   subtype ELECTRICAL_TYPE is FLOAT range 0.0..10.0;
   subtype FUEL_TYPE is FLOAT range 0.0..1.0;

   TEMPERATURE : TEMPERATURE_TYPE;
   PRESSURE    : PRESSURE_TYPE;
   ELECTRICAL  : ELECTRICAL_TYPE;
   FUEL        : FUEL_TYPE;

end SENSORS;
```

In this example, the four data objects and data types have the same names as in the previous package. The Ada compiler will be able to differentiate between objects of the same name having different data types in statements such as

```
if TEMPERATURE > 80.0 then
   START_AIR_CONDITIONER;
elsif TEMPERATURE < 60.0 then
   START_HEATER;
end if;
```

Since the TEMPERATURE object is a floating-point type instead of an enumeration type, Ada can differentiate between the objects.

To access the data and data types in a package, the package is compiled and placed in a program library. A program using the package names the package in **with** and **use** statements. The **with** statement accesses the package so that elements in the package can be used in the program such as in the next example, which calculates the average temperature from input data.

```
with TEXT_IO;
package FLOAT_IO is new TEXT_IO.FLOAT_IO (FLOAT);

with TEXT_IO, FLOAT_IO, SENSORS;
use  TEXT_IO, FLOAT_IO;
procedure AVERAGE is
   SUM : FLOAT := 0.0;
   AVERAGE_TEMPERATURE : SENSORS.TEMPERATURE_TYPE;
begin
   PUT_LINE (" Average temperature of sensor inputs ");
   for I in 1..10 loop
   -- FOR TEST USE TERMINAL INPUT
   -- REPLACE WITH SENSOR INPUT
     PUT (" Enter a temperature value "); NEW_LINE;
     GET (SENSORS.TEMPERATURE);
     SUM := SUM + SENSORS.TEMPERATURE;
   end loop;
   AVERAGE_TEMPERATURE := SUM / 10.0;
   PUT (" Average temperature is ");
```

```
      PUT (AVERAGE_TEMPERATURE, 3, 3, 0);
      NEW_LINE;
   end AVERAGE;
```

This program accesses the SENSORS package along with the TEXT_IO package and the FLOAT_IO package because of the **with** statement. The objects and data types in the program are fully qualified. The name of the package, SENSORS, precedes the name of the object in the package as in SEN-SORS.TEMPERATURE. To eliminate this qualification, we may add a **use** statement, which makes the names inside the package visible. For example, we can change the last example to

```
with TEXT_IO;
package FLOAT_IO is new TEXT_IO.FLOAT_IO (FLOAT);

with TEXT_IO, FLOAT_IO, SENSORS;
use  TEXT_IO, FLOAT_IO, SENSORS;
procedure AVERAGE is
   SUM : FLOAT := 0.0;
   AVERAGE_TEMPERATURE : TEMPERATURE_TYPE;
begin
   for I in 1..10 loop
   -- REQUEST INPUT TEMPERATURE FROM TERMINAL
      PUT (" Enter sensor temperature ");
      NEW_LINE;
      GET (TEMPERATURE);
      SUM := SUM + TEMPERATURE;
   end loop;
   AVERAGE_TEMPERATURE := SUM / 10.0;
   PUT (" Average temperature is ");
   PUT (AVERAGE_TEMPERATURE, 3, 3, 0);
   NEW_LINE;
end AVERAGE;
```

Now we can refer to the names within the package as TEMPERATURE and TEMPERATURE_TYPE. Some programmers believe that it is better to fully qualify names with the package name, and some believe it is more readable to use a **with** statement and the names as they appear in the package.

PROGRAM PACKAGES

Many applications will use packages to store related data. However, the most powerful use is to group related programs together such as a group of trigonometric functions, a group of TV games, or a group of text processing functions. Functions that are useful for a particular type of navigation equipment or for a particular display or for solving a particular type of equation should be placed in a package.

Simple examples of this type of package specification are

```
package GAMES is
   procedure SPACE_BLASTERS;
   procedure ASTRALS;
```

```
      procedure MISSION_TO_MARS;
      procedure BLACK_JACK;
   end GAMES;

   package TRIGONOMETRIC is

      PI : constant := 3.14159;
      subtype RADIAN is FLOAT range 0.0..2.0*PI;
      subtype UNIT_RANGE is FLOAT range -1.0..1.0;

      function SINE (ANGLE : RADIAN) return UNIT_RANGE;
      function COSINE (ANGLE : RADIAN) return UNIT_RANGE;

   end TRIGONOMETRIC;
```

In the first example, the package specification names a group of programs without parameters. The package body will contain the implementation of the programs and may contain other subprograms that the user of the package need not be concerned with.

The user of the package may receive an already compiled set of games with the specification. The user can then use these games, but not access the actual program that implements them. The actual program is contained in the package body, which is *hidden* from the user. The user cannot change the body or study it. This mechanism is useful for providing protection of the package body as well as for hiding details. It is analogous to our black box example. The designer of the black box does not want it altered but wants to make certain operations available to the user of the black box. By preventing attachments to the black box except at specified interfaces, the designer can prevent erroneous use of the black box as well as protect any proprietary design information. The designer may also at a future time change the internal implementation details of the black box and provide a new, improved black box that provides the same operations to the user of the black box.

In the second example, the package specifies two trigonometric functions. The range of values that are legitimate inputs and legitimate outputs are specified as subtypes. The package also contains a constant named PI, which is used in the package to define a subtype. Any user of the package has access to this type definition and to the constant. Ada will detect erroneous use of the package. For example, if a value is passed to the function not of type RADIAN or outside the range of 0 to 2*PI, an error will be detected. Errors will also be reported if a result is outside the range −1.0 to 1.0.

PROGRAM LIBRARY

Most compilers read a source program and produce a listing, reports on errors, and object code. This is illustrated in figure 10.1 by the box labeled *Brand X Compiler*. Ada compilers perform these same functions, but they have an important additional feature: They keep track not only of the program unit being compiled but other previously compiled units. This is done with the program library feature of Ada.

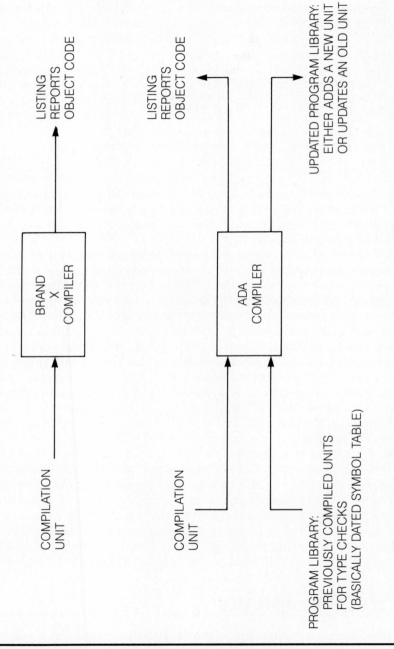

Figure 10.1   Ada Compiler compared to Brand X Compiler

In addition to the normal outputs from a compiler, an Ada compiler will provide information to be stored in a program library. This information includes interface information and the date of compilation. The date of compilation will be used by Ada to ensure that a good compilation order is used. In Ada, the program library enforces a reasonable compilation order. This is to prevent old subprograms being used when a new version has been put on the program library. Although this is not a serious problem in small examples, in the development of large programs it is difficult to keep track of the correct compilation order. Ada package libraries help in this task.

Consider the possible sequence of events listed in the table. First, a package implementing the trigonometric functions SINE and COSINE is prepared and compiled on January 15. A navigation package that uses the trigonometric package functions is prepared and compiled on February 1. If the interfaces between the two packages agree, both packages will reside in the program library.

If, on February 15, the trigonometric package is changed such that it now accepts negative angles, all the programs that use the trigonometric package will need to be recompiled. Depending on the user and the Ada environment, it may not be until February 20, when a change is made to the navigation package, that the user will be notified that it is necessary to recompile. In any case, Ada will prevent the use of out-of-date packages, as well as check that the interfaces between packages agree.

SEQUENCE OF EVENTS

JANUARY 15	COMPILE TRIGONOMETRIC PACKAGE CONTAINING SINE AND COSINE
FEBRUARY 1	COMPILE NAVIGATION PACKAGE USING TRIGONOMETRIC PACKAGE
FEBRUARY 15	CHANGE TRIGONOMETRIC PACKAGE
FEBRUARY 20	CHANGE NAVIGATION PACKAGE

PACKAGE BODIES

Another way of visualizing an Ada package is shown in figure 10.2. The two parts of the package are shown as the two parts of a window. The upper half of the window represents the package specification. It is transparent, so the specification is visible to all users. The lower half of the window is not visible since the curtain is drawn. It contains the package body, which implements the specification and which may be hidden from the user.

Package bodies can be hidden from the user by compiling them separately. The user of the package then has access to the specification and to the compiled object code but not to the source text. This feature of allowing for

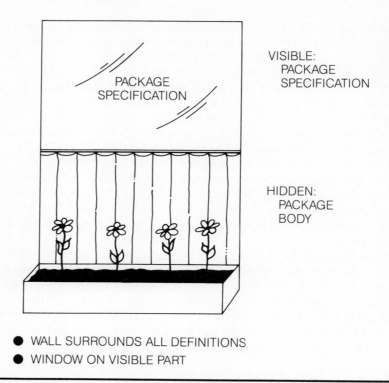

● WALL SURROUNDS ALL DEFINITIONS
● WINDOW ON VISIBLE PART

Figure 10.2   A window view of Ada packages

separate, hidden package bodies has important implications for the software industry.

The first important implication is that package specifications can be done in the software design phase of a project. These specifications can be checked by the Ada compiler for consistency and completeness before proceeding to the implementation of the package bodies. This use of Ada as a design language is very powerful—it means that the transition from design to implementation will not require using a different language or system. It also means that interface problems between parts of the program will be minimized if not eliminated.

The second implication is that a developer of a package need not expose the package implementation to potential users, which will give developers protection for proprietary software. Developers may also be able to offer several implementations satisfying the same package specification. For example, one implementation may conserve memory and another may conserve time.

An example of an Ada package specification and body is:

```
package TINY is          -- Smallest possible package
   procedure DO_NOTHING;  -- Procedure specification
end TINY;
```

```
package body TINY is          -- Package body for package TINY
  procedure DO_NOTHING is     -- Procedure implementation
  begin
    null;
  end DO_NOTHING;
end TINY;

with TINY;  use TINY;
procedure MAIN is                   -- Main program
begin
  DO_NOTHING;                       -- Use procedure in package
end MAIN;
```

In this simple example, the package TINY is defined and used in a main program, MAIN. The package specification for the package TINY contains one procedure specification for the procedure DO_NOTHING. The package body, which starts with the keywords **package body**, contains the implementation for the procedure DO_NOTHING. The implementation consists of a single **null** statement, which is the Ada statement to do nothing. MAIN uses the package named TINY by specifying it in a **with** and in an **use** statement. The main program has access to any data types, any data objects, and any subprograms specified in the package. In the example, the main program calls on the procedure named DO_NOTHING.

PACKAGE DESIGN

Packages can support a variety of design techniques, two of which are called *top-down* and *bottom-up* design. Top-down design is used when a new system of programs is to be designed. Bottom-up design is sometimes used when there is an existing base of software programmers want to use in the creation of a new system.

In a top-down design the names of the top level packages are specified, and the lower level details are specified later. For example, the start of the design of a digital flight control system might begin with

```
package DIGITAL_FLIGHT_SYSTEM is
  package NAVIGATION is
  end NAVIGATION;

  package AUTO_LAND is
  end AUTO_LAND;

  package PILOT_DISPLAY is
  end PILOT_DISPLAY;

end DIGITAL_FLIGHT_SYSTEM;

package body DIGITAL_FLIGHT_SYSTEM is
  package body NAVIGATION is
  end NAVIGATION;
```

```
package body AUTO_LAND is
end AUTO_LAND;

package body PILOT_DISPLAY is
end PILOT_DISPLAY;

end DIGITAL_FLIGHT_SYSTEM;
with DIGITAL_FLIGHT_SYSTEM;
use  DIGITAL_FLIGHT_SYSTEM;
procedure CHECK_PERFORMANCE is
begin
  null;
end CHECK_PERFORMANCE;
```

In this design, all the major functions for this system are placed in three packages: NAVIGATION, AUTO_LAND, and PILOT_DISPLAY. The packages are given the names of the major subdivisions of the system, but the package bodies are left to be defined later. The main program is given access to the packages, but does not do anything.

In a large program, each of the individual packages would be given to a designer whose responsibility would be to refine the package into subpackages. For example, the designer of the NAVIGATION package might provide a subdivision:

```
package NAVIGATION is
  package INERTIAL_NAVIGATION is
  end INERTIAL_NAVIGATION;

  package SATELLITE_NAVIGATION is
  end SATELLITE_NAVIGATION;

  package RADIO_NAVIGATION is
  end RADIO_NAVIGATION;

  package CELESTIAL_NAVIGATION is
  end CELESTIAL_NAVIGATION;

end NAVIGATION;
```

Again, the NAVIGATION package is broken down into packages, each of which need refining. This process continues until the bottom-level functions necessary to program the system are defined.

If a sizable group of designers is involved, they will meet after defining the individual functions in terms of program specifications, data types, and data objects to determine if any common functions have been defined. These functions will be brought together in a utility package for all the subsystems to use.

In the bottom-up approach to package design, the utility package for a system is defined first. The designers then define the next higher level functions until the entire system fits together. For example, a common set of utility functions could be a package of the trigonometric functions named within a package called MATH_FUNCTIONS. Then a higher level package could be designed to use the functions to calculate the great-circle distance between two points on the earth.

```
package TRIGONOMETRIC is

   PI : constant := 3.14159;
   subtype RADIAN is FLOAT range 0.0..2.0*PI;
   subtype UNIT_RANGE is FLOAT range -1.0..1.0;

   function SINE (ANGLE : RADIAN) return UNIT_RANGE;
   function COSINE (ANGLE : RADIAN) return UNIT_RANGE;

end TRIGONOMETRIC;

package body TRIGONOMETRIC is
   function SINE (ANGLE : RADIAN) return UNIT_RANGE is separate;
   function COSINE (ANGLE : RADIAN) return UNIT_RANGE is separate;
end TRIGONOMETRIC;

with TRIGONOMETRIC;
use  TRIGONOMETRIC;
package GREAT_CIRCLE_DISTANCE is
   subtype LATITUDE_IN_RADIANS  is FLOAT range -PI/2.0..PI/2.0;
   subtype LONGITUDE_IN_RADIANS is FLOAT range  0.0..2.0*PI;
   subtype DISTANCE_IN_KILOMETERS is FLOAT range 0.0..150_000.0;
   function GREAT_CIRCLE_DISTANCE (LATITUDE : LATITUDE_IN_RADIANS;
                                   LONGITUDE : LONGITUDE_IN_RADIANS)
                   return    DISTANCE_IN_KILOMETERS;

end GREAT_CIRCLE_DISTANCE;

package body GREAT_CIRCLE_DISTANCE is
   function GREAT_CIRCLE_DISTANCE (LATITUDE : LATITUDE_IN_RADIANS;
                                   LONGITUDE : LONGITUDE_IN_RADIANS)
                   return    DISTANCE_IN_KILOMETERS is separate;
end GREAT_CIRCLE_DISTANCE;
```

In either approach to design, checks are made as the design progresses that the interfaces between the different levels are consistent in type, in number of parameters, and in the use of parameters.

Another approach to Ada design is to define the objects that are to exist in the systems first. Then the types that these objects are to take on are defined, and, last, the functions that are to operate on these objects are defined. This is the *object-oriented* approach to system design. It works well when it is known what data exists in and out of a system. We will cover this technique when we look at real-time programming in chapter 20.

PACKAGE INITIALIZATION

Packages have an optional initialization section, which is executed once when
the package is declared. This section is useful for invoking initialization subprograms that are to execute only once.

```
package BANK_ACCOUNTS is
   subtype MONEY_TYPE is FLOAT range 0.0..40_000.0;
   type ACCOUNT_NUMBERS is range 1..50_000;
   type ACCOUNT_TYPE is array (ACCOUNT_NUMBERS) of MONEY_TYPE;

   procedure OPEN_ACCOUNT;
   procedure ADD_DEPOSIT (MONEY : MONEY_TYPE;
                          ACCOUNT : ACCOUNT_TYPE;
                          NEW_BALANCE : MONEY_TYPE);
   procedure SUBTRACT_WITHDRAWAL (MONEY : MONEY_TYPE;
                                  ACCOUNT : ACCOUNT_TYPE;
                                  NEW_BALANCE : MONEY_TYPE);
   end BANK_ACCOUNTS;

package body BANK_ACCOUNTS is
   procedure START_UP is separate;
   procedure OPEN_ACCOUNT is separate;
   procedure ADD_DEPOSIT (MONEY : MONEY_TYPE;
                          ACCOUNT : ACCOUNT_TYPE;
                          NEW_BALANCE : MONEY_TYPE) is separate;
   procedure SUBTRACT_WITHDRAWAL (MONEY : MONEY_TYPE;
                                  ACCOUNT : ACCOUNT_TYPE;
                                  NEW_BALANCE : MONEY_TYPE)
                                  is separate;
begin
   START_UP;
end BANK_ACCOUNTS;
```

Packages can hide underlying implementation details from a user and
can provide protection for low-level functions dealing with timing, interrupts,
or other operating system type functions a casual user might misuse.

There are several methods of hiding information in Ada. The simplest
is the use of local subprograms in a package body. A procedure placed in the
body of a package, but that does not appear in the specification part of the
package, is not available to the package's user. Rather, it is intended for use
by the package's programmer. Such subprograms are usually low-level functions that should not be used except by the programmer who wrote the package.

WHAT HAVE YOU LEARNED?

Packages are one of Ada's most important features.

Packages bring together groups of related subprograms, data, and data
types.

Packages have two parts: a specification part and a body.

The two parts of a package can be compiled separately.

A package containing only data and data types has no package body. A simple example:

```
package STATUS_PANEL is
-- Package for types and data
-- Describes data used for X-27 automobile dash instrumentation
-- Programmed by Chuck Glenn
   type TEMPERATURE_TYPE is (HOT, NORMAL, COLD);
   type PRESSURE_TYPE  is (HIGH, NORMAL, LOW);
   type ELECTRICAL_TYPE is (CHARGING, NORMAL, DISCHARGING);
   type FUEL_TYPE is (EMPTY, LOW, NORMAL, FULL);

TEMPERATURE  :  TEMPERATURE_TYPE;
PRESSURE     :  PRESSURE_TYPE;
ELECTRICAL   :  ELECTRICAL_TYPE;
FUEL         :  FUEL_TYPE;

end STATUS_PANEL;
```

To make use of the items in the package, we name the package in **with** and **use** statements. If we do not use a **use** statement, we fully qualify the name with

package name.object name

The most powerful use of Ada packages is to group related programs together with the data types and data objects to be used in the package. For example:

```
package GAMES is
   procedure SPACE_BLASTERS;
   procedure ASTRALS;
   procedure MISSION_TO_MARS;
   procedure BLACK_JACK;
end GAMES;
```

The Ada program library contains information on program interfaces and the date of compilation. The date of compilation ensures that a good compilation order is used.

Package bodies can be hidden from the user by compiling them separately. The user of the package then has access to the specification and to the compiled object code but not to the source text.

Packages can support a variety of design techniques. Included in these techniques are top-down, bottom-up, object-oriented, and data abstraction design.

Packages bodies have an optional initialization. The initialization part follows the **begin** of the package body.

```
package body package_name is
        -- implementation of subprograms
begin
        -- initialization part
end package_name;
```

PROBLEMS

1. Write a package specification for a set of subprograms to calculate a checking account report that can be printed once a month. Allow the interactive input of the data you want in the report.

2. Write the implementation of your package specification in problem 1. Use the initialization part of the package body to initialize the data in the package. Test the program with data from ten checks.

3. Write the package specification for data and subprograms that would be useful in writing a calendar program that prints the calendar for a year. You can look in an encyclopedia to determine what day January 1 falls on given the year.

4. Write the package body for the package in problem 3. Test your program by printing a calendar for this year.

5. Write the package specification for a bank that handles only saving accounts.

6. Write the package specification for a text editor. Use the specification to describe the data types, data objects, and functions of the text editor that you use to write programs.

7. Packages GREET, READ_IN, COMPUTE, and PRINT_OUT are all compiled at the same time. COMPUTE is then modified. Which packages will need to be recompiled to preserve the correct compilation order if the package dependencies are

   package COMPUTE uses package GREET.
   package PRINT_OUT uses package READ_IN and package COMPUTE.

8. Show the use of top-down design in the design of a package that performs the functions in an automated library.

CHAPTER
❖ 11 ❖

OVERLOADED OPERATORS

Ada allows you to define new operators for user-defined types. These new operators are particularly useful for string types, arrays, matrices, and records. It is often worthwhile to define a few new operators for each new application and to collect these operators together in a package. With new operators, an Ada program can often be made shorter and more understandable.

When we define new operators, we use the normal operator symbols, but *overload* the old operator. Because the assignment operator and the equality operator have special meanings in an Ada program, it is not possible to overload either one. However, almost all the other operators can be overloaded. Just as Ada can use types to distinguish between floating-point addition and integer addition, it uses types to determine when operator overloading is present for one of the new types.

New operators are designated by writing a function subprogram for the operator. We use a function subprogram with two parameters to define the binary operators that take two operands to produce a result. We use a function subprogram with one parameter to define unary operators that take one operand.

In our first example, the "–" operator is defined for arrays of type VEC-TOR. The function is written as if it were a function named SUBTRACT_ ARRAY with two parameters: A and B of type VECTOR. But instead of giving the function a name as we have done before, we give it the name of an operator by writing the operator's name within quotes in place of the name of the function. Otherwise, all the internals of the function are written as though the function had a normal name. The fact that it has the name of an operator allows it to be used in statements as a normal operator.

```
type VECTOR is array (INTEGER range <>) of FLOAT;
function "-" ( A, B : VECTOR ) return VECTOR is
   C: VECTOR (A'RANGE);
begin
   for I in A'RANGE loop
     C(I) := A(I) - B(I);
   end loop;
   return C;
end "-";
```

Any variable of type VECTOR can be subtracted from another of type VECTOR by using a simple expression. For example, if velocity is a vector with three components, we can write a program to compute the velocity gained in travel by taking the difference between the ending velocity and the beginning velocity. We might start by declaring

```
ENDING_VELOCITY, BEGINNING_VELOCITY,
      VELOCITY_GAINED_IN_TRAVEL : VECTOR (1..3);
```

and then writing the simple *assignment* statement

```
VELOCITY GAINED_IN TRAVEL := ENDING_VELOCITY -
                               BEGINNING_VELOCITY ;
```

The next program shows an example of this use.

```
with TEXT_IO;
package FLOAT_IO is new TEXT_IO.FLOAT_IO (FLOAT);
with TEXT_IO, FLOAT_IO; use TEXT_IO, FLOAT_IO;
procedure VELOCITY is
-- Unconstrained array type to represent vectors
type VECTOR is array (INTEGER range <>) of FLOAT;
-- Data for velocity
   ENDING_VELOCITY, BEGINNING_VELOCITY,
   VELOCITY_GAINED_IN_TRAVEL : VECTOR (1..3);
   function "-" (A, B : VECTOR) return VECTOR is
   -- Function to overload subtraction for objects of type vector
     C : VECTOR (A'FIRST..A'LAST);
   begin
     for I in A'RANGE loop
     C (I) := A(I) - B(I);
     end loop;
     return C;
   end "-";

procedure PUT (ITEM : VECTOR) is
begin
   for I in ITEM'RANGE loop
     PUT (ITEM (I), 5, 3, 0);
   end loop;
end PUT;
```

```
begin
   ENDING_VELOCITY := (50.0, 50.0, 25.0);
   BEGINNING_VELOCITY := (0.0, 10.0, 5.0);
   VELOCITY_GAINED_IN_TRAVEL := ENDING_VELOCITY -
                               BEGINNING_VELOCITY;
   PUT (" Velocity gained in travel = "); NEW_LINE:
   PUT (VELOCITY_GAINED_IN_TRAVEL);
end VELOCITY;
```

When the VELOCITY program executed, it produced the following output:

```
Velocity gained in travel =
   50.000   40.000   20.000
```

VARIABLE STRING OPERATIONS

Ada has left some features undefined so that you can supply these missing features with user-defined types and operations. One of these undefined features is the *variable string feature*.

In Ada, all strings are of fixed length, a characteristic suitable for only the simplest applications. But you can easily define a set of operators for variable strings to use in your programs.

Since STRING has been predefined, it is best to choose another name for the variable string type, for example, the name TEXT. To define a variable-length string, you use a record with two fields: The first field contains the string's length, the second field contains the string itself. This basic field uses the predefined data type STRING, and in this version of the definition we will give the string a maximum length of forty characters. In chapter 13, we will show how to define this maximum length at declaration time to be of various sizes.

```
type TEXT is record
   LENGTH : LENGTH_TYPE := 0;
   VARIABLE_STRING : STRING (1..40) := (others => ' ');
end record;
```

Every object of the type TEXT can store a string up to forty characters long. At the time of declaration, the string is blank and has zero length.

We can use the type TEXT to declare objects,

```
NAME : TEXT;
ADDRESS : TEXT;
```

The next question is, what operations do we want to perform on objects of type TEXT? A reasonable set of operations is:

input items of type TEXT

output items of type TEXT

assign to items of type TEXT

concatenate items of type TEXT

compare items of type TEXT

extract parts of type TEXT

search for a pattern in items of type TEXT

The operations that Ada provides us for items of type TEXT are assignment and tests for equality. Thus statements such as

```
NAME : = ADDRESS;
```

and

```
if NAME = ADDRESS then
    PUT (" Name found in address ");
end if;
```

are legal Ada statements.

We also have the ability to set an item of type TEXT using a record *aggregate* notation:

```
NAME : = ( 3, ( 'A', 'b', 'e', others => ' '));
```

Since we cannot overload assignment, we need to define a function such as ASSIGN to overcome this rather awkward notation. We can state

```
NAME : = ASSIGN ("Abe");
```

without needing to count the number of characters in the name.

We also want to state

```
PUT (NAME);   GET (NAME);
```

which are procedures instead of operators.

For this example, we will confine our overloading to the operations >, <, > =, < =, and &. All the operations except for & are relational operators. The & will overload the concatenation operator so that

```
NAME : = ASSIGN (" Abe" & " Lincoln");
```

will result in name being set to " Abe Lincoln".

Other useful operations include finding a substring that matches a pattern and replacing the match with another string. In our example, we will define these two operations as FIND and REPLACE. Their specifications will be

```
type SUBRANGE_TYPE is
    record
        FIRST_CHARACTER : NATURAL;
        SECOND_CHARACTER : NATURAL:
    end record;
```

```
function FIND ( A, B : TEXT) return SUBRANGE_TYPE:
function REPLACE (A: TEXT; B: SUBRANGE_TYPE; C: TEXT)
                    return TEXT;
```

SUBRANGE_TYPE keeps track of the two positions where the match occurred. If no match occurs, both values will be zero. The position can then be used in the REPLACE operation to make a string substitution.

Even in simple examples such as this one, procedures, functions, and operators can be overloaded to obtain a useful set of operations. We will create a package that defines a few of the operations useful for variable-length strings.

The first two procedures, GET and PUT, overload the standard procedures GET and PUT for the new type TEXT. The next operation would overload the assignment operator if we had the freedom to do so. As we saw, overloading assignment is not allowed, so we will define a function named ASSIGN to perform assignment between STRING and TEXT objects. We then define the four relational operators and the concatenation operator for TEXT objects. Finally, we specify the functions FIND and REPLACE.

In the package's body we see that the lower level functions and procedures for handling data of the predefined data types handle this new data type. The PUT operation outputs the data a character at a time up to the length of the text data. The GET operation uses the specified length of the string in the parameter to input a fixed length string, which is assigned to the TEXT data. The assign operation uses string assignment, filling in the extra characters with the blank character.

The relational operations become somewhat more complicated because we have to treat three cases: the first string being longer than the second string, the second string being longer than the first string, and the strings being of equal length. In the actual comparisons we use the array slice to compare between strings of equal length. Note that if one string is longer than another string, we compare the parts that are of equal length, and if they are equal or satisfy the relationship, the result is true. These functions are good examples of the use of BOOLEAN variables rather than **if** statements to solve problems in logic.

The two overloaded functions > and < define the functions for > = and < = . This is commonly done with overloaded functions where a higher level function uses a previously defined lower level function. In fact, a good sign that you have picked the right name for an overloaded function is when the same name or operation appears in the definition of the new function. This is the case for our new concatenation operation, the definition of which is based on the concatenation operation for strings. Note how the slice operation is used to build up the new TEXT string.

The two functions FIND and REPLACE are more sizable functions. The FIND function sets up a loop to search in the second TEXT string for the value in the first TEXT string. The slice establishes the portion of the TEXT string tested. As soon as the slice finds an equality, the function returns with the values of the indices, which point to the start and end of the match. These indices can then be used as the second parameter in the REPLACE function.

The REPLACE function makes extensive use of Ada's array slice feature to place characters in the proper position in the TEXT string on return. The best way to understand this function is to study Figure 11.1.

The first thing the program does is compute the length of the new string D.LENGTH. The new string length is the sum of the old string length and the difference between the new replacement string (A.LENGTH) and the old string (B.LAST_CHARACTER − B.FIRST_CHARACTER + 1). The rest of the program is one large assignment statement that uses the array slice operation to pick out the slices of interest. The first slice picks up the front part of the string from 1 to B.FIRST_CHARACTER−1. Note that if B.FIRST_CHARACTER is equal to 1, the range will be empty. The second slice sets the new TEXT string, A, into the character positions from B.FIRST_CHARACTER on. The third slice sets the remainder of the old TEXT string in place, and the last slice just fills the remaining positions with blanks.

By defining a set of procedures and functions for your application at the start of a project, you can make life simpler when you define more complex procedures. The example shown here is a demonstration of how a small set of functions and procedures can make string handing easier in Ada.

function REPLACE (A : TEXT; B: SUBRANGE; C: TEXT) return TEXT;

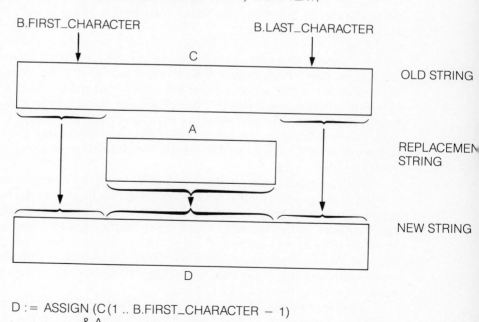

```
D := ASSIGN (C (1 .. B.FIRST_CHARACTER − 1)
             & A
             & C (B.LAST_CHARACTER + 1 .. A' LAST));
```

Figure 11.1   REPLACE operation

```
with TEXT_IO;
package INTEGER_IO is new TEXT_IO.INTEGER_IO (INTEGER);
with TEXT_IO, INTEGER_IO; use TEXT_IO, INTEGER_IO;
package VARIABLE_STRING is
  subtype LENGTH_TYPE is NATURAL;
  type TEXT is
    record
      LENGTH : LENGTH_TYPE := 0;
      VARIABLE_STRING : STRING (1..40) := (others => ' ');
    end record;

  type SUBRANGE_TYPE is
    record
      FIRST_CHARACTER : NATURAL;
      LAST_CHARACTER  : NATURAL;
    end record;

-- Input and output procedures
  procedure PUT (A : TEXT);
  procedure GET (A : out TEXT);
-- Assign operation
  function ASSIGN (A : STRING) return TEXT;
-- Relational operations
  function ">" (A, B : TEXT) return BOOLEAN;
  function "<" (A, B : TEXT) return BOOLEAN;
  function ">=" (A, B : TEXT) return BOOLEAN:
  function "<=" (A, B : TEXT) return BOOLEAN;
--Concatenation operation
  function "&" (A, B : TEXT) return TEXT;
--Find and replace functions
  function FIND (A, B : TEXT) return SUBRANGE_TYPE;
  function REPLACE (A : TEXT; B : SUBRANGE_TYPE;
                    C : TEXT) return TEXT;
end VARIABLE_STRING;

with TEXT_IO, INTEGER_IO; use TEXT_IO, INTEGER_IO;
package body VARIABLE_STRING is

-- Input and output procedures
  procedure PUT (A : TEXT) is
  -- Output character by character up to the length
  --of the string
  begin
    for I in 1..A.LENGTH loop
      PUT (A.VARIABLE_STRING (I));
    end loop;
  end PUT;

procedure GET (A : out TEXT) is
-- Reads a string of the length determined in
-- the parameter
begin
  GET_LINE (A.VARIABLE_STRING, A.LENGTH);
end GET;
```

```
-- Assign operation
  function ASSIGN (A : STRING) return TEXT is
    C : TEXT;
  begin
    C.LENGTH := A'LENGTH;
    C.VARIABLE_STRING := (others => ' ');
    C.VARIABLE_STRING (1..A'LAST) := A;
  return C;
  end ASSIGN;


-- Relational operations
  function ">" (A, B : TEXT) return BOOLEAN is
    C : BOOLEAN:
  begin
    if A.LENGTH = B.LENGTH then
      C := A.VARIABLE_STRING > B.VARIABLE_STRING;
    elsif A.LENGTH > B.LENGTH then
      C := A.VARIABLE_STRING (1..B.LENGTH) >= B.VARIABLE_STRING;
    else -- A must be shorter than B
      C := A.VARIABLE_STRING >= B.VARIABLE_STRING (1..A.LENGTH);
    end if;
    return C;
end ">";

function "<" (A, B : TEXT) return BOOLEAN is
  C : BOOLEAN;
begin
  if A.LENGTH = B.LENGTH then
    C := A.VARIABLE_STRING < B.VARIABLE_STRING;
  elsif A.LENGTH > B.LENGTH then
    C: = A.VARIABLE_STRING (1..B.LENGTH) <= B.VARIABLE_STRING;
  else -- A must be shorter than B
    C := A.VARIABLE_STRING <= B.VARIABLE_STRING (1..A.LENGTH);
  end if;
  return C;
end "<";

function ">=" (A, B : TEXT) return BOOLEAN is
begin
  return A = B or A > B;
end ">=";

function "<=" (A, B : TEXT) return BOOLEAN is
begin
  return A = B or A < B;
end "<=";

-- Concatenation operation
  function "&" (A, B : TEXT) return TEXT is
    C : TEXT;
  begin
    C.LENGTH := A.LENGTH + B.LENGTH;
    C.VARIABLE_STRING := (others => ' ');
    C.VARIABLE_STRING (1..A.LENGTH) := A.VARIABLE_STRING;
    C.VARIABLE_STRING (A.LENGTH + 1 .. C.LENGTH) := B.VARIABLE_STRING;
  end "&";
```

```
-- Find and replace functions
-- Find location of A in the string B
  function FIND (A, B : TEXT) return SUBRANGE_TYPE is
    J : NATURAL;
    C : SUBRANGE_TYPE := (0,0);
  begin
-- Find subrange for where A is in B
    for I in 1..B.LENGTH - A.LENGTH + 1 loop
      J := I + A.LENGTH - 1;
      if A.VARIABLE_STRING(1..A.LENGTH) = B.VARIABLE_STRING (I..J) then
        C := (I,J);
        return C;  -- early return on first find
      end if;
    end loop;
    return C;
  end FIND;

  function REPLACE (A : TEXT; B : SUBRANGE_TYPE;
                    C : TEXT) return TEXT is
    D : TEXT;
    L : NATURAL;
  begin
-- Put text in A in place of text in C for the
-- subrange in B
    L := B.FIRST_CHARACTER + A.LENGTH;
    D.LENGTH := C.LENGTH + L - B.LAST_CHARACTER - 1;
    D := ASSIGN (
        C.VARIABLE_STRING (1..B.FIRST_CHARACTER - 1) &
        A. VARIABLE_STRING(1..A.LENGTH) &
        C.VARIABLE_STRING (B.LAST_CHARACTER + 1 .. C.LENGTH));
    return (D);
  end REPLACE;
end VARIABLE_STRING;
```

The next program uses the VARIABLE_STRING package to do a common computer function known as *searching*. This program initializes an array containing a person's name and telephone number. Then the program enters a loop to ask for a name, search for the name in the list, and to display the telephone number for the name. Such a program can find reservations for a person, find a state's capital city given the state's name, or find any number of simple associations. The program does a *sequential search* of the data. More efficient searches are possible if the data are sorted, but it is usually worthwhile to sort the data and to use an efficient search only in applications having long lists such as a real telephone list.

```
with TEXT_IO, VARIABLE_STRING;
use  TEXT_IO, VARIABLE_STRING;
procedure VARIABLE_STRINGS is
  type TELEPHONE_TYPE is
    record
      NAME : TEXT;
      NUMBER : TEXT;
    end record;
```

```
     type TELEPHONE_LIST is
        array (POSITIVE range <>) of TELEPHONE_TYPE;
     FRIENDS_TELEPHONE : TELEPHONE_LIST (1..3);
     NAME : TEXT;
  begin
     PUT (" Variable string program is beginning "); NEW_LINE;
  -- Initialize list with names and numbers
     FRIENDS_TELEPHONE (1).NAME := ASSIGN ("Joseph Johnson");
     FRIENDS_TELEPHONE (1).NUMBER := ASSIGN ("805-964-1123");
     FRIENDS_TELEPHONE (2).NAME := ASSIGN ("David Douglas");
     FRIENDS_TELEPHONE (2).NUMBER := ASSIGN ("415-652-0328");

     FRIENDS_TELEPHONE (3).NAME : = ASSIGN ("Nancy Drew");
     FRIENDS_TELEPHONE (3).NUMBER := ASSIGN ("202-564-3095");

  -- After reading in a name, display the number
     loop -- forever loop
       PUT (" Type in a name to look up a telephone number ");
       NEW_LINE;
       GET (NAME); NEW_LINE;
       for I in FRIENDS_TELEPHONE'RANGE loop
         if NAME = FRIENDS_TELEPHONE (I).NAME then
           PUT (FRIENDS_TELEPHONE(I).NUMBER); NEW_LINE;
           exit;
         elsif I = FRIENDS_TELEPHONE'LAST then
           PUT (" Number not in list "); NEW_LINE;
         end if;
       end loop;
     end loop;
  end VARIABLE_STRINGS;
```

The last example shows how operators can support user-defined data types. However, strings are used so often in computer programs that such a definition is more like expanding the capability of Ada to do something that probably should have been defined in the language initially. Operators should also be defined for the ENUMERATION data types for functions that result in repeated code in a program.

In a navigation program, the compass points can be treated as an ENUMERATION type.

```
     type COMPASS_POINT_TYPE is ( NORTH, EAST, SOUTH, WEST );
```

In a boat, ship, or plane, it is also common to treat the directions of port and starboard as commands.

```
     type DIRECTION_TYPE is ( PORT, STARBOARD );
```

That is, if a ship heads north and is given the command to turn to port, its heading now will be west. Let us define a new operation such that adding a COMPASS_POINT_TYPE object to a DIRECTION_TYPE object will result in a new COMPASS_POINT type.

The program starts off setting the heading to north. A new order causes the program to go to a new heading by adding the order to the old heading.

At each pass through the loop the program asks for a new order and displays the new heading. The addition is handled as a new function definition. The addition operation uses two lower level functions named RIGHT_TURN and LEFT_TURN to perform the order. These functions are needed because the PRED and SUCC functions do not wrap around to the next value in the list.

```
with TEXT_IO; use TEXT_IO;
procedure SIMPLE_COMPASS is
   type COMPASS_POINT_TYPE is (NORTH, EAST, SOUTH, WEST);
   type DIRECTION_TYPE is (PORT, STARBOARD);

   package COMPASS_POINT_IO is new ENUMERATION_IO (COMPASS_POINT_TYPE);
   package DIRECTION_IO is new ENUMERATION_IO (DIRECTION_TYPE);
   use COMPASS_POINT_IO;
   use DIRECTION_IO;

HEADING : COMPASS_POINT_TYPE;
ORDER   : DIRECTION_TYPE;
   function RIGHT_TURN (A : COMPASS_POINT_TYPE)
     return COMPASS_POINT_TYPE is
     C : COMPASS_POINT_TYPE;
   begin
     if A = COMPASS_POINT_TYPE'LAST then
       C := COMPASS_POINT_TYPE'FIRST;
     else
       C := COMPASS_POINT_TYPE'SUCC (A);
     end if;
    return C;
   end RIGHT_TURN;

   function LEFT_TURN (A : COMPASS_POINT_TYPE)
     return COMPASS_POINT_TYPE is
     C : COMPASS_POINT_TYPE;
   begin
     if A = COMPASS_POINT_TYPE'FIRST then
       C := COMPASS_POINT_TYPE'LAST;
     else
       C := COMPASS_POINT_TYPE'PRED (A);
     end if;
     return C;
   end LEFT_TURN;

   function "+" (A : COMPASS_POINT_TYPE; B : DIRECTION_TYPE)
     return COMPASS_POINT_TYPE is
     C : COMPASS_POINT_TYPE;
   begin
     case B is
       when PORT => C := LEFT_TURN (A);
       when STARBOARD => C := RIGHT_TURN (A);
     end case;
     return C;
   end "+";
```

```
begin
  HEADING := NORTH;  -- Starting value
  loop -- loop forever
    PUT (" Current heading is ");  PUT (HEADING);
    PUT (" ENTER ORDER, PORT OR STARBOARD ");  NEW_LINE;
    GET  (ORDER);  NEW_LINE;
    HEADING := HEADING + ORDER;
  end loop;
end SIMPLE_COMPASS;
```

Two-dimensional arrays, or matrices, are often used with operators to perform addition, subtraction, and multiplication of the matrices. The addition and subtraction of matrices is similar to the addition and subtraction of vectors. Each element is operated on by the addition or subtraction operator and stored in the corresponding element. For example, addition is written as

```
C(I,J) := A(I,J) + B(I,J);
```

where the statement is placed in loops that vary I and J over all values.

Multiplication is somewhat more complicated in that the element of the resulting matrix is the result of adding up products. Multiplication is usually defined as

$$C(I,J) := \sum_{M} A(I,M) * B(M,J)$$

Since this is not an Ada statement it translates to a loop over M. C(I,J) is initially set to zero, and the loop adds the product of A(I,M) and B(M,J) to the previous sum in the loop.

```
for M in A'RANGE(2) loop
  C(I,J) := C(I,J) + A(I,M) * B(M,J);
end loop;
```

The following package defines operators for matrix addition and multiplication; it also contains procedures for input and output of matrices. This package is then used in the program MATRIX_EXAMPLE to show how two matrices can be multiplied together with the new operator *.

```
with TEXT_IO;
package FLOAT_IO is new TEXT_IO.FLOAT_IO (FLOAT);

with TEXT_IO, FLOAT_IO;
use TEXT_IO, FLOAT_IO;

package MATRIX_OPERATORS is
  type MATRIX is array (INTEGER range <>, INTEGER range <>) of
    FLOAT;
  function "+" (A, B : MATRIX) return MATRIX;
  function "*" (A, B : MATRIX) return MATRIX;
  procedure GET (A : out MATRIX);
  procedure PUT (A : in MATRIX);
end MATRIX_OPERATORS;
```

```
with TEXT_IO, FLOAT_IO;
use  TEXT_IO, FLOAT_IO;
package body MATRIX_OPERATORS is
   function "+" (A, B : MATRIX) return MATRIX is
      C : MATRIX (A'FIRST (1)..A'LAST (1),
                  A'FIRST (2)..A'LAST (2));
   begin
     for I in A'RANGE (1) loop
       for J in A'RANGE (2) loop
         C (I, J) := A(I, J) + B(I, J);
         end loop;
       end loop;
     return C;
   end "+";

   function "*" (A, B : MATRIX) return MATRIX is
      C : MATRIX (A'FIRST (1)..A'LAST (1),
                  B'FIRST (2)..B'LAST (2));
   begin
     for I in A'RANGE (1) loop
       for J in B'RANGE (2) loop
         C (I, J) := 0.0;
         for M in A'RANGE (2) loop
           C (I, J) := C (I, J) + A (I, M) * B (M, J);
           end loop;
         end loop;
       end loop;
     return C;
   end "*";

   procedure GET (A : out MATRIX) is
   begin
     for I in A'RANGE (1) loop
       for J in A'RANGE (2) loop
         GET (A (I, J));
         end loop;
       end loop;
     NEW_LINE;
   end GET;

   procedure PUT (A : in MATRIX) is
   begin
     for I in A'RANGE (1) loop
       for J in A'RANGE (2) loop
         PUT (A (I, J));
         end loop;
       NEW_LINE;
       end loop;
   end PUT;
end MATRIX_OPERATORS;

with TEXT_IO, MATRIX_OPERATORS;
use  TEXT_IO, MATRIX_OPERATORS;
procedure MATRIX_EXAMPLE is
   X, Y, Z : MATRIX (1..3, 1..3);
```

```
begin
   PUT (" Matrix example program is beginning. ");
   NEW_LINE;
   X := ((1.0,  0.0,  4.0),
         (6.0,  2.2,  1.2),
         (5.1,  1.1,  2.2));
   PUT (" The first matrix values are "); NEW_LINE;
   PUT (X);
   Y := ((6.7,  1.2,  2.2),
         (3.3,  4.4,  5.6),
         (7.2,  8.5,  1.6));
   PUT (" The second matrix values are "); NEW_LINE;
   PUT (Y);
   Z := X * Y;
   PUT (" The result of multiplying the two matrices is ");
   NEW_LINE;
   PUT (Z);
end MATRIX_EXAMPLE;
```

When the matrix example program executed, it produced the following output:

```
Matrix example program is beginning.
The first matrix values are
1.00000E+00 0.00000E+00 4.00000E+00
6.00000E+00 2.20000E+00 1.20000E+00
5.10000E+00 1.10000E+00 2.20000E+00
The second matrix values are
6.70000E+00 1.20000E+00 2.20000E+00
3.30000E+00 4.40000E+00 5.60000E+00
7.20000E+00 8.50000E+00 1.60000E+00
The result of multiplying the two matrices is
3.55000E+01 3.52000E+01 8.60000E+00
5.61000E+01 2.70800E+01 2.74400E+01
5.36400E+01 2.96600E+01 2.09000E+01
```

WHAT HAVE YOU LEARNED?

New operators are designated via the definition of a new function subprogram for the operator, which is named by the operation symbol within quotes.

Most operators can be overloaded. Exceptions are the assignment and the equality operations. (The equality operation can be renamed but this is rarely a good idea.) Other operators that cannot be overloaded are the short circuit logical operators (**and then, or then**) and the membership operators (**in, not in**). All the binary operators can be redefined using a function subprogram with two parameters. The unary operators can be redefined using a function subprogram that has one parameter.

Binary operators:

+ – * /	**and or not xor**	> >= < <=
** &		**mod rem**

Unary operators:

– (negation)	**not**	**abs**

Overloaded operators are usually placed in a package together with the data types for the operators.

Overloaded operators can be defined for user-defined data types whether the type is an enumeration, an array, or a record. Almost every application can benefit from the definition of a few overloaded operators and procedures.

PROBLEMS

1. Write a program that uses overloading of the addition operator for vectors. In the program read into the computer the values for the initial velocity and the velocity gained in travel. Use these quantities and your definition of the addition operator to compute the ending velocity. Display your result.

2. Add to the functions defined in the example in this chapter:

```
function FIND ( A: STRING; B: TEXT) return POSITIVE;
function REPLACE ( A:  TEXT;  B:  SUBRANGE_TYPE;  C:  STRING)
                                              return TEXT;
```

which will overload the previously defined procedures named FIND and REPLACE in the package VARIABLE_STRING. These new functions allow some of the parameters to be a string object where appropriate. We can use them in statements such as

```
SUB_RANGE : = FIND ("Mary" , NAME);
NAME      : = REPLACE ( NAME , SUB_RANGE, "Nancy");
```

so that if NAME contained the string "Mary Smith" before these statements, it would contain "Nancy Smith" after the statements. Write your program to alter your first name with these functions.

3. Write a function for the specification

```
function ASSIGN ( A: TEXT ) return STRING;
```

which will allow assignment of text objects to fixed string objects. Use such a function in a program that inputs data to a variable of type STRING, assigns the input data to a variable of type TEXT, assigns it back to a variable of type STRING, and then outputs the STRING data. Test the program with the names of the days of the week.

4. What happens in the VARIABLE_STRING program when a person enters a name that is not on the list? Change the program to present a message telling the user that the name is not on the list. Then let the user enter the name again or enter another name.

5. Define a new REPLACE function that does away with the FIND function by

```
function REPLACE ( A , B, C : TEXT) return TEXT;
```

where A is the text string to search for in B. If found, the result of the function will be to replace the matching text in B with the text in C. That is if

```
A := ASSIGN ( "Car" );
B := ASSIGN ( "Boat, Train, or Car" );
C := ASSIGN ( "Airplane" );
REPLACE     (A, B, C)  will have a value which represents "Boat, Train, or Airplane."
```

6. Write a function to rotate a text string.

```
ROTATE  ("abcd")  will result in a value "dabc".
```

7. A data type that is very useful in embedded applications is the bit string.

```
type BIT_STRING is array ( POSITIVE range < >) of BOOLEAN;
```

Define a set of operators to perform the logical operations **and**, **or**, and **xor** for data of type BIT_STRING.

8. Define a function for the data type DAY_TYPE so that you can add an integer to the day value and come up with the name of the day. For example, Monday + 2 will have the value Wednesday.

```
type DAY_TYPE is (SUNDAY,   MONDAY, TUESDAY, WEDNESDAY,
                  THURSDAY, FRIDAY, SATURDAY);
```

A good attribute to use in this example is 'POS.

9. Add a a "–" operation to the MATRIX_OPERATIONS package. Use the package to input two matrices, to take the difference between them, and to display the result.

10. A useful vector operation is called the *dot product*. In the dot product, each element of two vectors is multiplied together. Then the sum of the products is taken to result in a single number. For example, (1,2,3) dot (4,5,6) results in 4 + 10 + 18 or 32. Write a dot product operation using ∗ for the vector data type and test it with the example in this problem.

11. In the package MATRIX_OPERATIONS, the operation ∗ assumes that the number of columns in matrix A is the same as the number of rows in matrix B. Change the function to display an error message if this assumption is not correct.

CHAPTER
❖ 12 ❖

GENERIC SUBPROGRAMS

Ada is a strongly typed language, which means subprogram parameters must match exactly in number and type. In any large application, this limitation is overly restrictive. Ada solves this potential problem in an elegant manner by using *generic subprograms,* which can also eliminate another of Ada's restrictions, the ban against using subprograms as parameters.

You will want to use a generic procedure when your procedure operates on more than one data type. For example, in chapter 11 we examined an operation common to many applications—searching for a value in a list. In the example we searched a list of friends' names and ouput a friend's telephone number. We can write a subprogram to perform the search:

```
function SEARCH (NAME : TEXT; LIST : TELEPHONE_LIST)
                    return TEXT is
begin
  for I in TELEPHONE_LIST'RANGE loop
    if TELEPHONE_LIST(I).NAME = NAME then
      return TELEPHONE_LIST(I).NUMBER;
    elsif I=TELEPHONE_LIST'LAST then
        return TELEPHONE_LIST(I).NUMBER;
    end if;
  end loop;
end SEARCH;
```

But if we later want to search a list of states for a state name and return the name of its capital, we will have to write another search function with different types of parameters. The new search function's internal statements will perform the same operations as in the old program. To avoid this repetition of effort, such common functions as the search function can be generic.

Generic subprograms are classified by the types of parameters you use in the subprogram: private, enumeration, integer, floating-point, fixed, and limited private type parameters. We will discuss and look at an example of each parameter class.

PRIVATE PARAMETERS

The most general generic parameter—of the type name **private**, which is a reserved word—is used in subprogram statements that call on the assignment, equality, and inequality operators.

In our search subprogram, for instance, we used only the assignment and equality operators. Thus this subprogram is a candidate for becoming a generic subprogram. We can rewrite the function as a generic function:

```
generic
  type ITEM_TYPE is private;
  type KEY_LIST_TYPE is array  (POSITIVE range <>) of ITEM_TYPE;
  type DATA_LIST_TYPE is array (POSITIVE range <>) of ITEM_TYPE;
function SEARCH (KEY : ITEM_TYPE; KEY_LIST : KEY_LIST_TYPE;
                 DATA_LIST : DATA_LIST_TYPE)  return ITEM_TYPE;
function SEARCH (KEY : ITEM_TYPE; KEY_LIST : KEY_LIST_TYPE;
                 DATA_LIST : DATA_LIST_TYPE)  return ITEM_TYPE is
begin
  for I in KEY_LIST'RANGE loop
    if KEY = KEY_LIST (I) then
      return DATA_LIST (I);
    elsif I = KEY_LIST'LAST then
      return DATA_LIST (I);
    end if;
  end loop;
end SEARCH;
```

The generic subprogram starts off with the reserved word **generic**. Before the function or procedure specification, the generic parameters are listed in terms of their type definitions. After the type definitions and the procedure specification, the normal program follows with the parameters being used in the usual statements. You can think of each of the three statements as a parameter.

You can also think of the generic subprogram as a template with the blanks labeled **private**; these blanks are filled in when you use the program. In just the same way, to use a subprogram you fill in the blanks with type names. It is just as though you gave type definitions where the reserved word **private** appears in the generic definition. For example, instead of

```
type ITEM_TYPE is private;
type KEY_LIST_TYPE is array (POSITIVE range <>) of ITEM_TYPE;
type DATA_LIST_TYPE is array (POSITIVE range <>) of ITEM_TYPE;
```

you want to have

```
type ITEM_TYPE is TEXT;
type KEY_LIST_TYPE is TEXT_LIST;
type DATA_LIST_TYPE is TEXT_LIST;
```

To accomplish this transformation, you perform a *generic instantiation,* which means you substitute actual types for the types listed as private types in this definition of the generic subprogram.

To instantiate the function subprogram named SEARCH with the types that you want to use in your program, you write

```
function SEARCH is new SEARCH (TEXT, TEXT_LIST, TEXT_LIST);
```

You could even give a different name to the program if you wanted. For example,

```
function FIND is new SEARCH (TEXT, TEXT_LIST, TEXT_LIST);
```

The reserved word **new** and the list of types in the parameters causes the creation or instantiation of a program from the generic template. It is as if you had written the specification for the program as

```
function SEARCH ( NAME : TEXT;  KEY_LIST : TEXT_LIST;
                  DATA_LIST : TEXT_LIST) return TEXT;
```

ENUMERATION PARAMETERS

A second class of generic parameters, the *enumeration parameters,* allows the use of all the operators for enumeration types: the relational operators, $<$, $<=$, $>$, and $>=$; the SUCC operator; the PRED operator; and the membership operators **in** and **not in**. Our example for this type of parameter is a generic function named WRAP—we have seen this function defined for several types in chapter 11. This function is like the SUCC operator, but it wraps around to the first value in the list, which SUCC does not do. This function is useful for all enumeration types, so it is a good candidate for a generic function. Generic parameters of the enumeration type are specified as ($<>$). Thus,

```
generic
  type ENUMERATION is (<>);
function WRAP (A : ENUMERATION) return ENUMERATION ;
function WRAP (A : ENUMERATION) return ENUMERATION is
  B : ENUMERATION;
begin
  if A = ENUMERATION'LAST then
    B := ENUMERATION'FIRST;
  else
    B := ENUMERATION'SUCC(A);
  end if;
  return B;
end WRAP;
```

To instantiate WRAP to be our function RIGHT_TURN, which we used in chapter 11 for objects of type COMPASS_POINT_TYPE, write

```
function RIGHT_TURN is new WRAP (COMPASS_POINT_TYPE);
```

The function is created as though you had written all the lines in the RIGHT _TURN function for the proper type.

The general form for a generic instantiation of a function is

```
function identifier name is new generic name (type list);
```

INTEGER PARAMETERS

The third case of generic parameters is the type used with integer operations and the integer data types. The operations $+$, $-$, $*$, $/$, **rem, mod**, and $**$ can be used in addition to the operations of the enumeration type and the assignment and equality and inequality operations. To use these operations, the generic parameter is defined to be **range** $<>$. A simple generic function for the integer class of operations is a SUM function, which will sum the values in an array of any integer type.

```
generic
   type INDEX_TYPE is range <>;
   type ELEMENT_TYPE is range <>;
   type GENERIC_ARRAY is array (INDEX_TYPE) of
        ELEMENT_TYPE;
function SUM (A : GENERIC_ARRAY) return ELEMENT_TYPE;
function SUM (A : GENERIC_ARRAY) return ELEMENT_TYPE is
   S : ELEMENT_TYPE := 0;
begin
   for I in INDEX_TYPE loop
     S := S + A(I);
   end loop;
   return S;
end SUM;
```

To use this function we instantiate it by the statement

```
function ADD is new SUM (INTEGER, INTEGER,
                            INTEGER_ARRAY_TYPE);
```

Now we can use the instantiated function to sum up arrays where the element and the indices are of the same type.

```
function ADD is new SUM (PUPIL_NUMBER_TYPE, HEIGHT_TYPE,
                            HEIGHT_ARRAY_TYPE);
```

This form of the instantiated function can sum up arrays whose elements are of type HEIGHT_TYPE, which are indexed by integers.

The next program instantiates the generic SUM function to calculate the average height of students in a class.

```
with TEXT_IO; use TEXT_IO;
procedure AVERAGE_HEIGHT is
   type HEIGHT_TYPE is range 0..1000; -- upper bound for
        -- sum of 10 pupils each over 8 feet tall
   type PUPIL_NUMBER_TYPE is range 1..10;
   type HEIGHT_ARRAY_TYPE is array (PUPIL_NUMBER_TYPE) of
        HEIGHT_TYPE;
   HEIGHT_ARRAY    : HEIGHT_ARRAY_TYPE;
   TOTAL, AVERAGE : HEIGHT_TYPE;
   package HEIGHT_IO is new INTEGER_IO (HEIGHT_TYPE);
   use HEIGHT_IO;
   generic
      type INDEX_TYPE is range <>;
      type ELEMENT_TYPE is range <>;
      type GENERIC_ARRAY is array (INDEX_TYPE) of
         ELEMENT_TYPE;
   function SUM (A : GENERIC_ARRAY) return ELEMENT_TYPE;
   function SUM (A : GENERIC_ARRAY) return ELEMENT_TYPE is
      S : ELEMENT_TYPE := 0;
   begin
      for I in INDEX_TYPE loop
         S := S + A(I);
      end loop;
      return S;
   end SUM;
   function ADD is new SUM (PUPIL_NUMBER_TYPE, HEIGHT_TYPE,
                           HEIGHT_ARRAY_TYPE);

begin
   PUT (" Average height program beginning "); NEW_LINE;
   PUT (" Type in pupil height for each pupil "); NEW_LINE:
   for I in PUPIL_NUMBER_TYPE loop
      GET (HEIGHT_ARRAY(I));
   end loop;
   TOTAL := ADD (HEIGHT_ARRAY);
   AVERAGE := TOTAL/HEIGHT_ARRAY'LENGTH;
   PUT (" Average height is "); PUT (AVERAGE); NEW_LINE;
end AVERAGE_HEIGHT;
```

FLOATING-POINT PARAMETERS

The fourth type of generic parameter allows you to use floating-point operations. We can convert our last example to sum up arrays where the element type is one of the floating-point types merely by changing the generic parameter for the element type to **digits** <>. In this case the generic function would appear as

```
generic
   type INDEX_TYPE is range <>;
   type ELEMENT_TYPE is digits <>;
   type GENERIC_ARRAY is array (INDEX_TYPE) of
      ELEMENT_TYPE;
```

```
function SUM (A : GENERIC_ARRAY) return ELEMENT_TYPE;
function SUM (A : GENERIC_ARRAY) return ELEMENT_TYPE is
  S : ELEMENT_TYPE := 0.0;
begin
  for I in INDEX_TYPE loop
    S := S + A(I);
  end loop;
  return S;
end SUM;
```

The only changes to the SUM function are the initialization of the partial sum, S, to 0.0 instead of 0 and the definition of the ELEMENT_TYPE to

```
type ELEMENT_TYPE is digits <>;
```

FIXED AND LIMITED PRIVATE TYPE PARAMETERS

There are two other cases for the generic type parameters:

```
type SOME_TYPE is delta <>; -- for fixed-point types
type SOME_OTHER_TYPE is limited private; -- for types that
                    -- are intended to have all their
                    -- operations defined in a package
```

The fixed-point types are useful in computers without built-in floating-point operations. Some of the very small computers need to use fixed-point types to perform rapid calculations. We will discuss fixed-point types in chapter 20.

The **limited private** types are useful in restricting the available operations on an object. We will show examples of the use of these types in chapter 15.

PACKAGES AND PROCEDURES

All the examples in this chapter have been functions, but generic procedures and packages can also be defined. In fact, Ada's input and output mechanisms are defined in terms of generic packages—most useful subprograms in libraries will be defined in generic packages.

In chapters 1 and 3 we looked at ways to prepare useful input/output programs. At the time you were actually following directions for generic instantiation of packages in a package named TEXT_IO for some of the simple data types such as INTEGER, BOOLEAN, and FLOAT. Ada does provide input and output for characters and strings without requiring generic instantiation, but all the other data types do require it.

The following example shows how to create a package containing the input and output procedures for the predefined types INTEGER, FLOAT, and BOOLEAN.

```
with TEXT_IO;
package SIMPLE_IO is
   package INTEGER_IO is new TEXT_IO.INTEGER_IO (INTEGER);
   package FLOAT_IO is new TEXT_IO.FLOAT_IO (FLOAT);
   package BOOLEAN_IO is new TEXT_IO.ENUMERATION_IO (BOOLEAN);
end SIMPLE_IO;
```

The line in the package definition for BOOLEAN_IO allows input and output of the enumeration (FALSE, TRUE). If you wanted to input or output some other enumeration type such as

```
type STATUS_TYPE is (OFF, TRANSIENT, STABLE, ABNORMAL);
```

you can write an instantiation:

```
with TEXT_IO;
package STATUS_IO is new TEXT_IO.ENUMERATION_IO (STATUS_TYPE);
```

For example, the package we defined in chapter 11 to perform operations on matrices was useful only for matrices consisting of FLOAT and element INTEGER indices. A more general package requires the definition of a generic package. In fact, when writing a package, you should always think of ways to generalize it into a generic package so that it can be used with other data types. For example, to turn the MATRIX_OPERATORS package defined in the last chapter into a generic package, we can write the package specification:

```
with TEXT_IO;
use TEXT_IO;
generic
   type INDEX_TYPE is (<>);
   type ELEMENT_TYPE is digits <>;
   type MATRIX_TYPE is array (INDEX_TYPE range <>,
                              INDEX_TYPE range <>) of
                              ELEMENT_TYPE;
package MATRIX_OPERATORS is
   package MATRIX_IO is new TEXT_IO.FLOAT_IO(ELEMENT_TYPE);
   use MATRIX_IO;
   function "+" (A, B : MATRIX_TYPE) return MATRIX_TYPE;
   function "-" (A, B : MATRIX_TYPE) return MATRIX_TYPE;
   function "*" (A, B : MATRIX_TYPE) return MATRIX_TYPE;
   procedure GET (A : out MATRIX_TYPE);
   procedure PUT (A : in MATRIX_TYPE);
end MATRIX_OPERATORS;
```

We write the package body as before, remembering to use the attributes of the parameters. To use the package, instantiate it as in the next example, which adds two real matrices using the generic package.

```
with TEXT_IO, MATRIX_OPERATORS;
procedure ADD_MY_MATRICES is
   use TEXT_IO;
   type MY_MATRIX_TYPE is array (INTEGER range <>,
                                 INTEGER range <>) of FLOAT;
   package MY_OPERATIONS is new MATRIX_OPERATORS (INTEGER, FLOAT,
                              MY_MATRIX_TYPE);
```

```
    use MY_OPERATIONS;
    X : MY_MATRIX_TYPE (1..2, 1..3) := ((1.0, 2.0, 3.0), (4.0, 5.0, 6.0));
    Y : MY_MATRIX_TYPE (1..2, 1..3) := ((3.0, 7.0, 8.0), (1.0, 2.0, 3.0));
    Z : MY_MATRIX_TYPE (1..2, 1..3) ;
begin
    PUT (" Matrix generic program is beginning. ");
    NEW_LINE:
    PUT (" The first matrix values are "); NEW_LINE:
    PUT (X);
    PUT (" The second matrix values are "); NEW_LINE;
    PUT (Y);
    Z := X + Y;
    PUT (" The result of adding the two matrices is ");
    NEW_LINE;
    PUT (Z);
end ADD_MY_MATRICES;
```

The declaration statement initializes the two matrices, X and Y. Then an assignment statement sets the matrix Z to the sum of the two matrices. The assignment statement uses the overloaded operation for addition to add the two matrices. The instantiation of package MATRIX_OPERATIONS in the declaration part of the program allows you to use integer indices and floating-point elements. The instantiation of package FLOAT_IO in TEXT_IO allows the output of floating-point objects.

FORMAL PARAMETERS

Although variable-length strings are often implemented by records containing a length field and a string field, they can also be implemented by a generic procedure that defines a variable-length string type and the operations to be performed on that type.

This example shows another kind of parameter, the formal parameter, which has a value, and which can be used in a generic procedure or package. Generic procedures may be passed values or even expressions as a parameter.

```
    with TEXT_IO; use TEXT_IO;
    generic
      MAXIMUM_LENGTH : NATURAL;
    package VARIABLE_STRING is
      subtype LENGTH_TYPE is NATURAL;
      type TEXT is
        record
          LENGTH : LENGTH_TYPE := 0;
          VARIABLE_STRING : STRING (1..MAXIMUM_LENGTH) := (others => ' ');
        end record;

    -- Input and output procedures
      procedure PUT (A : TEXT);
      procedure GET (A : out TEXT);
    -- Assign operation
      function ASSIGN (A : STRING) return TEXT;
```

```
-- Concatenation operation
  function "&" (A, B : TEXT) return TEXT;
end VARIABLE_STRING;
```

To use such a package, you must decide on the maximum length of all the strings that the subprograms are to operate on and instantiate the package for a string of that length.

```
with VARIABLE_STRING;
package MY_STRINGS is new VARIABLE_STRING (100);
```

You then have available the operations defined in the package to define objects such as

```
LINE : TEXT;
```

in the declaration part of the program.

The advantage of defining variable-length strings as a record type having a discriminant is that there is no need to instantiate the package for different maximum-length strings. All you need to do is define the string and its maximum length in the definition for the variable string. Since all the operations defined for the variable string type will be valid for all variable-length strings, there is no need to rewrite another package of functions and procedures. Hence generic packages do not seem useful when a procedure is to operate on a constrained type. They are very useful when a procedure is to operate on different data types as the GET and PUT procedures do.

SUBPROGRAM PARAMETERS

Ada does not normally allow a subprogram to be a parameter to another subprogram, although this ability has been found useful in symbolic manipulation and mathematical integration. The language LISP is known for its expressive power mainly because a subprogram can be a parameter to another subprogram.

In Ada, a subprogram can be a parameter in generic subprograms. In the next example, we define a generic procedure that performs integration of a function defined as a parameter to the procedure. Function parameters are preceded by the keyword **with** in the specification of the generic parameters.

```
generic
  with function Y (X : FLOAT) return FLOAT;
procedure INTEGRATION (X_MINIMUM, X_MAXIMUM : FLOAT;
                       RESULT : out FLOAT);
procedure INTEGRATION (X_MINIMUM, X_MAXIMUM : FLOAT;
                       RESULT : out FLOAT) is
  STEP_SIZE : FLOAT := (X_MAXIMUM - X_MINIMUM)/10.0;
  X : FLOAT := X_MINIMUM;
begin
  RESULT := 0.0;
  for I in 1..10 loop
```

```
       RESULT : = RESULT + STEP_SIZE * Y(X);
       X : = FLOAT (I) * STEP_SIZE + X_MINIMUM;
    end loop;
  end INTEGRATION;
```

Now, say we want to integrate the function X^2 between $X = 0$ and $X = 1$. To do so, we first define the function for X^2 as

```
function Y(X : FLOAT) return FLOAT is
begin
   return X**2;
end Y;
```

We then instantiate the integration procedure by writing

```
function INTEGRATE_X_SQUARE is new INTEGRATION(Y);
```

This can be put in a package and used by a main program:

```
generic
  with function Y (X : FLOAT) return FLOAT;
package INTEGRATION_ROUTINE is
  procedure INTEGRATION (X_MINIMUM, X_MAXIMUM : FLOAT;
                           RESULT : out FLOAT;
end INTEGRATION_ROUTINE;
package body INTEGRATION_ROUTINE is
  procedure INTEGRATION (X_MINIMUM, X_MAXIMUM : FLOAT;
                           RESULT : out FLOAT) is
    STEP_SIZE : FLOAT : = (X_MAXIMUM − X_MINIMUM)/10.0;
    X : FLOAT : = X_MINIMUM;
begin
    RESULT : = 0.0;
    for I in 1..10 loop
      RESULT : = RESULT + STEP_SIZE * Y(X);
       X : = FLOAT (I) * STEP_SIZE + X_MINIMUM;
      end loop;
   end INTEGRATION;
end INTEGRATION_ROUTINE;

with TEXT_IO;
package FLOAT_IO is new TEXT_IO.FLOAT_IO (FLOAT);

with TEXT_IO, FLOAT_IO, INTEGRATION_ROUTINE;
use  TEXT_IO, FLOAT_IO;
procedure MAIN is
  RESULT : FLOAT;
  function Y (X : FLOAT) return FLOAT is separate;
  package INTEGRATE_X_SQUARE is new
            INTEGRATION_ROUTINE (Y);
  use INTEGRATE_X_SQUARE;
begin
  PUT (" Test integration routine "); NEW_LINE;
  INTEGRATION (0.0, 1.0, RESULT);
  PUT (" Integral of X squared over the interval 0 to 1 ");
  NEW_LINE;
  PUT (RESULT); NEW_LINE;
end MAIN;
```

```
separate (MAIN)
function Y (X : FLOAT) return FLOAT is
begin
   return X**2;
end Y;
```

Naturally we can also pass parameters such as a data type and a value by defining the generic package to have other parameters. For example, if we define the generic package as

```
generic
   type FLOAT_TYPE is digits <>;
   with function Y (X : FLOAT_TYPE) return FLOAT_TYPE;
package INTEGRATION_ROUTINE is
   procedure INTEGRATION (X_MINIMUM, X_MAXIMUM : FLOAT_TYPE;
                                RESULT : out FLOAT_TYPE);
end INTEGRATION_ROUTINE;
```

The instantiation of the package has two parameters. The first specifies the type and the second the function.

```
with TEXT_IO, INTEGRATION_ROUTINE;
use TEXT_IO;
procedure MAIN is
   type REAL is digits 4;
   RESULT : REAL;
   function Y ( X : REAL) return REAL is separate;
   package INTEGRATE_X_SQUARE is new
            INTEGRATION_ROUTINE (REAL, Y);
   use INTEGRATE_X_SQUARE;
   package REAL_IO is new TEXT_IO.FLOAT_IO (REAL);
   use REAL_IO;
begin
   PUT (" Test integration routine "); NEW_LINE:
   INTEGRATION (0.0, 1.0, RESULT);
   PUT (" Integral of X squared over the interval 0 to 1 ");
   NEW_LINE:
   PUT (RESULT); NEW_LINE;
end MAIN;
```

This example integrates variables of type REAL, which are defined to have 4 digit accuracy.

WHAT HAVE YOU LEARNED?

Use a generic procedure, function, or package when your subprogram can be used

on more than one data type
with functions as procedures
to make general packages

The form of a generic unit is

generic
   -- generic parameters
procedure *procedure name and parameters* **is**
   -- declarations that can be
   -- in terms of generic parameters
   -- along with other declarations
begin
   -- executable statements
end *procedure name;*

or

generic
   -- generic parameters
function *function name and parameters* **return** *function type;*
function *function name and parameters* **return** *function type* **is**
   -- declarations for the function
   -- which may be in terms of generic parameters
   -- along with other declarations
begin
   -- executable statements
end *function name;*

or

generic
   -- generic parameters
package *package name* **is**
   -- package specification
end *package name;*

Generic parameters can be

private
   -- to match any data type and have the operations of := , = , and /=
      available
   -- operations defined in other subunits can be passed as parameters to
      the generic unit
   -- probably the most useful generic parameter type
   -- to make NAME_TYPE a private parameter

```
type NAME_TYPE is private;
```

limited private
   -- to match any data type and to only have operations defined in the
      generic unit or passed as parameters available for use
   -- to make BANK_ACCOUNT_TYPE a **limited private** parameter

```
type BANK_ACCOUNT_TYPE is limited private;
```

enumeration
    -- to match any enumeration data type and to have the enumeration
         operations available
    -- characters and Booleans are enumeration types
    -- useful for expanding the repertoire of operations on enumeration types
    -- to make DAY_LIST an enumeration type parameters

```
type DAY_LIST is (<>);
```

integer
    -- to match any integer data type and to have the integer operations
         available
    -- useful for mathematical functions on integers
    -- to make SMALL_INTEGER an integer type parameter

```
type SMALL_INTEGER is range <>;
```

floating point
    -- to match any floating-point data type and to have the floating-point
         operations available
    -- useful for mathematical functions on floating-point numbers
    -- to make LARGE_FLOAT a floating-point type parameter

```
type LARGE_FLOAT is digits <>;
```

fixed point
    -- to match any fixed-point data type and to have the fixed-point oper-
         ations available
    -- useful for mathematical functions on fixed-point numbers
    -- to make DOLLAR_TYPE a fixed-point type parameter

```
type DOLLAR_TYPE is delta <>;
```

function
    -- to match any function including all the defined operations
    -- useful for passing functions as parameters, which includes defining
         operations to a generic subprogram defined in terms of private types
    -- to make INTEGRATION_FUNCTION a function type parameter

```
with function INTEGRATION_FUNCTION
        (any parameters for the function)
        return function type name;
```

PROBLEMS

1. Write a generic function to compute the average of an integer array. Test it by instantiating for an array that computes the average height of ten students.

2. Rewrite the MATRIX_OPERATORS package to contain input and output operations for objects of MATRIX_TYPE. Use the new package in a better

version of the program ADD_MY_MATRICES to replace the loops in the program with PUT(Z).

3. Write the generic package specification for a more complete set of text operations than the example shown in this chapter for package VARIABLE_STRINGS.

4. Write the generic package body for the package specification package VARIABLE_STRINGS. Use the package in a main program to assign a variable length string of type TEXT to the string

```
" It does not matter how long a string is " &
" as long as you can handle it. "
```

and display the result.

5. Write the generic package for the integration routine. Use it to integrate the function X**2 − X + 1 between 0 and 10.

6. Define a generic function predecessor so that the predecessor of an enumeration type is the same as the PRED operation, except that the predecessor of the first value in the list yields the last value in the list. Test the function by instantiating it for

```
type TIME_OF_DAY is (MORNING, AFTERNOON, EVENING);
```

and taking the predecessor of each value in the list.

7. Rewrite the generic function SUM so that the indices of the array can be any enumeration type. Test the function by defining an enumeration type and using it in the declaration of an array. Then instantiate the function and use it to sum up the elements of an array with enumeration type indices.

8. Write a generic package to contain the mathematical functions sine and cosine. Use the formulas

$$\mathbf{sine}\,(X) = X - \frac{X^3}{6} + \frac{X^5}{120}$$

$$\mathbf{cosine}\,(X) = 1 - \frac{X^2}{2} + \frac{X^4}{24}$$

Allow the parameter to be any floating-point type, and then use the package to compute **sine** (3.14159/6) and **cosine** (3.14159/3).

CHAPTER
❖ 13 ❖

DISCRIMINANTS

Ada provides a special form of the record type with parameters called *discriminants*, which have several uses. They can

- ◆ define various sizes for record fields,
- ◆ define various field names for record fields,
- ◆ define various shapes for records, and
- ◆ define various sets of values for record fields.

Ada provides some protection against the erroneous use of discriminants. Whenever you change the value of the discriminant, you must set the entire record to a consistent set of values.

SIZE SPECIFICATION

In chapter 7 we saw how a string is defined in terms of its length. A useful record type that handles variable-length strings is one that stores the actual length of the string in one field and the string in another field. A discriminant can specify the maximum length for the string in the declaration for any string variable.

In this example, the **record** type TEXT has a discriminant named MAX.

```
type TEXT (MAX: NATURAL) is
  record
    LENGTH: NATURAL := 0;
    VALUE:  STRING (1..MAX);
end record;
```

The two fields in the record are LENGTH and VALUE. The LENGTH field is initialized to zero; the VALUE field is a string of length MAX.

To declare a string using this record definition, we declare the variable with the type name followed by a parameter value:

```
DAY    : TEXT (9);
FRIDAY : constant TEXT := (9,6, "Friday   ");
```

This results in a variable named DAY, which can store strings up to nine characters in length. In chapter 11 we saw some useful procedures and functions for such a type. For the moment we will use the standard operations on the type TEXT such as assignment or test for equality.

```
DAY := (9, 6, "Monday   ");

if DAY = FRIDAY then
   PUT ("Go to TGIF");
   NEW_LINE;
end if;
```

In setting a record that has a discriminant, the first value in the definition is the discriminant. The named notation is probably better to use in this example:

```
DAY := (MAX => 9, LENGTH => 6, VALUE => "Monday   ");
```

or

```
DAY.LENGTH := 6;
DAY.VALUE  := "Monday   ";
```

The previous example can also be written using a subtype:

```
subtype DAY_TYPE is TEXT(9);
DAY    : DAY_TYPE;
FRIDAY : constant DAY_TYPE :=
            (MAX => 9, LENGTH => 6, Value => "FRIDAY   ");
```

FIELD NAME SPECIFICATION

A common use for discriminants is to allow you to select a field or group of fields in a record depending on the value of the discriminant. In the following example, the field PREGNANT is chosen depending on whether the value of the discriminant SEX is MALE or FEMALE.

```
type GENDER is (MALE, FEMALE);
subtype NAME_TYPE is STRING(1...5);
type PERSON (SEX : GENDER) is
  record
    NAME : NAME_TYPE;
    case SEX is
      when MALE => BALD : BOOLEAN;
      when FEMALE => PREGNANT : BOOLEAN;
    end case;
  end record;
```

In this form of the discriminant, the **case** statement in the record selects which field name is to be used—the case is always on the discriminant. All values of the discriminant must be specified in the list of **when** clauses, and the clause **when others** may be used to group together remaining values of the discriminant. Some examples of declarations using the preceding discriminant are:

```
-- John is a bald male
JOHN : PERSON (MALE) : = (MALE, "John ", TRUE);
-- Mary is a not pregnant female
MARY : PERSON (FEMALE) : = (FEMALE, "Mary ", FALSE);
```

These variables can be used in statements such as:

```
if JOHN.BALD then
  PUT ("John is bald");
  NEW_LINE;
else
  PUT ("John is not bald");
  NEW_LINE:
end if;
```

or

```
JOHN.BALD : = FALSE;  -- John got a transplant.
```

But a statement such as:

```
if JOHN.PREGNANT then
  PUT (" Schedule Maternity leave");
  NEW_LINE:
end if;
```

will be caught by Ada as being inconsistent with the value in the discriminant.

A better way of handling such records is to use subtypes:

```
subtype MALE is PERSON (MALE);
subtype FEMALE is PERSON (FEMALE):
JOHN : MALE : = (SEX => MALE, NAME => "JOHN ", BALD => TRUE);
MARY : FEMALE : = (SEX => FEMALE, NAME => "Mary ", PREGNANT => FALSE);
```

We can never change John to being a female in an assignment statement.

DEFAULT VALUES

Discriminants can have default values if you assign a value to the discriminant in its declaration. In the following example, the type PERSON will have a default value of FEMALE for the discriminant.

```
type PERSON (SEX : GENDER : = FEMALE) is
  record
    NAME : NAME_TYPE;
    case SEX is
      when MALE => BALD       : BOOLEAN;
      when FEMALE => PREGNANT : BOOLEAN;
    end case;
  end record;
```

We can still use the declaration as before to define John and Mary. However, we have the option of not filling in the discriminant value in the type specification for females:

```
MARY : PERSON : = (SEX => FEMALE, NAME => "Mary ", PREGNANT => FALSE);
```

In this example it is probably better to use subtypes rather than default values. Default values are suitable for situations when most of the data takes on a default value.

SETS OF VALUES

Discriminants can be used not only to select different field names but to select from among different sets of values.

In this example, the western states Arizona, California, and Nevada are listed with several of the political parties available to voters in each state. The discriminant, STATE, is used to select among the values.

```
type WESTERN is (CALIFORNIA, ARIZONA, NEVADA);
subtype NAME_TYPE is STRING (1..5);
type CALIFORNIA_PARTIES is (DEMOCRAT, REPUBLICAN, PEACE);
type ARIZONA_PARTIES is (DEMOCRAT, REPUBLICAN, LIBERTARIAN);
type NEVADA_PARTIES is (DEMOCRAT, REPUBLICAN, INDEPENDENT);
type VOTER_DATA (STATE : WESTERN) is
  record
    FIRST_NAME : NAME_TYPE;
    LAST_NAME  : NAME_TYPE;
    case STATE is
      when CALIFORNIA => CA_PARTY : CALIFORNIA_PARTIES;
      when ARIZONA    => AZ_PARTY : ARIZONA_PARTIES;
      when NEVADA     => NE_PARTY : NEVADA_PARTIES;
    end case;
  end record;
```

The declaration for a record that can hold information for a person in California:

```
VOTER : VOTER_DATA (CALIFORNIA);
```

Possible legal assignments to VOTER are:

```
VOTER := (CALIFORNIA, "Sam  ", "Smith", PEACE);
VOTER.FIRST_NAME := "Joan ";
VOTER.CA_PARTY := DEMOCRAT;
```

However, we cannot make an assignment to the discriminant:

```
VOTER.STATE := NEVADA;   -- illegal assignment
```

Subtypes are also useful in this example.

```
subtype CALIFORNIAN is VOTER_DATA (CALIFORNIA);
subtype ARIZONAN is VOTER_DATA (ARIZONA);
subtype NEVADAN is VOTER_DATA (NEVADA);
```

VARIOUS SHAPES

Discriminants can specify various shapes for a record. In the next example, the record has either two or three fields in addition to the discriminant field. As shown in figure 13.1, the thermometer has a record with three fields:

◆ the sensor name field,
◆ the time field, and
◆ the temperature field.

RECORD FOR TEMPERATURE SENSOR

THERMOMETER	TIME	TEMPERATURE

RECORD FOR PUMP SENSOR

PUMP	TIME	SPEED	PRESSURE

Figure 13.1   Records with different shapes

The pump has a record with four fields:

- ◆ the sensor name field,
- ◆ the time field,
- ◆ the speed field, and
- ◆ the pressure field.

The declaration for a record to handle both types of data is

```
type SENSOR_TYPE is (THERMOMETER, PUMP);
subtype TIME_TYPE is POSITIVE range 0..20000;
subtype SPEED_TYPE is POSITIVE range 0..4095;
subtype PRESSURE_TYPE is POSITIVE range 0..8191;
subtype TEMPERATURE_TYPE is POSITIVE range 0..1023;

  record
    TIME : TIME_TYPE;
    case INSTRUMENT is
      when THERMOMETER => TEMPERATURE : TEMPERATURE_TYPE;
      when PUMP         => SPEED       : SPEED_TYPE:
                           PRESSURE    : PRESSURE_TYPE;
    end case;
  end record;
```

Since you must write out each shape of the record type, you may wonder why one would use this feature to combine two or more record types in one type definition. For input and output over a single channel to a computer or to a single mass storage file, it may be necessary to combine various sources of data. The discriminant in the first field of each record can determine the form and amount of the rest of the data in a record. To set objects which have been declared as a RAW_DATA_TYPE as

```
RAW_DATA_PUMP : RAW_DATA_TYPE (PUMP);
RAW_DATA_THERMOMETER : RAW_DATA_TYPE (THERMOMETER);
```

we use assignment statements such as:

```
RAW_DATA_THERMOMETER := (THERMOMETER, 101, 75);
RAW_DATA_PUMP := (PUMP, 506, 3000, 2015);
```

A discriminant parameter can also constrain the shape of an array:

```
type SQUARE_ARRAY is array (POSITIVE range <>, POSITIVE range<>) of FLOAT;
type SQUARE_MATRIX (N:POSITIVE) is
record
SQUARE : SQUARE_ARRAY (1..N, 1..N);
end record:
```

These declarations can generate square matrices of various sizes:

```
CHESS_BOARD : SQUARE_MATRIX (8);
```

Discriminants can be used as an extra field of information to make programs more readable, as in these declarations for tabulating oil well information:

```
type STATE_TYPE is (OFF, ON);
subtype SPEED_TYPE is FLOAT range 0.0..2500.0;
subtype PRESSURE_TYPE is FLOAT range 0.0..500.0;
type PUMP_TYPE is
  record
    STATE : STATE_TYPE;
    SPEED : SPEED_TYPE;
  end record;
type LOCATION_TYPE is
  (GULF_OF_MEXICO, SANTA_BARBARA_CHANNEL, NORTH_SEA);

subtype BARREL_TYPE is INTEGER range 0..1E6;
type WELL (LOCATION : LOCATION_TYPE) is
  record
    BARRELS : BARREL_TYPE;
    PUMP    : PUMP_TYPE;
  end record;
subtype CHANNEL_WELL is WELL (SANTA_BARBARA_CHANNEL);
GETTY_PLATFORMS : array (1..5) of CHANNEL_WELL;
HOLLY : CHANNEL_WELL :=
            (LOCATION => SANTA_BARBARA_CHANNEL,
             BARRELS => 0,
             PUMP    => (OFF, 0.0, 0.0));
```

WHAT HAVE YOU LEARNED?

Discriminants are a special form of the record type that have parameters and can be used to define the size of arrays:

```
type TEXT (MAX: NATURAL) is
  record
    LENGTH: NATURAL := 0;
    VALUE: STRING (1..MAX);
  end record;
```

to vary record fields:

```
type PERSON (SEX : GENDER) is
  record
    NAME : NAME_TYPE;
    case SEX is
      when MALE   => BALD : BOOLEAN;
      when FEMALE => PREGNANT : BOOLEAN;
    end case;
  end record;
```

to vary sets of values on the same record:

```
type VOTER_DATA (STATE : WESTERN) is
  record
    FIRST_NAME: NAME_TYPE;
    LAST_NAME : NAME_TYPE;
```

```
      case STATE is
        when CALIFORNIA  => (DEMOCRAT, REPUBLICAN, PEACE);
        when ARIZONA     => (DEMOCRAT, REPUBLICAN, LIBERTARIAN);
        when NEVADA      => (DEMOCRAT, REPUBLICAN, INDEPENDENT);
      end case;
    case record;
```

to vary the amount of data in a record:

```
  type RAW DATA TYPE (INSTRUMENT : SENSOR_TYPE) is
    record
      TIME : TIME_TYPE;
      case INSTRUMENT is
        when THERMOMETER => TEMPERATURE : TEMPERATURE_TYPE;
        when PUMP        => SPEED       : SPEED_TYPE;
                            PRESSURE    : PRESSURE_TYPE;
    end case;
  end record;
```

Ada provides protection against the erroneous use of discriminants. The protection also allows the use a field only when its use is consistent with the value of the discriminant.

PROBLEMS

1. Change the declaration of NAME_TYPE in the example for the **record** type name PERSON to be TEXT (5). How would you define John not to be bald given the new type definition?

2. Rewrite the package VARIABLE_STRING as defined in chapter 11 to allow operations on the type TEXT defined in this chapter.

3. Determine whether the following statements are legal or illegal if the declaration DAY : TEXT (9); is given for the type TEXT as defined in this chapter.

   a. DAY := (6, 6, "Monday");

   b. DAY.LENGTH := 0;

   c. DAY.VALUE := "Monday";

   d. DAY := (LENGTH => 7,
              VALUE => "Tuesday");

4. Define a record for employee information for a business which has three types of employees: salaried, hourly, and consultants. The business is located in Massachusetts, but some employees live in New Hampshire. The employees in Mass. must have a deduction for Mass. income tax. Those who live in NH do not pay state income tax. The salaried and hourly workers can work overtime. Consultants are paid up to 8 hours a day. The record should contain information for the name, hours worked, state, federal tax, and state tax.

LisT PROCESSING

List processing is an extremely useful technique, and many applications having a variable amount of information use them—the list of passengers making reservations on an airplane flight is an example. Other applications, where the relationships between the information items are important, often use list processing techniques. Some examples include keeping track of genealogical relationships or keeping track of store inventories. Many games have a variable amount of information and varying relationships between the information, and such games are usually programmed using list processing techniques. Modeling or simulation systems use list processing and even the Ada compiler uses list processing. Almost all artificial intelligence applications such as chess playing programs and expert systems use list processing.

This chapter will not make you an expert on list processing—that would take another book. You will, however, be able to build a simple list structure by the end of the chapter.

CREATING A LIST

Ada has a special data type for use in list processing. This data type is the **access** data type, and it is used for accessing items in a list of data.

A *queue* is a list that has a head and a tail just as does the line at a grocery store checkstand. The queue has an order—the first object in the queue is at the head of the queue and the last object is at the tail of the queue. The order of objects in the queue can be alphabetical, by price, by size, by color, or by any ordering we wish. In our example, the order will be by time. We will use the package CALENDAR—one of the standard packages available on every Ada system—to access the time when the object entered in the queue and store the time away with the other information.

Our first example of creating a list will use a linear data structure called a *linked list* to represent the cars in inventory at a car dealer. In the list, we will store the type of the car, its price, its style, its color, and the date when the car entered the inventory.

To describe the information to be stored in the queue, we can write a record type:

```
type CAR_TYPE is (CHEVROLET, FORD, CHRYSLER);
type CAR_COLOR_TYPE is (RED, BROWN, YELLOW, GREEN, BLACK,
                        WHITE);
type STYLE_TYPE is     (SEDAN, CONVERTIBLE, HATCH_BACK,
                        STATION_WAGON);

subtype PRICE_TYPE is FLOAT range 0.0 .. 50_000.0;
type CAR_INVENTORY_TYPE is
  record
     BRAND : CAR_TYPE;
     COLOR : CAR_COLOR_TYPE;
     STYLE : STYLE_TYPE;
     PRICE : PRICE_TYPE;
     DATA  : TIME;  -- defined in package calendar
  end record;
```

This definition, shown in figure 14.1, allows the description of any car in a dealer's inventory to be stored. All we do is define an object of CAR_TYPE and fill in the fields in the record. We can also define an array of records

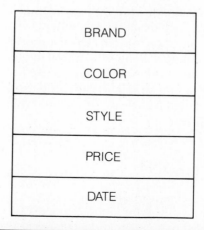

Figure 14.1   Record for CAR_TYPE

as we did in chapter 7 and store information on a group of cars. This approach has several drawbacks. For example, we need to determine how big the array should be. If we want to keep the cars in time order in the array, we will constantly need to move around the array every time a car is sold or entered into the array.

A list processing approach removes these drawbacks. A new entry into the list can be made every time a car is put into inventory, and a car can be removed from the list every time a car is sold or otherwise removed from the inventory.

To use such an approach we define a field in the record called a *link field*, which links together the cars in the inventory as shown in figure 14.2. External to the cars but used in processing the list are objects shown as HEAD and TAIL. These are objects of the **access** data type for this list.

When we start out, we will have no cars in our list, and by convention, we use the value **null** to represent nothing—the same keyword Ada uses to represent an empty list. HEAD and TAIL will have the value **null** at the beginning. The declarations that will be used to apply list processing to this example are

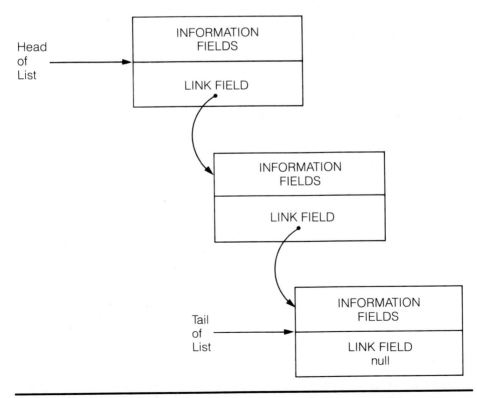

Figure 14.2   Linking together cars

```
type CAR_TYPE is (CHEVROLET, FORD, CHRYSLER);
type CAR_COLOR_TYPE is (RED,    BROWN,   YELLOW,   GREEN, BLACK,
                        WHITE);
type STYLE_TYPE is      (SEDAN, CONVERTIBLE,   HATCH_BACK,
                        STATION_WAGON);

subtype PRICE_TYPE is FLOAT range 0.0 .. 50_000.0;
type CAR_INVENTORY_TYPE;   -- incomplete definition
type CAR_ACCESS_TYPE is access CAR_INVENTORY_TYPE;
type CAR_INVENTORY_TYPE is
  record
    BRAND : CAR_TYPE;
    COLOR : CAR_COLOR_TYPE;
    STYLE : STYLE_TYPE;
    PRICE : PRICE_TYPE;
    DATE  : TIME;  -- defined in package calendar
    LINK  : CAR_ACCESS_TYPE;
  end record;
  HEAD, TAIL : CAR_ACCESS_TYPE := null;
```

The extra lines in this declaration appear in order to allow list processing operations to take place safely in Ada. An **access** type such as CAR_ACCESS TYPE can only be used with the data type CAR_INVENTORY_TYPE. Since we cannot use a type name before we define it, there is a line defining CAR_ INVENTORY_TYPE as a type before it is used in the definition for the access type. This definition, which states that CAR_INVENTORY_TYPE is a type without defining the record, is called an *incomplete definition*. Such a definition is necessary in most list processing examples because the record contains an **access** type used to access the record itself.

Once the definition of the types is complete, we define the objects HEAD and TAIL to be CAR_ACCESS_TYPE and set them both to **null.** To create our first object, we assign it to an object of the CAR_ACCESS_TYPE using the keyword **new** and fill in the fields with the information we want for the object.

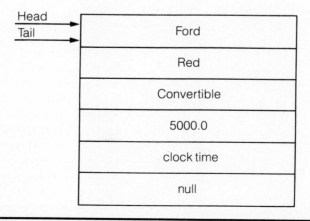

Figure 14.3   Creating the first record

```
TAIL := new CAR_INVENTORY_TYPE'(FORD, RED, CONVERTIBLE,
                           5000.00, CLOCK, null );
```

Such an assignment creates a record with the information as shown in figure 14.3. The convention **null** is used when the link does not join objects together. We will also assign HEAD to be

```
HEAD := TAIL;    -- both access types point to the car
```

At some later time we add to the inventory by assigning our object named TAIL to another car:

```
TAIL := new CAR_INVENTORY_TYPE'(CHRYSLER, BLACK, SEDAN,
                            8500.0, CLOCK, null );
```

This assignment results in the creation of a record as shown in figure 14.4.

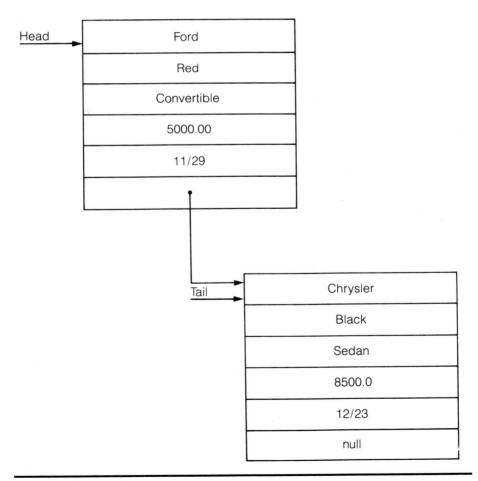

Figure 14.4   Linking together two cars

Now we have two records, one pointed to by TAIL and one pointed to by HEAD. The next step is to join these records together. This can be done by setting the access field of the record pointed to by TAIL. In our two-record example, this can be done with

```
HEAD.LINK : = TAIL;
```

which changes the value of the LINK field in the record accessed by HEAD to be equal to TAIL instead of **null.** The general form for a reference to a field in a record with an access type object is

access object name.field name

This example works fine in the two-record case but does not work so well when there are three or more cars. What we need to do is keep a place holder for the new object in the list and then link in the new object to the tail of the list. The best way to do this is to have another access type object named TEMPORARY and, instead of assigning TAIL to the new object, we assign TEMPORARY to the new object:

```
TEMPORARY : = new CAR_INVENTORY_TYPE'(CHEVROLET, YELLOW,
                    STATION_WAGON, 10000.0, CLOCK, null );
```

We then fix up the link fields by setting

```
TAIL.LINK : = TEMPORARY;
```

and setting the TAIL to be equal to TEMPORARY

```
TAIL : =   TEMPORARY;
```

These steps are portrayed in figure 14.5.

To see these statements in the context of a complete program, the following program adds objects to a car inventory list from keyboard entries. After the user enters the information for 4 cars, the program displays the information in the list.

```
with TEXT_IO, CALENDAR; use TEXT_IO, CALENDAR;
package CREATE_CAR_LIST is

   type CAR_TYPE is (CHEVROLET, FORD, CHRYSLER);
   type CAR_COLOR_TYPE is (RED, BROWN, YELLOW, GREEN, BLACK,
                   WHITE);
   type STYLE_TYPE      is (SEDAN, CONVERTIBLE, HATCH_BACK,
                   STATION_WAGON);

   subtype PRICE_TYPE  is FLOAT range 0.0 .. 50_000.0;
   type CAR_INVENTORY_TYPE;   -- incomplete definition
   type CAR_ACCESS_TYPE is access CAR_INVENTORY_TYPE;
   type CAR_INVENTORY_TYPE is
```

1. Create new record

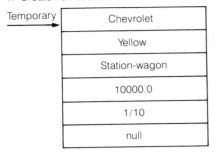

2. Fix up link fields

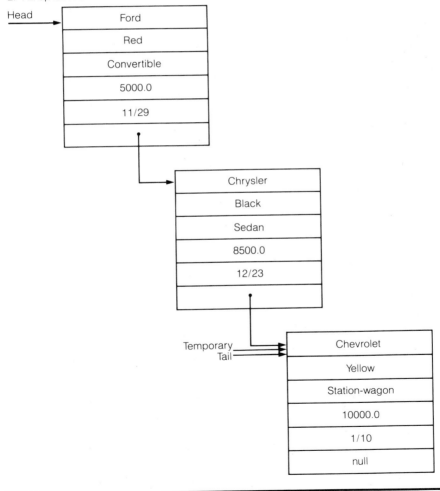

Figure 14.5   Linking more fields together

```
      record
        BRAND : CAR_TYPE        : = CHEVROLET;
        COLOR : CAR_COLOR_TYPE : = YELLOW;
        STYLE : STYLE_TYPE      : = STATION_WAGON;
        PRICE : PRICE_TYPE      : = 12000.0;
        DATE  : TIME;  -- defined in package calendar
        LINK  : CAR_ACCESS_TYPE;
      end record;

    procedure GET (CAR_INFORMATION : out CAR_INVENTORY_TYPE);
    procedure ADD_CAR_TO_LIST (CAR_INFORMATION : CAR_INVENTORY_TYPE);
    procedure PUT_LIST;

end CREATE_CAR_LIST;

with TEXT_IO, CALENDAR; use TEXT_IO, CALENDAR;
package body CREATE_CAR_LIST is

  HEAD, TAIL : CAR_ACCESS_TYPE : = null;

  -- instantiate IO packages
  package CAR_TYPE_IO is new ENUMERATION_IO (CAR_TYPE);
  package CAR_COLOR_TYPE_IO is new ENUMERATION_IO (CAR_COLOR_TYPE);
  package STYLE_TYPE_IO is new ENUMERATION_IO  (STYLE_TYPE);
  package PRICE_TYPE_IO is new FLOAT_IO (PRICE_TYPE);
  use CAR_TYPE_IO;
  use CAR_COLOR_TYPE_IO;
  use STYLE_TYPE_IO;
  use PRICE_TYPE_IO;
  procedure GET (CAR_INFORMATION : out CAR_INVENTORY_TYPE) is

  begin
    NEW_LINE;
    PUT (" Enter car type : Chevrolet, Ford, or Chrysler ");
    NEW_LINE;

    GET (CAR_INFORMATION.BRAND);
    NEW_LINE;
    PUT (" Enter car color : ");
    PUT (" Red, Brown, Yellow, Green, Black, White ");
    NEW_LINE;

    GET (CAR_INFORMATION.COLOR);
    NEW_LINE;
    PUT (" Enter car style : ");
    PUT (" Sedan, Convertible, Hatch_back, Station_wagon");
    NEW_LINE;

    GET (CAR_INFORMATION.STYLE);
    NEW_LINE;

    PUT (" Enter car price : ");
    NEW_LINE;
```

```
    GET (CAR_INFORMATION.PRICE);
    NEW_LINE:
    CAR_INFORMATION.DATE := CLOCK;

    CAR_INFORMATION.LINK := null;

end GET;

procedure ADD_CAR_TO_LIST (CAR_INFORMATION : CAR_INVENTORY_TYPE) is
    TEMPORARY : CAR_ACCESS_TYPE;
begin
    TEMPORARY := new CAR_INVENTORY_TYPE'(CAR_INFORMATION);
    -- test for empty list case
    if TAIL /= null then
        TAIL.LINK := TEMPORARY;
        TAIL := TEMPORARY;
    else
        TAIL := TEMPORARY;
        HEAD := TAIL;
    end if;
end ADD_CAR_TO_LIST;
procedure PUT_LIST is
    -- displays information in list in time order from
    -- oldest in list to newest in list

    TEMPORARY : CAR_ACCESS_TYPE;

begin

    TEMPORARY := HEAD;

    PUT ( " CAR INVENTORY ");
    NEW_LINE;
    PUT ( " BRAND       STYLE       COLOR       PRICE ");
    NEW_LINE;
    while TEMPORARY /= null loop -- loop till end of list

        PUT (TEMPORARY.BRAND); SET_COL (13);
        PUT (TEMPORARY.STYLE); SET_COL (27);
        PUT (TEMPORARY.COLOR); SET_COL (37);
        PUT (TEMPORARY.PRICE); NEW_LINE;

        TEMPORARY := TEMPORARY.LINK;

    end loop;
 end PUT_LIST;
end CREATE_CAR_LIST;

with TEXT_IO, CREATE_CAR_LIST; use TEXT_IO, CREATE_CAR_LIST;
procedure MAIN is
    CAR_DATA : CAR_INVENTORY_TYPE;

begin
```

```
PUT (" car inventory example "); NEW_LINE:
PUT (" Enter information for 4 cars ");
NEW_LINE;
for I in 1..4 loop
  NEW_LINE;
  GET (CAR_DATA);
  NEW_LINE;
  ADD_CAR_TO_LIST (CAR_DATA);
end loop;
PUT_LIST;
end MAIN;
```

Manipulating a List

Creating a list is only the first step in list processing. Very often we want to add to the list, delete from the list, find something in the list, or rearrange the list in some order such as alphabetical order.

To delete an object from a singly linked list, we move the **access** around the object. For example, if we wanted to remove all Chevrolets from the list we created, we go down the list from the head to the tail, and each object with the BRAND Chevrolet is removed from the list by moving the link field to point around the object with the Chevrolet brand. We have to be careful about deleting the objects making up the head and the tail of the list; we also have to take care of the case when no objects remain in the list. The subprogram DELETE_CAR does this for Chevrolets.

Although the program DELETE_CAR removes the car from the list, it still occupies space in the computer. Ada is not required to perform garbage collection on list elements and so they will occupy space until the subprogram which contains the declaration for the list finishes executing.

```
procedure DELETE_CAR is
  -- deletes all Chevrolets from the created list
  TEMPORARY : CAR_ACCESS_TYPE;
  FOLLOWER  : CAR_ACCESS_TYPE;
begin
  TEMPORARY : = HEAD;
  FOLLOWER  : = HEAD;
  while TEMPORARY /= null loop -- loop till end of list
    -- test if object is a Chevrolet
    if TEMPORARY.BRAND = CHEVROLET then
      --    delete object
      if TEMPORARY = HEAD then
        -- case for head object being deleted
        HEAD : = TEMPORARY.LINK;
        FOLLOWER : = HEAD;
      elsif TEMPORARY = TAIL then
        -- case for tail object being deleted
        TAIL : = FOLLOWER;
        TAIL.LINK : = null;
```

```
        else
           -- case for middle object being deleted
           FOLLOWER.LINK := TEMPORARY.LINK;
        end if;
     else
        FOLLOWER := TEMPORARY;
     end if;
     TEMPORARY := TEMPORARY.LINK;  -- move to next object
   end loop;
end DELETE_CAR;
```

In DELETE_CAR we used a follower to the access object that moves through the list. We need such a follower in a singly linked list because there is no way to go backward to link up with the previous object unless we keep track of the object behind. This program does not need to test for the empty list case because the loop on the variable named TEMPORARY will terminate immediately if the value of HEAD is **null.**

One way to avoid the need for a follower access object is to have a backward-pointing field in the linked list. This has the advantage of making it easier to manipulate the list but the disadvantage that it takes up more storage. However, in a list with many fields, the increase in storage for the extra link may not be significant.

The additional field makes the list into a doubly linked list. Figure 14.6 shows an example of such a list. The declaration that can be used for this list is

```
type CAR_INVENTORY_TYPE is
  record
     BRAND         : CAR_TYPE;
     COLOR         : CAR_COLOR_TYPE;
     STYLE         : STYLE_TYPE;
     PRICE         : PRICE_TYPE;
     DATE          : TIME;  -- defined in package calendar
     FORWARD_LINK  : CAR_ACCESS_TYPE;
     BACKWARD_LINK : CAR_ACCESS_TYPE;
  end record;
```

Sometimes there are even triply and quadruply linked lists.

TREES

One of the most useful linked list structures is the *tree*. In computer programs, the most common tree structure is the binary tree, in which each node in the tree has two links or branches. Any tree such as a family tree can be expressed as a binary tree. Binary trees are also good for keeping records in a sorted form as the records are added to the list.

Figure 14.7 shows an example of a conventional family tree. As can be seen, the tree has many branches indicating the complex arrangements that can exist in a family tree. In figure 14.8, the tree is redrawn as a binary tree.

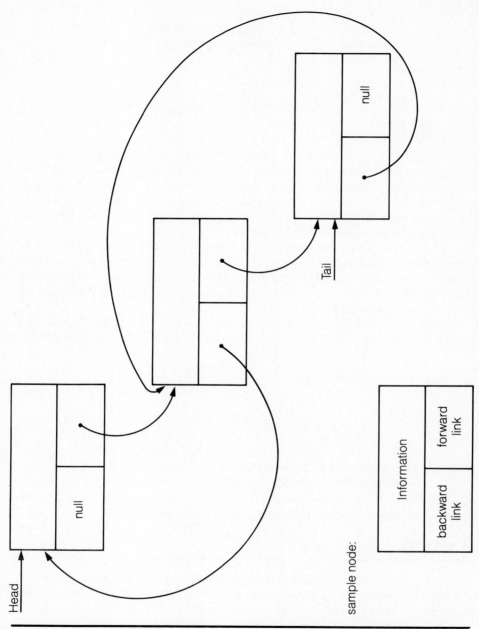

Figure 14.6   Doubly linked list

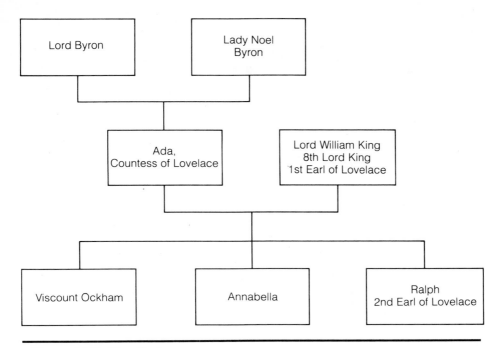

Figure 14.7   Family tree

In the binary form, the first descendant becomes the left branch, and the siblings become the right branch. The spouse becomes a field in the record.

To create such a tree, we first declare a record containing the information we want to store plus the links for the left and the right branch. An example of how this information might be represented in Ada follows for the information shown in figure 14.8 where the parents' names and the number of immediate descendants is stored. The siblings are shown in links to the right. Children are shown as links to the left. This is obviously a partial family tree since Ada's children had children.

```
type FAMILY_TREE_RECORD;   -- incomplete definition
type LINK_TYPE is access FAMILY_TREE_RECORD;
subtype NAME_TYPE is STRING (1..10);
subtype DESCENDANT_TYPE is INTEGER range 0..100;
type FAMILY_TREE_RECORD is
  record
    NAME        : NAME_TYPE;
    SPOUSE      : NAME_TYPE;
    DESCENDANTS : DESCENDANT_TYPE;
    LEFT_LINK   : LINK_TYPE;
    RIGHT_LINK  : LINK_TYPE;
  end record;
```

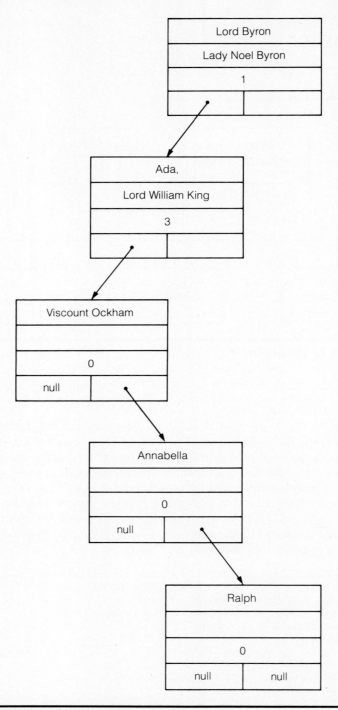

FIGURE 14.8   Family tree as a binary tree

Once the record type for the element in a binary tree has been defined, the remaining steps are not too different from the steps used to create the car list shown previously. In the family tree case, there are several additional decisions to be made, mostly to determine whether to add the new information to the left or to the right of the node. Information can be added to a tree so that one level is complete before going down one link to the left or it can be added down all the links to the left until the end of the tree is defined to the left before filling in the links to the right.

Since a family is created level by level, we will use this method in creating a family tree. The program CREATE_FAMILY_TREE can create the family tree shown in figure 14.8. It can also create a tree for your family. The most complex part of this program is the search for the parent, which makes use of a technique called *recursion*, a procedure that invokes itself. Handling trees is best done with recursive procedures. The procedure keeps calling itself looking to the left and to the right in the tree until the parent is found or until nothing can be found.

One common use of binary trees is keeping all information in the tree in sorted order. For example, all objects that come before the root object's key value will be found to the left of the root. All objects that come after the root object's key value will be to the right of the root. The order can be alphabetical or numeric.

```
with TEXT_IO;
package CREATE_FAMILY_TREE is
  type FAMILY_RECORD;  -- incomplete definition
  type LINK_TYPE is access FAMILY_RECORD;
  subtype NAME_TYPE is STRING (1..10);
  subtype DESCENDANT_TYPE is INTEGER range 0..100;
  type FAMILY_RECORD is
    record
      NAME          : NAME_TYPE;
      SPOUSE        : NAME_TYPE;
      DESCENDANTS   : DESCENDANT_TYPE;
      LEFT_LINK     : LINK_TYPE;
      RIGHT_LINK    : LINK_TYPE;
    end record;
  procedure GET (FAMILY_INFORMATION : out FAMILY_RECORD);
  procedure ADD_PERSON_TO_TREE (FAMILY_INFORMATION : FAMILY_RECORD);
end CREATE_FAMILY_TREE;

with TEXT_IO;
package body CREATE_FAMILY_TREE is
  ROOT : LINK_TYPE := null;
  PARENT_NAME : NAME_TYPE;
  use TEXT_IO; -- instantiate IO packages
  package DESCENDANT_TYPE_IO is new INTEGER_IO (DESCENDANT_TYPE);
  use DESCENDANT_TYPE_IO;
  procedure GET (FAMILY_INFORMATION : out FAMILY_RECORD) is
  begin
    PUT (" Name of new family member: "); NEW_LINE;
    GET (FAMILY_INFORMATION.NAME); NEW_LINE;
```

```
      PUT (" Enter name of spouse, or blanks if no spouse: ");
      NEW_LINE;
      GET (FAMILY_INFORMATION.SPOUSE);
      NEW_LINE;

      PUT (" Enter number of descendants for new family member : ");
      NEW_LINE;
      GET (FAMILY_INFORMATION.DESCENDANTS);
      NEW_LINE;

      PUT (" Enter name of parent for new family member : ");
      NEW_LINE;
      GET (PARENT_NAME);
      NEW_LINE,

      FAMILY_INFORMATION.LEFT_LINK  : = null;
      FAMILY_INFORMATION.RIGHT_LINK : = null;

   end GET;

   procedure SEARCH_PARENT (NAME : NAME_TYPE; WHERE : in out LINK_TYPE) is
   begin
      if WHERE = null or WHERE.NAME = NAME then  --  stop search
        null;
      else -- continue search
      -- first look to left
        if WHERE.LEFT_LINK /= null then
          SEARCH_PARENT (NAME, WHERE.LEFT_LINK);
        else
          SEARCH_PARENT (NAME, WHERE.RIGHT_LINK);
        end if;
      end if;
      return;
   end SEARCH_PARENT;

   procedure ADD_PERSON_TO_TREE (FAMILY_INFORMATION : FAMILY_RECORD) is
      WHO, TEMPORARY : LINK_TYPE;
      T : LINK_TYPE;
   begin
      TEMPORARY : = new FAMILY_RECORD'(FAMILY_INFORMATION);
            -- test for empty tree case
      if ROOT /= null then
        -- search for parent to add new member
        WHO : = ROOT;
        SEARCH_PARENT (PARENT_NAME, WHO);
        -- who points to parent node
        if WHO = null then
          -- parent was not found, ask for entry again
          PUT (" Please enter data again for the  ");
          PUT (" last person. The parent was not found. ");
        else
          -- now go down tree to right to add new member
          T : = WHO;
          while T.RIGHT_LINK /= null loop
            T : = T.RIGHT_LINK;
          end loop;
```

```
              -- add in new member
           T.RIGHT_LINK : = TEMPORARY;
        end if;
     else  -- empty tree case
        ROOT : = TEMPORARY;
        WHO  : = ROOT;
     end if;
  end ADD_PERSON_TO_TREE;
end CREATE_FAMILY_TREE;

with CREATE_FAMILY_TREE, TEXT_IO;
use CREATE_FAMILY_TREE, TEXT_IO;
procedure MAIN is
     FAMILY_INFORMATION : FAMILY_RECORD;
begin
  PUT (" Family Tree Example "); NEW_LINE;
  PUT (" Enter information on 5 family members ");
  NEW_LINE:
  for I in 1..5 loop
    GET (FAMILY_INFORMATION);
    ADD_PERSON_TO_TREE (FAMILY_INFORMATION);
  end loop;
end MAIN;
```

WHAT HAVE YOU LEARNED?

The **access** data type is a special data type for creating and manipulating lists.

A *queue* is a list with a head and a tail just like the line at a grocery store checkstand. The first object in the queue is at the head of the queue and the last object is at the tail of the queue. The order of objects in the queue can be alphabetical, by price, by size, by color, or by any ordering we wish.

Ada uses the keyword **null** to represent an empty list. In building a simply linked list, HEAD and TAIL will have the value **null** at the beginning. These declarations can be used in a simple list:

```
type LIST_NODE;   -- incomplete definition
type LIST_ACCESS_TYPE is access LIST_NODE;
type INFORMATION_TYPE is STRING (1..5);
type LIST_NODE is
  record
    INFORMATION : INFORMATION_TYPE;
    LINK        : LIST_ACCESS_TYPE;
  end record;
HEAD, TAIL: LIST_ACCESS_TYPE : = null;
```

Ada requires a partial definition of a data type when an access type is contained in a record. This helps allow list processing operations to take place safely. An access type such as LINK_ACCESS_TYPE can only be used with the data type LIST_NODE. Since we cannot use a type name before we define it, there is a line defining LIST_NODE as a type before it is used in the definition for the access type.

Once the definition of the types is complete, we define the objects HEAD and TAIL to be LIST_ACCESS_TYPE and set them both to **null**. To create our first object, we assign it to an object of the LIST_ACCESS_TYPE using the keyword **new** and filling in the fields with the information we want for the object.

```
TAIL : = new LIST_NODE'( "Sam  ", null);
```

Such an assignment creates a new record with the information filled in. The convention **null** is used when the link does not join objects together. We can also assign HEAD to be

```
HEAD : = TAIL;  -- both access types point to the same node
```

At some later time we can add to the list by assigning our object named TAIL to another object:

```
TAIL : = new LIST_NODE'( "Eric ", null );
```

The general form for a reference to a field in a record with an access type object is

access object name.field name

The general form to create a new record with an access type object is

*access object name : = **new** record type name'(values for fields);*

A temporary access type object is used as a place holder in a singly linked list to add new objects to the end of a list and to insert in the middle of a list. When creating a new object to be added to the end of a list, assign the new object to the temporary access type object and then link it into the list.

```
TEMPORARY : = new LIST_NODE'( "John ", null);
```

We then fix up the link fields by setting

```
TAIL.LINK : = TEMPORARY;
```

and setting the TAIL to be equal to TEMPORARY

```
TAIL : =  TEMPORARY;
```

To delete an object from a singly linked list, we need to move the access to the object to go around the object. For example, if we wanted to remove all the nodes with the name Eric from the list we had created, we would go down the list from the head to the tail, and each object that had the information field set to "Eric " would be removed from the list by moving the link field to point around the object with that name. We have to be careful about deleting the objects that make up the head and the tail of the list, and we have to take care of the case when no objects remain in the list.

Sometimes there are even doubly, triply, and quadruply linked lists. Such lists are easier to manipulate at the expense of extra room for the links in the list.

One of the most useful doubly linked list structures is called a *binary tree*. Binary trees are good for

-- showing relationships
-- keeping records in a sorted form

To create a binary tree, we first declare a record containing the information we want to store plus the links for the left and the right branch. For example,

```
type BINARY_TREE_RECORD;   -- incomplete definition
type LINK_TYPE is access BINARY_TREE_RECORD;
type INFORMATION_TYPE is STRING (1..10);
type BINARY_TREE_RECORD is
  record
    INFORMATION : INFORMATION_TYPE;
    LEFT_LINK   : LINK_TYPE;
    RIGHT_LINK  : LINK_TYPE;
end record;
```

Once the record type for the element in a binary tree has been defined, the remaining steps are not too different from the steps used to create a singly linked list. In the binary tree, there are several additional decisions to be made, mostly to determine whether to add the new information to the left or to the right of the node. Information can be added to a tree so that one level is complete before going down one link to the left or it can be added down all the links to the left until the end of the tree is defined to the left before filling in the links to the right. Recursive procedures are the best way to search a binary tree.

PROBLEMS

1. Alter the create car list example to have a procedure that can add a specified percentage to the price of the cars as a result of input from the keyboard. Test your program by inputting information on three cars and then increasing the price of the cars by 10%.

2. Rewrite the create car list example to be a generic package. Instantiate it for the car type record and test it on information on three cars.

3. Incorporate the DELETE_CAR procedure in a main program that reads in list of three cars and then deletes all Chevrolets from the list.

4. Write a create car list program to add cars to a doubly linked list.

5. Add a print program to print the information in the family tree created by the program CREATE_FAMILY_TREE. Use it to print the information in the tree created by the program.

6. Write the declaration for a record that could be used to describe the information shown in figure 14.9.

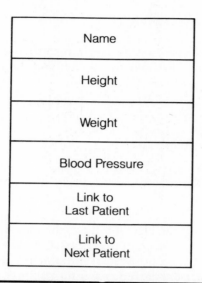

| Name |
| Height |
| Weight |
| Blood Pressure |
| Link to Last Patient |
| Link to Next Patient |

Figure 14.9   Record layout for doubly linked list

7. Create a binary tree that receives the following values {5, 0, 1, 10, 8}. As you create the tree, keep the smaller values to the left and the larger values to the right.

8. Print out the nodes of the tree created in problem 7 in order, from smallest to largest.

9. Write a package consisting of procedures to insert new nodes, delete old nodes, and search for a node in a list made up of the doubly linked list structure shown in figure 14.9.

10. Write a package to operate on a tree data structure. Include in the package procedures to add a node, delete a node, print out the contents of the tree.

CHAPTER

❖ 15 ❖

PRIVATE TYPES

❖ A private type is a type that is divided into two parts: the part that the user has access to and the part that the implementer has access to. Private types are useful for protecting data structures from erroneous use. This is because the user of a private type can only apply a restricted set of operations to the type. One of the most common problems with data structures is the erroneous setting of links in a linked list, hence it is advisable to protect a linked list with private types. The user can then add nodes to the list or delete nodes from the list, but cannot alter the links. Private types are also useful in protecting against erroneous use of input and output data areas and it is recommended that data areas used for input or output be treated as a private type. In fact, some believe that almost every data structure should be a private type.

To define the type for a data structure as a private type, it must be in a package. We first name the type as a private type in the package specification part of the package. Then, after all the other types and subprograms are defined in the package, we define the private part of the package after the keyword **private.** We define the type in the normal manner, and in the package body the implementation is written as if the type were not hidden. The following program shows the placement of the definitions for a private type named DATA_STRUCTURE_TYPE.

```
package PRIVATE_EXAMPLE is
  MAXIMUM_SIZE : constant INTEGER : = 100;
  type DATA_STRUCTURE_TYPE is private;
  procedure ADD_TO_STRUCTURE (A : DATA_STRUCTURE_TYPE);
  procedure LIST_STRUCTURE   (A : DATA_STRUCTURE_TYPE);
private
  type DATA_STRUCTURE_TYPE is
    array (INTEGER range 1..MAXIMUM_SIZE) of INTEGER;
end PRIVATE_EXAMPLE;
```

When we define a data structure as a private type and we place all the operations that are needed for that data structure in a package, we say that we have *encapsulated* the data structure.

The major difference between a type which is not private and a private type is the limitation on operations for private types. Private types have the operations of assignment, equality, and those operations defined in the package where the type is defined because the intention was to limit the operations on the private type to those defined in the package. In this way, the operations can be well tested on the data structure and users of the package cannot destroy the integrity of the data structure by forgetting to set links in the structure.

For example, in the following package the record type, CAR_INVENTORY _TYPE, and the access type, CAR_ACCESS_TYPE, are declared to be private types. This means that data can be assigned to a record of CAR_INVENTORY TYPE and tests for equality can be made on these records. Anyone who wants to declare records of CAR_INVENTORY_TYPE will use the packaged procedures: GET, ADD_TO_LIST, and PUT_LIST to operate on the data. In the original version of this package in chapter 14 we could have access to any field in the data structure from the main program. That is, we could have made statements such as

```
NEW_CAR  : =  new  CAR_INVENTORY_TYPE'(FORD, RED, SEDAN,
                        8000.00, null);
NEW_CAR.CAR_INVENTORY_TYPE.COLOR : =  BLUE;
```

in the main procedure.

In the version of the program that makes CAR_INVENTORY_TYPE a private type, we cannot make an assignment to the color field, but we can still make an assignment to the whole record as was done in the statement that allocated a new record. Hence the first of these two statements would be legal, but the second would be illegal outside the package. We also made the access type a private type so that it would be protected from use outside the packaged procedures. This is a good practice to follow for all access types

```
with TEXT_IO, CALENDAR; use TEXT_IO, CALENDAR;
package CREATE_CAR_LIST is

  type CAR_TYPE is (CHEVROLET, FORD, CHRYSLER);

  type CAR_COLOR_TYPE is (RED, BROWN, YELLOW, GREEN, BLACK,
                        WHITE);
```

```
   type STYLE_TYPE is    (SEDAN, CONVERTIBLE,  HATCH_BACK,
                           STATION_WAGON);
   subtype PRICE_TYPE is FLOAT range 0.0 .. 50_000.0;
   type CAR_INVENTORY_TYPE is private;
   type CAR_ACCESS_TYPE is private;
   procedure GET (CAR_INFORMATION : out CAR_INVENTORY_TYPE);
   procedure ADD_CAR_TO_LIST (CAR_INFORMATION : CAR_INVENTORY_TYPE);
   procedure PUT_LIST;
private
   type CAR_ACCESS_TYPE is access CAR_INVENTORY_TYPE;
   type CAR_INVENTORY_TYPE is
     record
       BRAND : CAR_TYPE        : = CHEVROLET;
       COLOR : CAR_COLOR_TYPE  : = YELLOW;
       STYLE : STYLE_TYPE      : = STATION_WAGON;
       PRICE : PRICE_TYPE      : = 12000.0;
       DATE  : TIME;   -- defined in package calendar
       LINK  : CAR_ACCESS_TYPE;
     end record;
end CREATE_CAR_LIST;
```

In the original main program we did not use any partial assignment; in fact, all we used were the subprograms defined in the package. This is the best approach. To follow a design principle called *data abstraction*, you define your data type as a private type. You also define the operations on that data type in a single package together with the data type.

Data abstraction is a simple concept that helps greatly in maintaining programs over a long period of time. In data abstraction, we first define the types that we need to solve a problem. Then we define the operations on the types. We put the types and the operations on these types together in packages such that the types are private types.

It is advisable to limit even the assignment and equality operations. For example, in our car inventory problem, the assignment to a new record allows the assignment of an access type. This is always dangerous. In order to avoid this, we go one step further and define the type as a limited private type. A type declared as a limited private type cannot be operated on by any operation other than those defined in the package. It is the only type that does not even have an assignment operation. We can change our example program so that CAR_INVENTORY_TYPE and CAR_ACCESS_TYPE are limited private types by changing the declaration statements to be

```
   type CAR_INVENTORY_TYPE is limited private;
   type CAR_ACCESS_TYPE is limited private;
```

The rest of the package remains the same. The actual types are defined after the keyword **private** and the implementation of the package body remains unchanged. Since we made no assignment or tests on the types in our main program, it will operate the same for the limited private type version as for our original version.

Private types are also useful in applications that do not use access types. The idea of restricting operations on data structures to a few small, carefully tested operations is an excellent approach to the development of reliable programs. All data structures should be considered as candidates for private types. Many should even be considered as candidates for limited private types. All data structures involved with input and output, whether to a terminal or to an auto-land system for an airplane, should be private types and probably even limited private types.

In chapter 11 a number of packages were defined for data structures commonly used in computer programming. Among these was a package named VARIABLE_STRING. In this package a type named TEXT was defined to represent a variable string and several operations were defined on this type. Such a type is a prime candidate for a private type.

The package specification from chapter 11 is easily transformed to allowing TEXT to be a private type as shown in the next program. The package body would not change. We would, however, need to perform more changes if we were to make TEXT a limited private type because the test for equality is used in the main program named VARIABLE_STRINGS.

One area where it is especially important to use private types is in the transfer of information from an external device. It is also important to keep the actual interface hidden from the user of the interface.

The user of an interface should receive information from a device via a high-level subprogram such as GET or PUT on an Ada data type. At a low level, actual physical implementation of the interface will be hidden from the user.

```
with TEXT_IO;
package INTEGER_IO is new TEXT_IO. INTEGER_IO (INTEGER);
with TEXT_IO, INTEGER_IO; use TEXT_IO, INTEGER_IO;
package VARIABLE_STRING is
      type TEXT is private;
      subtype LENGTH_TYPE is NATURAL;
      type SUBRANGE_TYPE is
       record
          FIRST_CHARACTER : NATURAL;
          LAST_CHARACTER : NATURAL;
        end record;
  --   input and output procedures
      procedure PUT (A : TEXT);
      procedure GET (A : out TEXT);
  --   assign operation
      function ASSIGN (A : STRING) return TEXT;
  --   relational operations
      function ">" (A, B : TEXT) return BOOLEAN;
      function "<" (A, B : TEXT) return BOOLEAN;
      function ">=" (A, B : TEXT) return BOOLEAN;
      function "<=" (A, B : TEXT) return BOOLEAN;
  --   concatenation operation
      function "&" (A, B : TEXT) return TEXT;
  --   find and replace functions
      function FIND (A, B : TEXT) return SUBRANGE_TYPE;
      function REPLACE (A : TEXT; B: SUBRANGE_TYPE; C: TEXT)
                    return TEXT;
```

```
private
  type TEXT is
    record
      LENGTH : LENGTH_TYPE : = 0;
      VARIABLE_STRING : STRING (1..40) : = (others => ' ');
    end record;
end VARIABLE_STRING;
```

Many of the predefined items in an Ada system are private types. For example, the first declaration in package TEXT_IO is

```
type FILE_TYPE is limited private;
```

This is intended to restrict the operations on objects of type FILE_TYPE to the ones contained in the package. It is also to hide the underlying implementation of the type. It is hoped that this will aid portability of programs from one computer to another.

Also in the package CALENDAR, the first declaration is

```
type TIME is private;
```

This is because time is very often handled differently on different computers. One computer might count time in units of milliseconds and another computer might count time in units of microseconds. The package, however, has functions that return the time in terms of seconds no matter which computer the program executes on.

These last two examples show a different use of private types. One that can aid portability across computers comes from hiding the low-level information in the computer, such as the way the computer calculates time and the manner in which it names its files. You will also find this use of private types valuable in hiding low-level data structures. In fact, the variable string example is an example where the low-level data structure using a fixed-length string and an integer are used to create a new higher level data structure. The user of the package need not be concerned with the form of the low-level data structure.

Because the = operation is not defined for the limited private data type, it can be defined in a package for any limited private type defined in that package. However, you cannot define /= because it is always the opposite of = and you might make another definition. Inequality is considered defined when you define equality without any extra effort on your part.

Assignment is handled differently. You cannot define the := operation ever, even for limited private types. Even though a limited private type does not have the assignment operation, you will use the assignment operation in the package where the data type is defined and you will pass an object of the limited private type as a parameter to functions or procedures. To eliminate confusion, the designers of Ada forbid defining a function for the assignment operator. Usually what is done is to name a function such as

```
function ASSIGN (A, B : SOME_TYPE) return SOME_TYPE;
```

WHAT HAVE YOU LEARNED?

Private types are useful for protecting data structures, such as those used in linked lists and in input and output.

   To define a data structure as a private type, name the type as a private type in the package specification part of the package. Then, after all the other types and subprograms are defined in the package, define the private part of the package after the keyword **private.** In the private part, define the type in the normal manner. Write the package body the same as if the type were not private. The general form of a package specification with a private type is

```
package PACKAGE_NAME is
   type TYPE_NAME is private;
      -- other declarations
private
   type TYPE_NAME is digits 4; -- some type definition
end PACKAGE_NAME;
```

Private types have the operations of assignment, equality, and those operations defined in the package where the type is defined.

   To use data abstraction in Ada, first define the types that are needed to solve the problem. Then define the operations on the types. Put the types and the operations on these types together in packages such that the types are private types. If possible, limit even the assignment and equality operations by making the types limited private. Limited private types have only those operations defined in the package where the type is defined.

   The general form of a limited type specification is

```
type TYPE_NAME is limited private;
```

   An important use of private types is hiding the underlying implementation of the type. This may aid portability of Ada programs.

   Because the = operation is not defined for the limited private data type, it can be defined in a package for any limited private type defined in that package. However, you cannot define /= because it is always the opposite of = and is automatically defined when you define =.

   You cannot define the := operation ever, even for limited private types. You can name a function such as

```
function ASSIGN (A, B : SOME_TYPE) return SOME_TYPE;
```

to perform assignment on limited private types.

PROBLEMS

1. Change the car inventory program to use limited private types. Do not allow the use of any access types external to the package.

2. Write a package incorporating the overloaded functions in procedure SIMPLE_COMPASS (Chapter 11). Make the type COMPASS_POINT_TYPE a limited private type. Test the package with a newly written procedure that performs the operations of the old SIMPLE_COMPASS program.

3. Write a package that alters the package MATRIX_OPERATORS (Chapter 11) to have MATRIX be a private type. Test the program with a program to replace procedure MATRIX_EXAMPLE. Note that you will have to put some of the main program in a new operation to display the contents of the matrix. Why?

4. Rewrite the VARIABLE_STRING package so that TEXT is a limited private type. Test it with the rewritten main program from Chapter 11.

5. Write a package that performs complex addition and subtraction. Make the complex data type a private data type.

6. Rewrite the package in problem 9, chapter 14 to have the doubly linked list node and the access types be limited private types.

7. Rewrite the family tree package of chapter 14 to have the tree and the access types be limited private types.

8. Rewrite the tree package of chapter 14, problem 10, to have the tree and the access types be limited private types.

C H A P T E R

❖ 16 ❖

USING ADA FOR DESIGN

Before you write an Ada program you will design the program. Ada makes an excellent design language, that is, its features aid you in designing efficient, correct programs. Ada supports design activities in that Ada can:

- record the design process through program libraries, which can store designs as well as programs;

- serve as a communication medium between the designer of a program and the programmer who implements the program through the package specification;

- support various design methodologies, such as top-down design, bottom-up design, and object-oriented design, without imposing a particular methodology on the designer;

- provide a mechanism for a design review process, particularly if the package has been well documented;

- check for consistency between formal and actual parameters by the compiler; and

- easily check that a program's design matches the implementation.

Furthermore the design can serve as a program skeleton which can be expanded into a complete Ada program.

In the previous chapters we gave some guidelines on the most efficient ways to program in Ada as the language's various features were introduced. These guidelines are also applicable to designing programs using Ada as a design language.

MODULARITY

The primary reason Ada makes a good design language is the package construct. Some programmers define their data types first when they design a program, other progammers define their subprograms first. You can do either with Ada. Whichever you do first, you create a package specification containing either data types or subprogram specifications that will be compiled separately from the package body. In fact, in designing a program, you are writing package specifications without the package body.

Many program designers find it easiest to draw a program's design as a block diagram showing the major data paths that go between parts of the program. They then name the data objects and the data types making up the program. Others find it easiest to think of the data objects and data types in a program and give no thought at first to the functions the program is meant to perform.

A package should contain related data types. If you have a large program with many different types of data, you probably should not put all the data type definitions in a single package, but you should place related data and data types together. You should also try to incorporate the functions that operate on a particular data type in the same package as the type definition. Keeping the data types and the operations on the data types together in the same package allows for better control of changes to the operations as the design progresses.

HIGH-LEVEL DESIGN

When you design an application, you start by giving a description of the entire program, leaving out details. This is called a high-level design. You need to go from an overall description to a detailed design or lower-level design by adding details. In approaching a high-level design, you put together design fragments. As you develop the design you will want to show consistency, document beyond what is possible with the Ada language, and provide a skeleton for implementers, a test plan outline for testers, a change history for maintainers, and a project history that tracks the design process.

In a high-level description of an application you describe the design by giving

◆ the name of the application,

◆ what is being input,

◆ what is being output,

◆ the paragraph in the requirements document that this part of the design applies to, and

◆ an English description of the function.

At a subsequent lower-level description, you will want to provide

◆ the type of the design element appropriate in an Ada program: procedure, package, function, or task;

◆ the data types appropriate to the interfaces; and

◆ the organization of the data in the interface: parameters, global data in a package, private data in a package.

At a still lower level of detail, you will specify

◆ the range of the data types in the interfaces;

◆ the physical units of the data in the interfaces; and

◆ the control structure in a design element.

An Ada compiler can always be used to check a design for correct syntax; it will take a connected design (one that has interfaces defined between all the parts of the design) to allow the compiler to check for correct interfaces. The compiler will not be able to check that all the inputs to the design are used and all the outputs from the design are generated—this takes manual analysis. Other needed checks are that the organization of data into packages, parameters, and local data is appropriate. Most design data should be placed in packages. It is the job of the implementer to specify local data needed for particular algorithms.

Figure 16.1 shows a block diagram approach to a high-level design of a data collection program. This program reads time and temperature information, records the maximum and average temperature over specified interval of time on a direct access disk, and displays the information on a terminal when the operator requests it to do so with a button push.

The high-level description of this design is accomplished by

◆ naming the system:
   REAL_TIME_DATA_COLLECTION

◆ naming the sources of data into the system:
   OPERATOR_BUTTON
   TIME_SYSTEM
   TEMPERATURE_SENSOR

◆ naming the places where data go out of the system:
   TERMINAL_DISPLAY
   DIRECT_ACCESS_DISK

◆ naming the location of the requirements for the system:
   chapter 16 high level design paragraph 1, figure 1

◆ providing a top-level description of the system

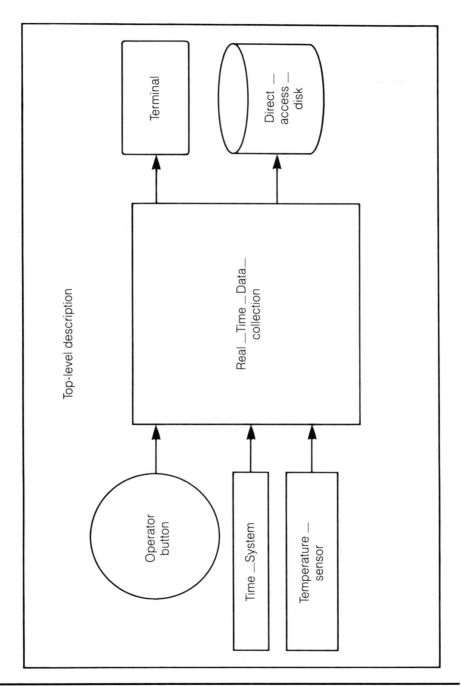

Figure 16.1 High-level design block diagram

The program reads time and temperature information. It records the maximum and average temperature every second on a direct access disk. It displays the information on a terminal when the operator pushes a button.

This high-level description transformed into Ada:

```
--  sources of data into the system
package OPERATOR_BUTTON is
end OPERATOR_BUTTON;
package TIME_SYSTEM is
end TIME_SYSTEM;
package TEMPERATURE_SENSOR is
end TEMPERATURE_SENSOR:
-- destinations of data out from the system
package TERMINAL_DISPLAY is
end TERMINAL_DISPLAY;
package DIRECT_ACCESS_DISK is
end DIRECT_ACCESS_DISK;
with OPERATOR_BUTTON, TIME_SYSTEM, TEMPERATURE_SENSOR,
    TERMINAL_DISPLAY, DIRECT_ACCESS_DISK;
procedure REAL_TIME_DATA_COLLECTION is
-- requirements
    -- chapter 16 high level design paragraph 1, figure 1
-- description
    -- The program reads time and temperature information. It
    -- records the maximum and average temperature every second
    -- on a direct access disk. It displays the information on
    -- a terminal when the operator pushes a button
begin
  null;
end REAL_TIME_DATA_COLLECTION;
```

Transforming the textual description and the block diagram into Ada flows naturally. Where Ada syntax does not adequately handle the description, use comments. Other comments useful in a design are designer name; design date, and version number. These can easily be added along with other useful information at the top of the design.

There are several ways to proceed once you have established a high-level design. The following sections describe several of these approaches.

TOP-DOWN DESIGN

In a top-down design you decompose the high-level design into smaller pieces that look more like the final implementation.

As a possible first decomposition of our high-level design, we can redraw figure 16.1 as shown in figure 16.2, which divides the block REAL_TIME_DATA COLLECTION into three blocks: INPUT_PROCESSING, DATA_REDUC-TION, and UPDATE_DISPLAY. These blocks can be packages, procedures or tasks; let us for now make them procedures placed in the high-level design.

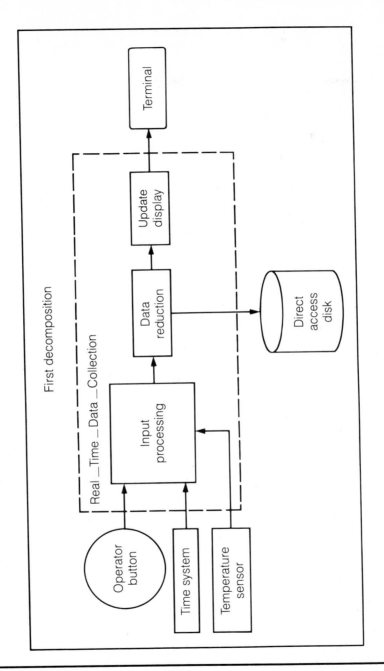

Figure 16.2   Top-down decomposition

As a result of the decomposition, we have other interfaces between the procedures, and we should name the interfaces for each of the connections between the blocks. These interfaces will take the form of Ada packages.

```
--  sources of data into the system
package OPERATOR_BUTTON is
end OPERATOR_BUTTON;
package TIME_SYSTEM is
end TIME_SYSTEM;
package TEMPERATURE_SENSOR is
end TEMPERATURE_SENSOR;
--  destinations of data out from the system
package TERMINAL_DISPLAY is
end TERMINAL_DISPLAY;
package DIRECT_ACCESS_DISK is
end DIRECT_ACCESS_DISK;
with OPERATOR_BUTTON, TIME_SYSTEM, TEMPERATURE_SENSOR,
      TERMINAL_DISPLAY, DIRECT_ACCESS_DISK;
procedure REAL_TIME_DATA_COLLECTION is
-- requirements
  -- chapter 16 high level design paragraph 1, figure 1
-- description
    -- The program reads time and temperature information. It
    -- records the maximum and average temperature every second
    -- on a direct access disk. It displays the information on
    -- a terminal when the operator pushes a button
  procedure INPUT_PROCESSING is separate;
  procedure DATA_REDUCTION is separate;
  procedure UPDATE_DISPLAY is separate;
begin
  null;
end REAL_TIME_DATA_COLLECTION;

package DATA_REDUCTION_INTERFACE is
end DATA_REDUCTION_INTERFACE;

with OPERATOR_BUTTON, TIME_SYSTEM, TEMPERATURE_SENSOR;
with DATA_REDUCTION_INTERFACE;
separate (REAL_TIME_DATA_COLLECTION)
procedure INPUT_PROCESSING is
  -- uses packages for operator button, time system, and
  -- temperature sensor
  use OPERATOR_BUTTON, TIME_SYSTEM, TEMPERATURE_SENSOR;
  -- also has interfaces to data reduction procedure
  use DATA_REDUCTION_INTERFACE;
begin
  null;
end INPUT_PROCESSING:

package UPDATE_DISPLAY_INTERFACE is
end UPDATE_DISPLAY_INTERFACE;

with DIRECT_ACCESS_DISK;
with DATA_REDUCTION_INTERFACE, UPDATE_DISPLAY_INTERFACE;
separate (REAL_TIME_DATA_COLLECTION)
```

```
procedure DATA_REDUCTION is
   -- uses interface to INPUT_PROCESSING
   use DATA_REDUCTION_INTERFACE;
   -- also uses interfaces to direct access disk and
   -- to update display
   use DIRECT_ACCESS_DISK, UPDATE_DISPLAY_INTERFACE;
begin
   null;
end DATA_REDUCTION;

with TERMINAL_DISPLAY, UPDATE_DISPLAY_INTERFACE;
separate (REAL_TIME_DATA_COLLECTION)
procedure UPDATE_DISPLAY is
   -- uses interface to data reduction
   use UPDATE_DISPLAY_INTERFACE;
   -- and interface to terminal display
   use TERMINAL_DISPLAY;
begin
   null;
end UPDATE_DISPLAY;
```

The additional packages we have defined must be specified as

```
package DATA_REDUCTION_INTERFACE is
end DATA_REDUCTION_INTERFACE;
package UPDATE_DISPLAY_INTERFACE is
end UPDATE_DISPLAY_INTERFACE;
```

As the next step in the decomposition the data interfaces and the data types that will be used with these interfaces should be defined for the appropriate packages. For example, we will expand the TIME_SYSTEM package to include a time record for the TIME_TYPE:

```
type TIME_TYPE is
   record
      YEAR    : YEAR_TYPE;
      MONTH   : MONTH_TYPE;
      DAY     : DAY_TYPE;
      HOUR    : HOUR_TYPE;
      MINUTE  : MINUTE_TYPE;
      SECOND  : SECOND_TYPE;
   end record;
```

At first you might try to lay out all the types in the records without defining such lower level type names as YEAR_TYPE. However, to use the Ada compiler it will be necessary for you to define all the types down to the implementation level. You should define the representation specification for the types if it is necessary to do so for a physical interface.

After you have defined the types for each package, the next level of detail will introduce functional order and the organization of data, data types, and functions into packages.

The top-down approach makes each processing element a separate procedure and each interface a separate package. Each processing element will appear as in figure 16.3.

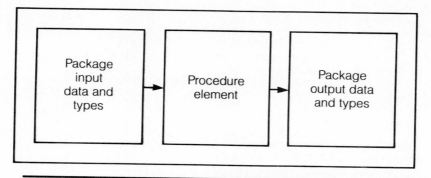

Figure 16.3   A single processing element

In the decomposition process, all higher level data is brought down to the lower level, so a decomposition will appear as in figure 16.4.

Top-Down Versus Data Oriented Decomposition

There are at least two problems with the top-down approach. One is that the higher level process will not usually input or output data; instead, the lower level elements will do so. The higher element will usually control only the order of operation of the lower elements. The second problem is that there might be data types and data common to more than one package. Such data types and data should be grouped separately in a package accessible to all subelements. The data-oriented approach attempts to solve these problems by defining the data types first.

As designer, you must organize the data and processing elements in an accessible package. You can group all data, data types, and processing elements together in a single package or place each interface and each processing element in a separate package.

Since you have grouped related data and functions, you have several choices. Figure 16.5 shows two organizations that might result from looking at the problem we have been tracking from two different views.

In the first view, the broken lines reflect the top-down design approach that we have been taking. The solid lines show a grouping of packages that might better satisfy data flow needs. This organization aims at grouping similar data types together in the same package. A good designer will take both design approaches to see which results in a cleaner design.

Our data oriented decomposition appears as

```
procedure REAL_TIME_DATA_COLLECTION is
  package BUTTON_PACKAGE is
  end BUTTON_PACKAGE;
  package DATA_PACKAGE is
  end DATA_PACKAGE;
```

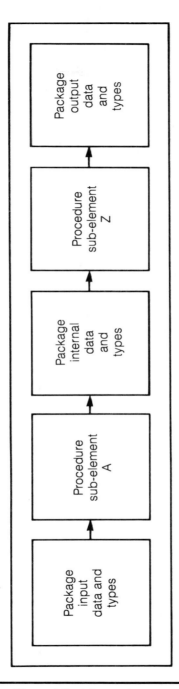

Figure 16.4   Decomposition of the element

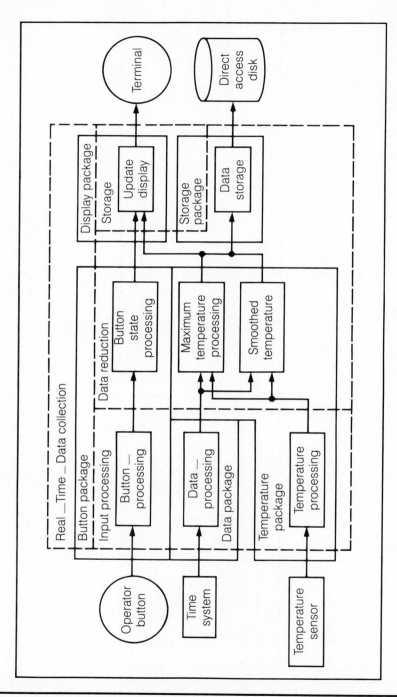

Figure 16.5 Two design views

```
   package TEMPERATURE_PACKAGE is
   end TEMPERATURE_PACKAGE;
   package DISPLAY_PACKAGE is
   end DISPLAY_PACKAGE;
   package STORAGE_PACKAGE is
   end STORAGE_PACKAGE;
begin
   null;
end REAL_TIME_DATA_COLLECTION;
```

The button package contains the button processing block and the interface to the operator button as well as to the button-state processing block.

After choosing the decomposition, the elements we have labeled as procedures should be defined as procedures, functions, or tasks. If defined as a task, the coordination via an interrupt entry or a rendezvous entry will be specified as well as the accept parameters. In the case of a procedure or function, the heading will be specified.

Place the data and data types in packages that reflect interfaces based on a top-down design. As with functions, this grouping might not be natural to a data-flow design—data types in separate packages might be better organized in a single package. Data composed of different data types might be better described in terms of the same data type. After you have categorized the data types, the data based on them can be assigned to the package in which the data type was defined or to a function package.

In a low-level design you insert control structures and English text to describe operations and their order. The expressions in the control structures can be English phrases or legal Ada expressions for which data have or have not been declared. The output of the low-level design should be an indented program skeleton; at implementation the program skeleton will fill out to be a complete program.

At some stage in the design process, the design will appear as in the following Ada example. The expansion to the low-level design will replace the **null** statement with English text; which reflects the control structure of the design in comments showing the control structure of the program. At this stage you will have specified the procedure name, its data, and its data types. In the low-level design you will concentrate on the Ada control structures and operators.

```
   package TIME_DATA is
   end TIME_DATA;
   package TEMPERATURE_DATA is
   end TEMPERATURE_DATA;
   with TIME_DATA, TEMPERATURE DATA;
   use TIME_DATA, TEMPERATURE_DATA;
   procedure MAXIMUM_TEMPERATURE_PROCESSING is
   -- description:  the maximum temperature over one second
   -- designer   :  Bob Wallace
   -- date       :  July 1984
   -- version    :  1.0
   -- status     :  new
   -- requirement:  4.5.1
```

```
-- inputs from:   DATA_PROCESSING, TEMPERATURE_PROCESSING
-- outputs to :   UPDATE_DISPLAY, DATA_STORAGE
begin
  null;
end MAXIMUM_TEMPERATURE_PROCESSING;
```

You will want to use statements that cannot be handled by Ada such as

```
if time to start then
    turn on motor
else
    turn off motor
end if;
```

In this case you will have to turn each non-Ada statement into a comment. The implementer will leave the comments in when turning the design into a complete Ada program.

BOTTOM-UP DESIGN

There are often existing sets of packages and programs developed over many years. Writing these packages requires such enormous effort, whether they are written in assembly language or some high-level language, that it will be uneconomical to discard the effort and start fresh with a complete new design.

In trying to work up from existing software, take the bottom-up approach. Organize the existing software into packages. The data types for this software must be declared in Ada; the subprograms must be defined appropriately as Ada functions or procedures using the interface **pragma** to define the original language in which they are written. The procedures that invoke these subprograms are then defined and new data types and data objects are introduced in new packages. You then build up the program into more sophisticated subprogram units until you have defined a complete system.

Ada does not enforce a design methodology upon you. If the bottom-up design approach is the more appropriate one to use, then feel free to use it.

WHAT HAVE YOU LEARNED?

Ada is an excellent design language

- ◆ serving as a communication medium between designers and implementers
- ◆ supporting various design methodologies: top-down design, bottom-up design, and object-oriented design
- ◆ providing a mechanism for design reviews
- ◆ allowing for consistency checks
- ◆ resulting in a program skeleton which can be expanded into a full implementation

One approach to design is to draw a block diagram showing the major data paths between parts of a program. Then name the data objects and the data types which make up the program.

Another approach is to define the data objects and data types for the program. Then add the functions which are to operate on the data types.

Use the package to contain related data types. Try to incorporate the functions that operate on a particular data type in the same package as the type definition.

Start off a design by giving

♦ the name of the application

♦ the names of the inputs

♦ the names of the outputs

♦ the references to other documents which are driving the design such as the requirements

♦ a brief description of the application

For the next step, you provide

♦ the type of design element appropriate to the program: procedure, package, function, or task

♦ the data types appropriate to the interface

♦ the organization of the data in the interface: parameters, global data in a package, private data in a package

For an even lower level of detail, you specify

♦ the range of the data types in the interfaces

♦ the physical units of the data

♦ the control structure in each design element

PROBLEMS

1. Design a program to automate a gas station. The gas station automation program should keep track of inventory, prices, expenses, and profit. The gas station sells three kinds of fuel: regular, unleaded, and super. Salaries, rent, and fuel make up the expenses. Prices for the fuel can fluctuate on a daily basis.

2. Design an airline reservation system for a small commuter airline which has 10 flights a day on two aircraft each of which has 16 seats.

3. Design a payroll system for a small company of 50 employees. Each person on the payroll receives a salary for which Federal and State income tax are withheld. Other deductions which are accounted for are social security, insurance, charity contributions, and credit union payments. The payroll

system should keep track of hours worked, hours taken in vacation, and hours taken in sick leave.

4. Design an automatic landing system for an aircraft. The system receives deviations from the glideslope and calculates commands in terms of roll, pitch, and yaw. When any command exceeds a predetermined threshold, the pilot is notified via a warning light.

5. Design a traffic control system for a busy intersection which has left turn lights and controls for walk/don't walk lights. Sensors are available for each direction so that the light will not turn green if no car is present at the intersection. Once green, the light will stay green until no cars approach the intersection for 10 seconds or if the light has been green for a preset length of time.

6. Design an air-conditioner control system for a building. The air-conditioner will turn on when the temperature goes above a preset value on a thermostat. It will stay on until the temperature drops 2 degrees below a preset value. In the evening, the thermostat will be ignored. The air-conditioner will turn on only when the temperature goes above 80 degrees and it will stay on until the temperature drops to 77 degrees.

CHAPTER
❖ 17 ❖
FILES

❖ All our input and output has been done using a keyboard as the input
device and the display as the output device. This is fine for small quantities of data, but most programs need to store data for long periods of time
and update that data as a result of computations. For example, an airline
reservation system needs to keep track not only of today's flights but flights
up to a year in advance for those people who reserve far in advance. This
large amount of information is too large to keep in the computer's memory
and so it is stored in *files.*

Ada allows us to send and receive information from two types of files,
sequential files and *random files.* In either case you can think of a file as a collection of records which contain information.

Sequential files are usually easier for a computer to handle, but they are
somewhat restricted in their use. In a sequential file the computer starts
processing records at the beginning of the file and processes each record until
you stop processing or reach the end of the file. It must read every record in
sequence, even if you do not intend to do anything with it. While sequential
files are easier for the computer to read, they are not good for very many
applications. This is because you usually do not want to read every record in
a file.

Most applications use random access files, which are called *direct files* in
Ada. A computer can read one particular record in the random access file
without reading any other record. The file will have an index number indi-

241

cating its location. It is up to you to associate this index number with some meaningful look-up information.

Ada was not meant to work much with files and it does not have all the facilities of a language such as COBOL. However, the facilities that it does have are adequate for handling simple file structures. All the file-handling facilities are placed in two predefined packages SEQUENTIAL_IO and DIRECT_IO. It is also possible to treat a file containing textual information as a sequential file with some of the procedures in TEXT_IO.

ASSOCIATING NAMES WITH FILES

Every computer system today has its own mechanism for naming files; it is unlikely that the names that your computer operating system uses are legal Ada names. It is more likely that the names will look something like these:

```
chapter 20.txt
financial.data
$trail.
```

In working with files, the first thing you have to do is tell Ada the name of the file as it exists in the system naming scheme and the name of the file that Ada will use in accessing the file. If the file already exists, you use the OPEN procedure to associate the Ada name with the system name.

```
OPEN (MY_FILE, OUT_FILE, "chapter20.txt");
```

If the file does not exist, you use the CREATE procedure to associate the Ada name with the system name and to create the file.

```
CREATE (MY_NEW_FILE, OUT_FILE, "salary.data");
```

In the first example, an existing file named chapter20.txt is given the Ada name MY_FILE. In the second example, a new file named salary.data is given the Ada name MY_NEW_FILE. In both examples, the second parameter is given the value OUT_FILE, which means that the file can be used as an output file. Other values that could be given to the second parameter are dependent on the type of file that is being opened or created. The possible values are

FOR OPENING DIRECT_IO
```
IN_FILE
OUT_FILE
INOUT_FILE
```

FOR OPENING SEQUENTIAL_IO AND TEXT_IO
```
IN_FILE
OUT_FILE
```

FOR CREATING DIRECT_IO
```
OUT_FILE
INOUT_FILE
```

FOR CREATING SEQUENTIAL_IO AND TEXT_IO
```
OUT_FILE
```

It is possible to create a file for temporary usage during a program with the command

```
CREATE (MY_TEMPORARY_FILE, INOUT_FILE);
```

which does not assign a value to the system name parameter. Errors, called *exceptions*, will be raised if the file is already open and a procedure tries to open it again. Hence it is good policy to open the files you are going to use at the start of your program.

Files must be declared in a declaration statement as a FILE_TYPE before they are used. Hence before we can use an OPEN or CREATE statement, we need to make declarations such as

```
MY_FILE : FILE_TYPE;
MY_NEW_FILE : FILE_TYPE;
MY_TEMPORARY_FILE : FILE_TYPE;
```

to make the files known to Ada.

SEQUENTIAL FILES

The package SEQUENTIAL_IO is a generic package for the management, reading, and writing of sequential files. Before any of the procedures are used on a sequential file, the package needs to be instantiated for the type of data that are to be read or written to the file. For example, if we had defined a record type named MY_INFORMATION, which is to be written to a sequential file, we would instantiate SEQUENTIAL_IO as

```
package MY_SEQUENTIAL_IO is new SEQUENTIAL_IO (MY_INFORMATION);
```

Then to have access to the types and procedures in the package, we write

```
use MY_SEQUENTIAL_IO;
```

The complete package specification for SEQUENTIAL_IO is given in Appendix C, but we will cover some of the most useful procedures in this chapter. If you want to read about all the procedures which can be used to manipulate sequential files, then you should read chapter 14 of the Ada Language Reference Manual after reading this chapter.

You may notice that in creating a file, there was a fourth parameter which was not used. This fourth parameter, the form parameter, will not be used in most computer systems, but it is there to take care of special requirements for some operating systems.

The usual sequence of operations in working with a sequential file is to

```
-- create the file for writing
-- write some information to be saved on the file
-- close the file for writing
-- open the file for reading
-- read the information from the file
-- process the information
-- close the file for reading
```

Very often the creation of the file and the reading of information from the file are found in two different programs that may execute on different days.

Another common sequence of operations used with sequential files involves merging two existing sequential files into one new sequential file in some new order. For example, the list of students who have graduated from a school might be updated on a yearly basis with the list of students who have newly graduated. Both lists might have been prepared in alphabetical order and the new list should be prepared in alphabetical order too.

The sequence of operations for merging such files:

```
-- open the file of old grads
-- open the file of new grads
-- create the file of all grads
-- read from the old grads and the new grads
-- keeping the records in alphabetical order
-- write to the file of all grads
-- when all records have been processed
-- close the file of old grads
-- close the file of new grads
-- close the file of all grads
```

The common operations to these two applications will be found time and again in many programs. We have covered the OPEN and CREATE procedures. At the end of programs, we will want to close the open files. This is done with the CLOSE procedure, which has only one parameter, the name of the file.

For example,

```
CLOSE (MY_FILE);
```

will close the file named MY_FILE. Closing the file usually involves some housekeeping to let the computer know it has a new file. It also serves to let the Ada program switch from having a file be a newly created OUT_FILE to being an existing IN_FILE for more processing.

The other most useful procedures in processing files are the READ and WRITE procedures. If we had a record named MY_RECORD, which was of type MY_INFORMATION, we can write the record on a sequential file by

```
WRITE (MY_FILE, MY_RECORD);
```

Later on, when the file has been opened as an IN_FILE, we can then retrieve the record with the statement

```
READ (MY_FILE, MY_RECORD);
```

A BOOLEAN function used in **while** loops tests for the end of the file. Most sequential file handling programs read a single record at a time and process it. At each pass through the loop, the program tests if it has read an end of file with the function END_OF_FILE. For example, a common structure is

```
OPEN (MY_FILE, IN_FILE, "salary.data");
while not END_OF_FILE (MY_FILE) loop
   READ (MY_FILE, MY_RECORD);
   -- do something with the record
```

```
    end loop;
    CLOSE (MY_FILE);
```

To demonstrate how all this fits together, we will write a program that creates a file containing employee data. We will use a simple record of the employee's name, social security number, and salary. The input to the file will come from the keyboard until the person entering the data wants to take a break and enters an end of file—control-Z on many computers. At that point the program will stop inputting and will display the data that have been entered on the terminal.

```
package EMPLOYEE_DATA is
   subtype SALARY_TYPE is FLOAT range 0.0 .. 100000.0;
   type EMPLOYEE_RECORD_TYPE is
     record
       NAME                  : STRING (1..10);
       SOCIAL_SECURITY       : POSITIVE;
       SALARY                : SALARY_TYPE;
     end record;
end EMPLOYEE_DATA;

with EMPLOYEE_DATA, TEXT_IO, SEQUENTIAL_IO;
use  EMPLOYEE_DATA;
package MY_IO is
   package FLOAT_IO is new TEXT_IO.FLOAT_IO (FLOAT);
   package INTEGER_IO is new TEXT_IO.INTEGER_IO (INTEGER);
   package MY_FILE_IO is new SEQUENTIAL_IO (EMPLOYEE_RECORD_TYPE);
   use MY_FILE_IO;
   MY_FILE : FILE_TYPE;
end MY_IO;

with EMPLOYEE_DATA, TEXT_IO, MY_IO;
use  EMPLOYEE_DATA, TEXT_IO, MY_IO;
procedure CREATE_EMPLOYEE_DATA is
   use MY_IO.FLOAT_IO, MY_IO.INTEGER_IO, MY_IO.MY_FILE_IO;
   EMPLOYEE_RECORD : EMPLOYEE_RECORD_TYPE;
begin
   PUT (" program to create employee data file ");
   NEW_LINE;
   CREATE (MY_FILE, OUT_FILE, "employee.dat");
   while not END_OF_FILE loop
     PUT (" Enter employee name : ");
     NEW_LINE;
     GET (EMPLOYEE_RECORD.NAME);
     NEW_LINE;
     PUT (" Enter employee social security number ");
     NEW_LINE;
     GET (EMPLOYEE_RECORD.SOCIAL_SECURITY);
     NEW_LINE;
     PUT (" Enter employee salary ");
     NEW LINE;
     GET (EMPLOYEE_RECORD.SALARY);
     WRITE (MY_FILE, EMPLOYEE_RECORD);
   end loop;
   CLOSE (MY_FILE);
```

```
                -- display data in file
                OPEN (MY_FILE, IN_FILE, "employee.dat");
                PUT (" Employee Data File - Employee.Dat ");
                NEW_LINE;
                PUT (" Name          Social Security          Salary ");
                while not END_OF_FILE (MY_FILE) loop
                  READ (MY_FILE, EMPLOYEE_RECORD);
                  NEW_LINE;
                  PUT (EMPLOYEE_RECORD.NAME);
                  PUT (EMPLOYEE_RECORD.SOCIAL_SECURITY);
                  PUT ("         ");
                  PUT (EMPLOYEE_RECORD.SALARY);
                end loop;
                CLOSE (MY_FILE);
              end CREATE_EMPLOYEE_DATA;
```

Our next example, a merging example, assumes that files already exist for the names, addresses, and graduation year of old grads and the names, addresses, and the graduation year of new grads. Both these files are sorted alphabetically by the name field; we want a new file that will contain the names of all grads sorted alphabetically.

```
              package GRADUATE_DATA is

                subtype YEAR_TYPE is INTEGER range 1800..3000;
                type    GRADUATE_RECORD_TYPE is
                  record
                    NAME :            STRING (1..20);
                    STREET_ADDRESS :  STRING (1..20);
                    CITY           :  STRING (1..20);
                    STATE          :  STRING (1..20);
                    COUNTRY        :  STRING (1..20);
                    YEAR           :  YEAR_TYPE;
                  end record;
              end GRADUATE_DATA;

              with SEQUENTIAL_IO, GRADUATE_DATA;
              use GRADUATE_DATA;
              package MERGE_IO is
                package GRADUATE_IO is new SEQUENTIAL_IO (GRADUATE_RECORD_TYPE);
                use     GRADUATE_IO;
                OLD_GRADS : FILE_TYPE;
                NEW_GRADS : FILE_TYPE;
                ALL_GRADS : FILE_TYPE;
              end MERGE_IO;

              with GRADUATE_DATA, TEXT_IO, MERGE_IO;
              use  GRADUATE_DATA, TEXT_IO, MERGE_IO;
              procedure MERGE is
                use MERGE_IO.GRADUATE_IO;
                OLD_GRADUATE_RECORD : GRADUATE_RECORD_TYPE;
                NEW_GRADUATE_RECORD : GRADUATE_RECORD_TYPE;
                OLD_VALID : BOOLEAN := FALSE;
                NEW_VALID : BOOLEAN := FALSE;
              begin
                -- open the file of old grads
```

```
    OPEN (OLD_GRADS, IN_FILE, "oldgrad.dat");
    -- open the file of new grads
    OPEN (NEW_GRADS, IN_FILE, "newgrad.dat");
    -- create the file of all grads
    CREATE (ALL_GRADS, OUT_FILE, "allgrad.dat");
    -- read from the old grads and the new grads
    -- keeping the records in alphabetical order
    -- write to the file of all grads
    while not END_OF_FILE (OLD_GRADS) and not END_OF_FILE (NEW_GRADS) loop

        if not OLD_VALID and not NEW_VALID then
            READ (NEW_GRADS, NEW_GRADUATE_RECORD);
            READ (OLD_GRADS, OLD_GRADUATE_RECORD);
            OLD_VALID : = TRUE;
            NEW_VALID : = TRUE;
        elsif not OLD_VALID and NEW_VALID then
            READ (OLD_GRADS, OLD_GRADUATE_RECORD);
            OLD_VALID : = TRUE;
        elsif OLD_VALID and not NEW_VALID then
            READ (NEW_GRADS, NEW_GRADUATE_RECORD);
            NEW_VALID : = TRUE;
        end if;
        if NEW_GRADUATE_RECORD.NAME > OLD_GRADUATE_RECORD.NAME then
        -- write out old graduate record and read another
            WRITE (ALL_GRADS, OLD_GRADUATE_RECORD);
            OLD_VALID : = FALSE;
        else
        -- write out new graduate record and read another
            WRITE (ALL_GRADS, NEW_GRADUATE_RECORD);
            NEW_VALID : = FALSE;
        end if;
    end loop;
    if OLD_VALID then
        WRITE (ALL_GRADS, OLD_GRADUATE_RECORD);
        OLD_VALID : = FALSE;
    elsif NEW_VALID then
        WRITE (ALL_GRADS, NEW_GRADUATE_RECORD);
        NEW_VALID : = FALSE;
    end if;
    -- make sure remaining records are copied to the all grads file
    while not END_OF_FILE (NEW_GRADS) loop
        READ (NEW_GRADS, NEW_GRADUATE_RECORD);
        WRITE (ALL_GRADS, NEW_GRADUATE_RECORD);
    end loop;
    while not END_OF_FILE (OLD_GRADS) loop
        READ (OLD_GRADS, OLD_GRADUATE_RECORD);
        WRITE (ALL_GRADS, OLD_GRADUATE_RECORD);
    end loop;
    -- when all records have been processed
    -- close the file of old grads
    CLOSE (OLD_GRADS);
    -- close the file of new grads
    CLOSE (NEW_GRADS);
    -- close the file of all grads
    CLOSE (ALL_GRADS);
end MERGE;
```

The merge program opens all the files and reads one record from each of the two input files. It then tests the records to determine which record to write to the merged file, ALL_GRADS. After writing a record, it replenishes the record to be tested. At one of the files ending, it writes all the remaining files to the merged file. It makes use of the fact that the **while** loop will not execute if the end of file has been reached for the file being tested.

RANDOM FILES

The second and only other type of file available to an Ada programmer is random access files or direct files. Direct files are used in such applications as picking up the credit record on someone given that person's license number.

Direct files are opened and closed in the same way as sequential files. Direct files have one advantage over sequential files in Ada in that they can be opened for both input and output with the use of INOUT_FILE as a second parameter in the OPEN or CREATE procedure. The SEQUENTIAL_IO programs written in the previous section could be rewritten to use DIRECT_IO with only a simple change of the package being instantiated. This is because direct files can be used sequentially but not vice versa.

The major difference between sequential files and direct files is the presence of an INDEX of type POSITIVE_COUNT. This INDEX starts with a value of 1 for the first record in a file and continues up to the number of records in the file or the *size* of the file. You can determine the size of a direct file by using the function SIZE in a statement such as

```
SIZE_MY_FILE  : = SIZE (MY_FILE);
```

The INDEX can be used to read or to write a particular record without going through all the records in the file. To make use of the INDEX we need some way of associating the INDEX with the record we want. This is often done with a sorted array on the field of interest versus the INDEX in the direct file. Or we can sort the direct file itself by some field of interest such as name and perform a search on the information in the file. We will show an example of this last method by searching a phone list for a name and presenting the name and phone number on the display.

The form of the READ and WRITE operations that use an INDEX are

```
-- to read record number denoted by index
READ  (MY_FILE,  RECORD_ELEMENT,  INDEX_COUNT);

-- to write at the record number denoted by index
WRITE (MY_FILE, RECORD_ELEMENT, INDEX_COUNT);
```

Additional procedures and functions useful in testing and manipulating the INDEX are

```
-- to position the INDEX
SET_INDEX (MY_FILE, INDEX_COUNT);

-- to determine the location of the current index

I := INDEX (MY_FILE);
```

In an efficient search method known as a binary search, we look at the middle of the file and determine if the name is greater or less than the name stored at that location. If it is less, we have divided the possibilities in two; the item we are searching for must be in the bottom half of the file. We continue to narrow the search until we find the item.

```
package TELEPHONE_FILE_DATA is
   type TELEPHONE_RECORD_TYPE is
   record
      NAME    : STRING (1..10);
      NUMBER  : STRING (1..10);
      ADDRESS : STRING (1..20);
   end record;
end TELEPHONE_FILE_DATA:

with DIRECT_IO, TELEPHONE_FILE_DATA;
use  TELEPHONE_FILE_DATA;
package MY_TELEPHONE_IO is
   package MY_IO is new DIRECT_IO (TELEPHONE_RECORD_TYPE);
   use     MY_IO;
   MY_FILE         : FILE_TYPE;
   BOTTOM_COUNTER  : COUNT;
   TOP_COUNTER     : COUNT;
   COUNTER         : COUNT;
   INDEX_COUNT     : POSITIVE_COUNT;
end MY_TELEPHONE_IO;

with TELEPHONE_FILE_DATA, MY_TELEPHONE_IO, TEXT_IO;
use  TELEPHONE_FILE_DATA, MY_TELEPHONE_IO, TEXT_IO;
procedure BINARY_SEARCH is
   use MY_TELEPHONE_IO.MY_IO;
   SEARCH_NAME       : STRING (1..10);
   DONE              : BOOLEAN;
   TELEPHONE_RECORD  : TELEPHONE_RECORD_TYPE;
begin
   OPEN (MY_FILE, IN_FILE, "TELE.DAT");
   loop -- infinite loop for operator
      PUT (" Enter name to search for ");  NEW_LINE;
      GET (SEARCH_NAME);
      DONE := FALSE;
      BOTTOM_COUNTER := 1;
      TOP_COUNTER    := SIZE (MY_FILE);
```

```
while not DONE loop
   COUNTER := (BOTTOM_COUNTER + TOP_COUNTER + 1)/2;
   READ (MY_FILE, TELEPHONE_RECORD, COUNTER);
   if TELEPHONE_RECORD.NAME < SEARCH_NAME then
      BOTTOM_COUNTER := COUNTER;
   elsif TELEPHONE_RECORD.NAME > SEARCH_NAME then
      TOP_COUNTER := COUNTER - 1;
   else
      -- found
      DONE := TRUE;
   end if;

   DONE := DONE or TOP_COUNTER = BOTTOM_COUNTER;
   if TOP_COUNTER = BOTTOM_COUNTER then
      COUNTER := (BOTTOM_COUNTER + TOP_COUNTER + 1)/2;
      READ (MY_FILE, TELEPHONE_RECORD, COUNTER);
   end if;
end loop;
if TELEPHONE_RECORD.NAME = SEARCH_NAME then
   PUT (TELEPHONE_RECORD.NAME);       NEW_LINE;
   PUT (TELEPHONE_RECORD.NUMBER);     NEW_LINE;
   PUT (TELEPHONE_RECORD.ADDRESS);    NEW_LINE;
else
   PUT (" Exact name not found, closest name is ");
   NEW_LINE;
   PUT (TELEPHONE_RECORD.NAME);       NEW_LINE;
   PUT (TELEPHONE_RECORD.NUMBER);     NEW_LINE;
   PUT (TELEPHONE_RECORD.ADDRESS);    NEW_LINE;
end if;
   end loop;
end BINARY_SEARCH;
```

What Have You Learned?

Ada has two types of files, sequential files and random files.

In a sequential file you process each record starting with the beginning of the file until you stop processing or you reach the end of the file.

In a random or direct access file you can read one particular record in the file without reading any other record. The file has an index number indicating its location.

All the facilities to work with files are placed in two predefined packages, SEQUENTIAL_IO and DIRECT_IO. It is also possible to treat a file containing textual information as a sequential file with some of the procedures in TEXT_IO.

If the file already exists, you use the OPEN procedure to associate the Ada name with the system name.

```
OPEN (MY_FILE, OUT_FILE, "chapter 20.txt");
```

If the file does not exist, you use the CREATE procedure to associate the Ada name with the system name and to create the file.

```
CREATE (MY_NEW_FILE, OUT_FILE, "salary.data");
```

The possible values of the second parameter in the CREATE and OPEN procedures are

FOR OPENING DIRECT_IO
```
IN_FILE
OUT_FILE
INOUT_FILE
```

FOR OPENING SEQUENTIAL_IO AND TEXT_IO
```
IN_FILE
OUT_FILE
```

FOR CREATING DIRECT_IO
```
OUT_FILE
INOUT_FILE
```

FOR CREATING SEQUENTIAL_IO AND TEXT_IO
```
OUT_FILE
```

It is possible to create a file for only temporary usage during a program with the command

```
CREATE (MY_TEMPORARY_FILE, INOUT_FILE);
```

Files must be declared in a declaration statement as a FILE_TYPE to make the files known to Ada before they are used:

```
MY_FILE           : FILE_TYPE;
MY_NEW_FILE       : FILE_TYPE;
MY_TEMPORARY_FILE : FILE_TYPE;
```

The package SEQUENTIAL_IO is a generic package for the management, reading, and writing of sequential files. We can instantiate SEQUENTIAL_IO as

```
package MY_SEQUENTIAL_IO is new SEQUENTIAL_IO (MY_INFORMATION);
use MY_SEQUENTIAL_IO;
```

At the end of programs we can close the open files. This is done with the CLOSE procedure.

```
CLOSE (MY_FILE);
```

We can write a record on a sequential file:

```
WRITE (MY_FILE, MY_RECORD);
```

When a file has been opened as an IN_FILE, we can retrieve the record with the statement

```
READ (MY_FILE, MY_RECORD);
```

The test for an end of the file is a BOOLEAN function often used in **while** loops. A common processing structure in using sequential files is

```
OPEN (MY_FILE, IN_FILE, "salary.data");
while not END_OF_FILE (MY_FILE) loop
  READ (MY_FILE, MY_RECORD);
  -- do something with the record
end loop;
CLOSE (MY_FILE);
```

Direct files are opened and closed in the same way as sequential files. Direct files have one advantage over sequential files in Ada in that they can be opened for both input and output with the use of INOUT_FILE as a second parameter in the OPEN or CREATE procedure.

Direct files have an INDEX of type POSITIVE_COUNT. This INDEX starts with a value of 1 for the first record in a file and continues up to the number of records in the file, known as the *size* of the file. The function SIZE yields the size of a direct file

```
SIZE_MY_FILE  : = SIZE (MY_FILE);
```

The form of the READ and WRITE operations that use an INDEX are

```
-- to read record number denoted by index
READ  (MY_FILE, RECORD_ELEMENT, INDEX_COUNT);

-- to write at the record number denoted by index
WRITE (MY_FILE, RECORD_ELEMENT, INDEX_COUNT);
```

Additional procedures and functions that are useful in testing and manipulating the INDEX are

```
-- to position the index
SET_INDEX (MY_FILE, INDEX_COUNT);

-- to determine the location of the current index
I : = INDEX (MY_FILE);
```

PROBLEMS

1. Write a BOOLEAN function called STILL_MORE_TO_READ to use in a looping construct such as

   ```
   while STILL_MORE_TO_READ (MY_FILE) loop
   ```

   instead of the usual expression

   ```
   while not END_OF_FILE (MY_FILE) loop
   ```

2. Write a program that adds to the employee data file created by the program CREATE_EMPLOYEE_DATA. Have the program merge the old contents of the file with new input from the keyboard. Test the program by entering data with the original program. Then add records with your program and display the entire file.

3. Write a program to create an old grads file and a new grads file that can be used with the merge program. Add statements to the merge program to display the contents of the files.

4. Write a program to create a telephone information file that can be used with the binary search program. Add statements to display the contents of the file after it is created.

CHAPTER
❖ 18 ❖
TASKING

❖ One of Ada's most powerful features, unavailable in most high-level languages, is *tasking*, which is needed for real-time programs and operating systems. Tasking means that more than one program can be executing in a computer at the same time—if you are sharing a computer with others, you may well be using a multitasking system. It is a good chance that the system will have been programmed in assembly language and is difficult to change as a result. Therefore, future multitasking systems may be written in Ada.

Ada has a number of forms of tasking. They can be categorized as

- totally independent,
- synchronized with busy wait,
- synchronized with optional communication points,
- synchronized with timeout, or
- synchronized with checks on availability of data or equipment.

All the forms of synchronization use the *rendezvous technique*, which can be thought of as a meeting between the tasks.

TOTALLY INDEPENDENT TASKS

The simplest form of tasking is when the tasks are totally independent and do not communicate with each other in any way.

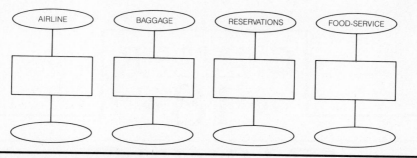

Figure 18.1   Fly by night airlines

Figure 18.1 shows four such tasks representing the operations at Fly by Night Airlines. This airline's computer program manages the airline, the baggage, the reservations, and the food service. None of these tasks coordinates with the others and none sends information between the others. Such a task structure can be programmed as

```ada
with TEXT_IO; use TEXT_IO;
procedure AIRLINE is
  task BAGGAGE;
  task RESERVATIONS;
  task FOOD_SERVICE;
  procedure CHECK_LUGGAGE is separate;
  procedure LOSE_LUGGAGE is separate;
  procedure TAKE_RESERVATION is separate;
  procedure CANCEL_RESERVATION is separate;
  procedure MAKE_MEAL is separate;
  procedure TAKE_COMPLAINTS is separate;
  procedure MISMANAGE is separate;
  procedure TAKE_VACATION is separate;
  task body BAGGAGE is
  begin
    loop
      CHECK_LUGGAGE;
      LOSE_LUGGAGE;
    end loop;
  end BAGGAGE;

  task body RESERVATIONS is
  begin
    loop
      TAKE_RESERVATION;
      CANCEL_RESERVATION;
    end loop;
  end RESERVATIONS;

  task body FOOD_SERVICE is
  begin
    loop
      MAKE_MEAL;
      TAKE_COMPLAINTS;
    end loop;
  end FOOD_SERVICE;
```

```
begin
   MISMANAGE;
   TAKE_VACATION;
end AIRLINE;
```

The procedure named AIRLINE is called a *main task*—you have been writing main tasks every time you wrote a main program. Embedded in the main task are three other tasks: BAGGAGE, RESERVATIONS, and FOOD_SERVICE. First the tasks are declared as tasks in the task declarations

```
task BAGGAGE;
task RESERVATIONS;
task FOOD_SERVICE;
```

These declarations specify that there are three additional tasks to the main task in the program. The definition of what is to be done in the tasks is shown in the task body, which can be separately compiled, although this example showed them nested in the main task. In fact, just like procedures, tasks can be placed in a package, where the task declaration goes in the specification part of the package and the task body goes in the package body.

An independent task is written just like a procedure without any parameters. Tasks can be nested so that the subprograms we made as procedures can also be made into independent tasks. It is inadvisable to have such complex tasking structures. Try to keep your tasking structures very simple; it will save you from much grief in debugging your program.

When tasks are declared to be part of a main task, they all start operating in parallel the moment that the **begin** of the main task is reached. They all continue to execute in parallel until terminated. In our example, the tasks are all in infinite loops, so they will not terminate unless one of the subprograms has an error that causes a termination. The main task does not have an infinite loop so it will execute and then wait at the **end** statement for the other tasks to terminate. If they all terminate, the main task will terminate.

Although not too many useful applications use totally independent tasks, some do. You can see that it is relatively simple to program such a tasking structure in Ada. Figure 18.2 shows a possible time line for the execution of these tasks. Conceptually, we show the tasks all executing at the same time, even though the computer can really do only one task at a time and must switch between tasks at appropriate points. This is called *scheduling* the tasks. How Ada manages to schedule between the tasks on a single computer is not defined. The designer of the Ada run-time system can make several choices to make it appear that the computer is executing the tasks in parallel.

SYNCHRONIZED WITH WAIT

In the second version of our program we will improve the communication between our tasks. Fly by Night Airlines has brought in management consultants. After extensive study they noticed that there was no coordination between the reservation department and the food service department. The

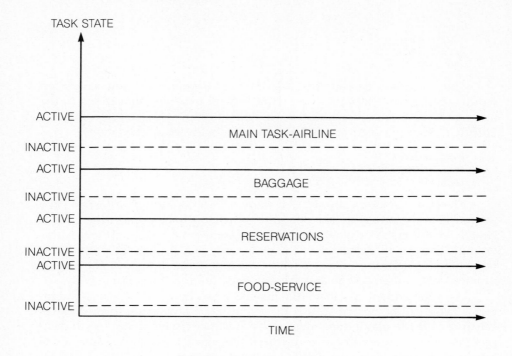

Figure 18.2   Time line for independent tasks

consultants suggested that considerable savings would be possible if the reservation department notified the food service department how many meals
to make for every flight. The consultants also suggested hiring a new chef to
cut down on complaints about the food preparation. Management agreed with
the suggestions and had another idea: do away with recording the complaints
since there was little that was done with them.

To incorporate these changes in the airline's computer program, we will
make use of the rendezvous technique to send information from the reservations department to the food service department. Figure 18.3 shows this
communication path; the line representing a rendezvous is drawn between
the block labeled *send order to food service* and the block labeled *receive food order.*

The major change we make to the program is to name the communication
point in the declaration of the task FOOD_SERVICE. The communication point
is called an *entry* in the task. We can have many such entries, but will have
only one in this example. The declaration becomes

```
task FOOD_SERVICE is
  entry ORDER (FOOD : MEAL_TYPE);
end FOOD_SERVICE;
```

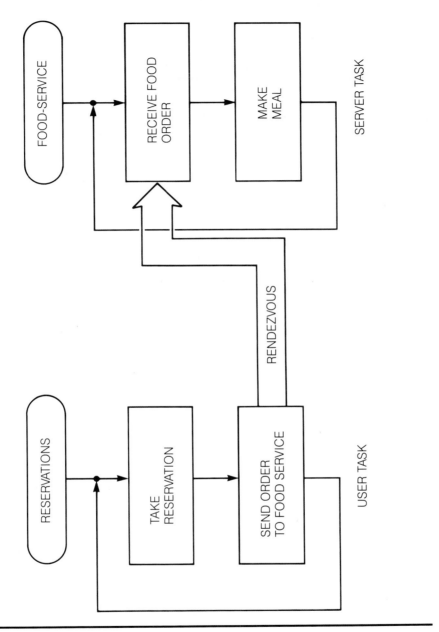

Figure 18.3   Communicating tasks

The declaration of the entry is much like a procedure specification: It states the name of the entry point and the parameters and their types and modes. Since we have not specified the mode, it is taken as an input parameter just as in a procedure parameter.

The task without the entry point invokes the task entry in the same manner as a procedure invocation. We see that in the reservations task there is a statement

```
FOOD_SERVICE.ORDER (MEAL);
```

This is an invocation to the rendezvous point in the other task.

The rewritten example appears as

```
with TEXT_IO; use TEXT_IO;
procedure AIRLINE is
  type MEAL_TYPE is (BREAKFAST, LUNCH, DINNER);
  task BAGGAGE;
  task RESERVATIONS;
  task FOOD_SERVICE is
    entry ORDER (FOOD : MEAL_TYPE);
  end FOOD_SERVICE;
  procedure CHECK_LUGGAGE is separate;
  procedure LOSE_LUGGAGE is separate;
  procedure TAKE_RESERVATION (MEAL : out MEAL_TYPE) is separate;
  procedure CANCEL_RESERVATION is separate;
  procedure MAKE_MEAL is separate;
  procedure MISMANAGE is separate;
  procedure TAKE_VACATION is separate;

  task body BAGGAGE is
  begin
    loop
      CHECK_LUGGAGE;
      LOSE_LUGGAGE;
    end loop;
  end BAGGAGE;

task body RESERVATIONS is
  MEAL : MEAL_TYPE;
begin
  loop
    TAKE_RESERVATION (MEAL);     -- sets meal
    FOOD_SERVICE.ORDER (MEAL);   -- rendezvous
  end loop;
end RESERVATIONS;
```

```
task body FOOD_SERVICE is
  procedure MAKE_BREAKFAST is
  begin
    PUT (" MAKE_BREAKFAST "); NEW_LINE;
  end MAKE_BREAKFAST;
  procedure MAKE_LUNCH is
  begin
    PUT (" MAKE_LUNCH "); NEW_LINE;
  end MAKE_LUNCH;
  procedure MAKE_DINNER is
  begin
    PUT (" MAKE_DINNER "); NEW_LINE;
  end MAKE_DINNER;
begin
  loop
    accept ORDER (FOOD : MEAL_TYPE) do
      case FOOD is
      when BREAKFAST => MAKE_BREAKFAST;
      when LUNCH     => MAKE_LUNCH;
      when DINNER    => MAKE_DINNER;
      end case;
    end ORDER;
  end loop;
  end FOOD_SERVICE;
begin
  MISMANAGE;
  TAKE_VACATION;
end AIRLINE;
```

In the body of the FOOD_SERVICE task the entry point appears in an **accept** statement. You can think of the **accept** statement as the procedure body for the communication point. The **accept** statement has parameters that are the same as specified in the entry point declaration. What happens is that all the tasks start executing in parallel as before. However, the two tasks that are to communicate, the RESERVATIONS task and the FOOD_SERVICE task, will execute down to the rendezvous point. Whichever task reaches the rendezvous point first will wait for the other task. When they are both at the rendezvous point, the invoking task or the *user task* will wait until the statements in the **accept** statement are executed before continuing on. After the statements in the invoked task or the *server task* are executed, the tasks will once again continue in parallel.

It is a good policy to keep the number of statements in the **accept** statement to a minimum because the other task is suspended from operating while the statements in the **accept** statement are being executed. While you can nest **accept** statements within **accept** statements, try to stay away from such complex structures unless it is very necessary. Usually the **accept** statement body just copies the parameter into a variable that is local to the task for some later operation.

The problem with this solution is that it makes one task wait for another. Although we can avoid waiting periods with a more complex structure, many applications continue to use the wait technique because of its simpler structure. It is the most popular tasking construct in real-time applications, which usually use a clock interrupt to start off a task sequence.

The next program shows a typical avionics program structure, which uses two clock interrupts to cause two different program sequences to be executed. The one sequence is called a SLOW_CLOCK_SEQUENCE and the other sequence is called a FAST_CLOCK_SEQUENCE. The slow clock operates 10 times per second and performs calculations that do not have to be done at a fast rate. The FAST_CLOCK_SEQUENCE operates at 100 times per second and performs calculations that need to be performed at a high rate. The main task just does error diagnostics in the background to make sure that everything is reasonable. Each of the two sequences and the error diagnostics are contained in subprograms. The two sequences are invoked by interrupts at the locations specified in the **for use** statements.

When a program is driven by a time clock interrupt such as this, the program must be finished before the next interrupt that invokes the program arrives again. A possible good time line for the program sequence is shown in the top half of figure 18.4. A bad time line sequence is shown in the lower half of the figure.

The program shows that there is a priority assigned to each of the two interrupts by Ada. Thus if the two interrupts arrive at the same time, the higher priority assigned with the statement

```
pragma PRIORITY (10);
```

will cause the FAST_CLOCK_SEQUENCE entry to be executed before the SLOW_CLOCK_SEQUENCE. Use is also made of the **pragma** INLINE for the collection of procedures that make up the programs to execute after the interrupt is received. The INLINE **pragma** eliminates the overhead associated with procedure invocation. It will be used extensively in real-time programs that are concerned with time deadlines.

All the pragmas are listed in Appendix E—you should beware that some compilers may not offer all the pragmas. They are not part of the standard required features for Ada.

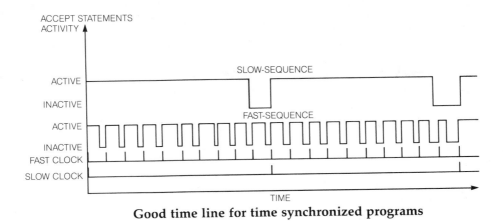

Good time line for time synchronized programs

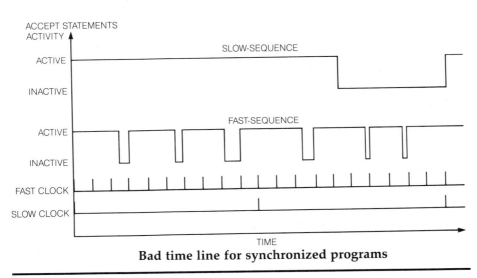

Bad time line for synchronized programs

Figure 18.4   Time lines for synchronized programs

```
with TEXT_IO; use TEXT_IO;
procedure AVIONICS is
  task SLOW is
    entry SLOW_CLOCK_SEQUENCE;
    for   SLOW_CLOCK_SEQUENCE use at 16#20#;
    pragma PRIORITY (5);
  end SLOW;
  task FAST is
    entry FAST_CLOCK_SEQUENCE;
    for   FAST_CLOCK_SEQUENCE use at 16#30#;
    pragma PRIORITY (10);
  end FAST;
  procedure ERROR_DIAGNOSTICS is separate;
  procedure SLOW_PROCEDURES is separate;
  procedure FAST_PROCEDURES is separate;
  pragma INLINE (SLOW_PROCEDURES);
  pragma INLINE (FAST_PROCEDURES);
  pragma INLINE (ERROR_DIAGNOSTICS);
  task body SLOW is separate;
  task body FAST is separate;
begin
  loop
    ERROR_DIAGNOSTICS;   -- perform background checks
  end loop;
end AVIONICS;

separate (AVIONICS)
task body SLOW is
begin
  loop
    accept SLOW_CLOCK_SEQUENCE;
    SLOW_PROCEDURES;
  end loop;
end SLOW;
separate (AVIONICS)
task body FAST is
begin
  loop
    accept FAST_CLOCK_SEQUENCE;
    FAST_PROCEDURES;
  end loop;
end FAST;
```

While this synchronous approach to real-time tasks is the most popular, reliable approach to tasking, it is sometimes felt that it wastes time between the interrupts and that people are overly conservative in their design, trying to make every path of the program stay within limits. The next section contains an approach called the *asynchronous* approach. It tries to eliminate this concern about staying synchronized.

SYNCHRONIZED WITH OPTIONAL COMMUNICATION POINTS

Figure 18.5 shows a block diagram of a simple real-time system. There are two sensors in this system. The sensor input can be a temperature gauge and the actuator output can be a control to a heater. When the temperature gets too low, the heater will be turned on and when the temperature gets too high the heater will be turned off. The actual software interface is represented by the blocks labeled *interface process*. The receiver process and the transmitter process will serve as buffers for the data between the software interface process. Such buffers are needed when the timing cannot be guaranteed between processes.

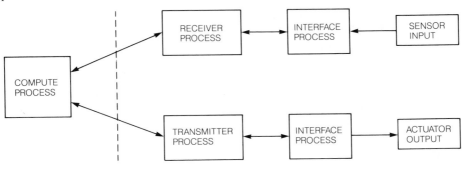

Figure 18.5   Tasking with optional communication points

Ada has a statement called the **select** statement, used to program tasks that have optional communication points. In such a case, the program does not wait on one entry in a task but accepts the first request to the task.

There are many ways to organize tasks. One of the main considerations is which tasks should be server tasks and which tasks should be user tasks. In our example the COMPUTE process will be the user task and we will have it invoke the RECEIVE task and the TRANSMIT task.

Based on the figure, we can write the task specification for this system:

```
with TEXT_IO; use TEXT_IO;
package OPTIONAL_COMMUNICATION is
  subtype TEMPERATURE_TYPE is INTEGER range 0..1024;
  type CONTROL_TYPE is (OFF, ON);
  task COMPUTE;
  task RECEIVE is
    entry INPUT (DATA : out TEMPERATURE_TYPE);
    entry SENSOR_INTERFACE (RAW_DATA : in TEMPERATURE_TYPE);
  end RECEIVE;
```

```
    task TRANSMIT is
      entry OUTPUT (DATA : in CONTROL_TYPE);
      entry ACTUATOR_INTERFACE (RAW_CONTROL : out CONTROL_TYPE);
    end TRANSMIT;
  end OPTIONAL_COMMUNICATION;
```

The package specification for this example uses two entry points for each of the server tasks. One of the entry points is used to communicate with the COMPUTE task and the other entry point communicates with the external device, sensor or actuator. We have assumed that the sensor and actuator notify the computer when the data is ready to receive or send. The program will then copy the data out of the interface into the location, which saves the data until the compute process requests to receive or send data.

A possible package body for this specification follows. The server tasks use the **select** statement in an infinite loop. Each path of the **select** statement contains an **accept** statement. With an **accept** statement, the task will perform whichever rendezvous comes first; it will not just wait on the first possible rendezvous. Hence, if the interrupt to read the control data comes before the compute program has calculated the first value, the initial value of the control data will be sent out of the computer. For this reason it is very important to make sure that all data values are initialized since the order of operations in such an arrangement is not known.

```
with TEXT_IO; use TEXT_IO;
package body OPTIONAL_COMMUNICATION is
  task body COMPUTE is
    INPUT_TEMPERATURE     : TEMPERATURE_TYPE;
    OUTPUT_CONTROL        : CONTROL_TYPE : = OFF;
    REGULATED_TEMPERATURE : constant TEMPERATURE_TYPE : = 440;
    SLACK_TEMPERATURE     : constant TEMPERATURE_TYPE : = 2;
  begin
    loop
      PUT (" COMPUTE READY TO RECEIVE "); NEW_LINE;
      RECEIVE. INPUT (INPUT_TEMPERATURE);
      if INPUT_TEMPERATURE > REGULATED_TEMPERATURE +
                             SLACK_TEMPERATURE then
        OUTPUT_CONTROL : = OFF;
      elsif INPUT_TEMPERATURE < REGULATED_TEMPERATURE -
                             SLACK_TEMPERATURE then
        OUTPUT_CONTROL : = ON;
      end if:
      PUT (" COMPUTE READY TO TRANSMIT "); NEW_LINE;
      TRANSMIT. OUTPUT (OUTPUT_CONTROL);
    end loop;
  end COMPUTE;
```

```
  task body RECEIVE is
    LATEST_DATA : TEMPERATURE_TYPE  : = 440;
  begin
    loop
      select
        accept INPUT (DATA : out TEMPERATURE_TYPE) do

          DATA : = LATEST_DATA;
          PUT (" RECEIVE ACCEPTS INPUT "); NEW_LINE;
        end INPUT;
      or
        accept SENSOR_INTERFACE (RAW_DATA : in TEMPERATURE_TYPE) do
          LATEST_DATA : = RAW_DATA;
          PUT (" RECEIVE ACCEPTS SENSOR "); NEW_LINE;
        end SENSOR_INTERFACE;
      end select;
    end loop;
  end RECEIVE;
  task body TRANSMIT is
    LATEST_CONTROL : CONTROL_TYPE : = OFF;
  begin
    loop
      select
        accept OUTPUT (DATA : in CONTROL_TYPE) do
          LATEST_CONTROL : = DATA;
          PUT (" TRANSMIT ACCEPTS OUTPUT "); NEW_LINE;
        end OUTPUT;
      or
        accept ACTUATOR_INTERFACE (RAW_CONTROL : out CONTROL_TYPE) do
          RAW_CONTROL : = LATEST_CONTROL;
          PUT (" TRANSMIT ACCEPTS ACTUATOR "); NEW_LINE;
        end ACTUATOR_INTERFACE;
      end select;
    end loop;
  end TRANSMIT;
end OPTIONAL_COMMUNICATION;

with TEXT_IO, OPTIONAL_COMMUNICATION;
use  TEXT_IO, OPTIONAL_COMMUNICATION;
procedure MAIN_TASK is
  T : TEMPERATURE_TYPE;
  C : CONTROL_TYPE;
begin
  loop
    PUT (" MAIN READY TO RECEIVE "); NEW_LINE;
    RECEIVE.SENSOR_INTERFACE (T);
    PUT (" MAIN READY TO TRANSMIT "); NEW_LINE;
    TRANSMIT.ACTUATOR_INTERFACE (C);
    if C = ON then
      PUT (" ON ");
    else
      PUT (" OFF ");
    end if;
    NEW_LINE;
  end loop;
end MAIN_TASK;
```

One possible problem with this simple program is that there is only one data location used for input and output. The compute program may miss data values that come from the temperature sensor if they come in faster than the compute task asks for data. This is not usually a serious problem in a temperature control system, but it could be if instead of a temperature system, we had a telephone system sending and receiving data. In such a case we do not want to miss information by writing over a single location that is reserved for data. Instead, we set up buffers to let one process work faster than another.

In our next example we will receive a stream of characters from a telephone interface. The input will be stored in a circular buffer, which the receive task will manage. The compute process will read a single character at a time from the circular buffer to form a message line that will be displayed every time a carriage return or a line feed is received.

The program uses a **select when accept** construct to decide whether to allow an **accept** to occur. The reasons for the tests are twofold—not to send data to the main program if no new data has been received—to stop receiving data if the buffer is full. This latter condition is an error condition we will treat in the next chapter. We have left the other side of this program for you to do as an exercise.

```ada
with TEXT_IO; use TEXT_IO;
package TELEPHONE_COMMUNICATION is
  BUFFER_SIZE : constant := 10;
  subtype BUFFER_LENGTH_TYPE is INTEGER range 1..BUFFER_SIZE;
  type BUFFER_TYPE is array (BUFFER_LENGTH_TYPE) of CHARACTER;
  task COMPUTE_PROCESS;
  task RECEIVE is
    entry INPUT (DATA : out CHARACTER);
    entry TELEPHONE_RECEIVE_INTERFACE (RAW_DATA : in CHARACTER);
  end RECEIVE;
end TELEPHONE_COMMUNICATION;

with TEXT_IO; use TEXT_IO;
package body TELEPHONE_COMMUNICATION is
  task body COMPUTE_PROCESS is
    C          : CHARACTER;
    LINE       : STRING (1..5);
    BLANK_LINE : STRING (1..5) := (others => ' ');
  begin
    LINE := BLANK_LINE;
    loop
      for I in LINE'RANGE loop
        RECEIVE.INPUT (C);
        LINE (I) := C;
        PUT (C); PUT (" C "); NEW_LINE;
        exit when C = ASCII.LF or C = ASCII.CR;
      end loop;
      PUT (LINE); NEW_LINE;
    end loop;
  end COMPUTE_PROCESS;
```

```
task body RECEIVE is
  subtype COUNT_TYPE is INTEGER range 0..BUFFER_SIZE;
  BUFFER        : BUFFER_TYPE;
  BUFFER_START  : BUFFER_LENGTH_TYPE := 1;
  BUFFER_STOP   : BUFFER_LENGTH_TYPE := 1;
  COUNT         : COUNT_TYPE := 0;
begin
  loop
    select
      when COUNT > 0 =>  -- something there
        accept INPUT (DATA : out CHARACTER) do
          DATA := BUFFER (BUFFER_START);
          BUFFER_START := BUFFER_START mod BUFFER_SIZE + 1;
          COUNT := COUNT - 1;
          PUT (DATA); PUT (" DATA "); NEW_LINE;
        end INPUT;
    or
      when COUNT < BUFFER_SIZE =>
        accept TELEPHONE_RECEIVE_INTERFACE (RAW_DATA : in CHARACTER) do
          COUNT := COUNT + 1;
          BUFFER (BUFFER_STOP) := RAW_DATA;
          BUFFER_STOP := BUFFER_STOP mod BUFFER_SIZE + 1;
          PUT (RAW_DATA); PUT (" RAW_DATA "); NEW_LINE;
        end TELEPHONE_RECEIVE_INTERFACE;
    end select;
  end loop;
end RECEIVE;
end TELEPHONE_COMMUNICATION;
```

TIMEOUTS

When everything goes as planned, it is possible to write the tasking structures we have seen so far. However, it is very rare that things go as planned—provision must be made for erroneous sequences of tasks so that the computer does not come to a halt in any program. Such a halt is called a *deadlock*.

The traditional way of preventing deadlocks is to have a timeout, when you decide what to do. One thing that can be done is reload the program and start over. Another thing that can be done is to reinitialize the program from some predetermined starting point. It is up to the program designer which of these and possibly other techniques to use. Whatever happens, you should notify the operator that a timeout has occurred—it could be a signal that things are not going well and the computer should be tested. It could also be a signal that there is a timing error of some sort in the program and if it happens often enough, some time should be spent finding out why the timeout happens.

Let us change the telephone receive task so that it has a timeout path. We will include a timeout of one second in the assumption that the telephone should have sent us some data or the compute process should have taken some data in that time.

```
task body RECEIVE is
  subtype COUNT_TYPE is INTEGER range 0..BUFFER_SIZE;

  BUFFER         : BUFFER_TYPE;
  BUFFER_START   : BUFFER_LENGTH_TYPE := 1;
  BUFFER_STOP    : BUFFER_LENGTH_TYPE := 1;
  COUNT          : COUNT_TYPE := 0;
begin
  loop
    select
      when COUNT > 0 =>   -- something there
        accept INPUT (DATA : out CHARACTER) do
          DATA := BUFFER (BUFFER_START);
          BUFFER_START := BUFFER_START mod BUFFER_SIZE + 1;
          COUNT := COUNT - 1;
        end INPUT:
      or
        when COUNT < BUFFER_SIZE =>
          accept TELEPHONE_RECEIVE_INTERFACE (RAW_DATA : in CHARACTER) do
            COUNT := COUNT + 1;
            BUFFER (BUFFER_STOP) := RAW_DATA;
            BUFFER_STOP := BUFFER_STOP mod BUFFER_SIZE + 1;
          end TELEPHONE_RECEIVE_INTERFACE;
      or
        delay 1.0;
        PUT (" Shutting down for repairs due to timeout ");
        NEW_LINE;
        exit;
    end select;
  end loop;
end RECEIVE;
```

The RECEIVE_PROCESS task will terminate by exiting the loop if one of the two other paths have not been taken in one second. Once this task has terminated, the other tasks will also terminate because they use the task.

The designer can also use a **terminate** statement to stop a task; sometimes, an **abort** statement will be used instead. It will be very rare to use an **abort** statement because it not only stops the task, it stops the entire program. There is no possibility of recovery with an **abort** statement, so it should be used only when all else fails. The form of the **abort** statement is the same as the **terminate** statement:

```
terminate;
abort;
```

Either the **terminate** statement or the **abort** statement can be used in any path of a **select** statement. For example, we could add a path for a receive process:

```
or
    when COUNT >= BUFFER_SIZE =>
        terminate;
end select;
```

This would cause the task to terminate if the buffer was to overflow. The **select** statement may also have an **else** part. The **else** part can contain any data statement except for the **delay, terminate** or **abort,** statements. The **else** part is meant to execute if no other part of the **select** paths can execute. The **else** part is good to use if it is known that a rendezvous is always immediately possible in one of the optional paths.

TASK TYPES

If you find yourself writing the same task structure for several tasks, you will want to use a task type. Task types are particularly useful for assigning input controllers to distinct terminals that all have the same interface. Communication equipment with different channels and telephone interfaces should probably all be handled with task types instead of tasks.

To define a task type we write

```
task type COMMUNICATION_CHANNEL is
   entry INPUT (DATA : out DATA_TYPE);
end COMMUNICATION_CHANNEL;
```

and then we write the task body for the COMMUNICATION_CHANNEL just as though it were a single task. Now we treat the task type as a template. For example, if there were thirty-six communication channels, we could have an array of tasks:

```
type COMMUNICATION_ARRAY_TYPE is array (1..36) of
                              COMMUNICATION_CHANNEL;
COMMUNICATION_CHANNELS : COMMUNICATION_ARRAY_TYPE;
```

A task type is a limited private type. It cannot be assigned to or tested for equality. It is a program that is meant to execute concurrently with other programs and so it makes sense not to allow any operation other than invocations on a task.

An array of tasks is invoked by the notation used in arrays such as

```
COMMUNICATION_CHANNELS(25).INPUT (DATA);
```

There can also be records of different tasks and tasks that have different names but the same task type. An example of the latter is

```
RADIO_CHANNEL      : COMMUNICATION_CHANNEL;
TELEVISION_CHANNEL : COMMUNICATION_CHANNEL;
```

To invoke the entry of the RADIO_CHANNEL task we would write

```
RADIO_CHANNEL.INPUT (INFORMATION);
```

Task types can also be used to activate tasks dynamically by using access types and the **new** operation:

```
type LINK_TO_TASK is access COMMUNICATION_CHANNEL;
type GROUP_OF_TASK_TYPE is array (1..20) of LINK_TO_TASK;
GROUP_OF_TASKS : GROUP_OF_TASK_TYPE;

for I in GROUP_OF_TASKS'RANGE loop
  GROUP_OF_TASKS (I) := new COMMUNICATION_CHANNEL;
end loop;
```

This is good for applications where the number of tasks that should be active is unknown in advance.

WHAT HAVE YOU LEARNED?

Ada has a number of forms of tasking:

◆ totally independent,

◆ synchronized with wait,

◆ synchronized with optional communication points,

◆ synchronized with timeout,

◆ synchronized with checks on availability of data or equipment.

All the synchronization forms use the rendezvous technique.

The simplest form of tasking is totally independent tasks. Such a task structure can be organized as

```
procedure MAIN is
  task A;
  task B;
  task body A is
  begin
   -- sequential statements for A
  end A;
  task body B is
  begin
  -- sequential statements for B
  end B;
begin
  -- sequential statements for main task
end MAIN;
```

When tasks are declared to be part of a main task, they all start operating in parallel the moment that the **begin** of the main task is reached. They all continue to execute in parallel until terminated. The main task does not terminate until all the nested (also called dependent) tasks terminate.

To communicate between tasks, we use the rendezvous technique. First we name the communication point in the declaration of the task. The communication point is called an entry in the task. We can have many such entries. For example,

```
task FOOD_SERVICE is
  entry ORDER (FOOD : MEAL_TYPE);
end FOOD_SERVICE;
```

The declaration of the entry is like a procedure specification. It states the name of the entry point and the parameters and their types and modes. Since we have not specified the mode, it is taken as an input parameter just as in a procedure parameter.

The task without the entry point invokes the task entry in the same manner as a procedure invocation.

```
FOOD_SERVICE.ORDER (BREAKFAST);
```

This is an invocation to the rendezvous point in the FOOD_SERVICE task.

In the body of the FOOD_SERVICE task the entry point appears in an **accept** statement. The **accept** statement is like the procedure body for the communication point.

When a task has an **accept** statement, all the tasks start executing in parallel as before. However, the two tasks which are to communicate execute down to the rendezvous point. Whichever task reaches the rendezvous point first waits for the other task. When they are both at the rendezvous point, the invoking task or the *user task* waits until the statements in the **accept** statement are executed before continuing. After the statements in the invoked task or the *server task* are executed, the tasks once again continue in parallel.

The form of the **accept** statement is

```
accept entry name (parameter declarations) do
    -- statements for rendezvous point
end entry name;
```

It is a good policy to keep the number of statements in the **accept** statement to a minimum because the other task suspends operation while the statements in the **accept** statement are being executed.

External interrupts are handled with a special form of the task declaration that names the interrupt location. It is common practice to give a priority to the interrupt with the **pragma** PRIORITY.

```
task SLOW is
  entry SLOW_CLOCK_SEQUENCE;
  for SLOW_CLOCK_SEQUENCE use at 16#20#;
  pragma PRIORITY (5);
end SLOW;
```

The use of **accept** statements alone causes one task to wait for another task. To avoid this the **select** statement is used. With the **select** statement the program does not wait on one entry in a task but accepts the first request to the task. A common tasking structure using the **select** statement is

```
task body TASK_NAME is
  LATEST_DATA : TEMPERATURE_TYPE;
begin
  loop
    select
      accept INPUT (DATA : out TEMPERATURE_TYPE) do
        DATA := LATEST_DATA;
      end INPUT;
```

```
    or
      accept SENSOR_INTERFACE (RAW_DATA : in TEMPERATURE_TYPE) do
        LATEST_DATA : = RAW_DATA;
      end SENSOR_INTERFACE;
    end select;
  end loop;
end TASK_NAME;
```

The **select when accept** construct is useful for putting conditions on entering a rendezvous point

```
select
  when COUNT >0 =>     -- something there
    accept INPUT (DATA : out CHARACTER) do
      DATA : = BUFFER (BUFFER_START);
      BUFFER_START : = BUFFER_START mod BUFFER SIZE + 1;
      COUNT : = COUNT - 1;
    end INPUT;
  or
  when COUNT < BUFFER_SIZE
    accept TELEPHONE_RECEIVE_INTERFACE (RAW_DATA : in CHARACTER) do
      COUNT : = COUNT + 1;
      BUFFER (BUFFER_STOP) : = RAW_DATA;
      BUFFER_STOP : = BUFFER_STOP mod BUFFER_SIZE + 1;
end select;
```

Timeouts are used to protect against tasking errors. The timeout can use the **delay** statement as one of the paths in a **select** statement. If no other path is taken, in the time specified in the **delay** statement, the statements following the **delay** statement are executed.

```
  or
    delay 1.0;
    PUT (" Shutting down for repairs due to timeout ");
    exit;
  end select;
```

Ada tasks can be stopped with the **terminate** statement. Although it will be very rare, an **abort** statement can be used to make all the tasks in a program stop.

```
terminate;  -- task stops
abort;  -- everything stops
```

Either the **terminate** statement or the **abort** statement can be used in any alternative of a **select** statement. **Select** statements may also have **else** parts which will execute if none of the alternative paths can execute.

Task types are particularly useful for assigning input controllers to distinct terminals sharing the same interface.

To define a task type we write

```
task type COMMUNICATION_CHANNEL is
  entry INPUT (DATA : out DATA_TYPE);
end COMMUNICATION_CHANNEL;
```

and then we write the task body for the COMMUNICATION_CHANNEL just as though it were a single task. However, we now treat the task type as a template.

For example, if we had thirty-six communication channels, we could have an array of tasks:

```
type COMMUNICATION_ARRAY_TYPE is array (1..36) of
                            COMMUNICATION_CHANNEL;
COMMUNICATION_CHANNELS : COMMUNICATION_ARRAY_TYPE;
```

A task type is a limited private type.

There can also be records of different tasks and tasks that have different names but are the same task type. An example of the latter is

```
RADIO_CHANNEL      : COMMUNICATION_CHANNEL;
TELEVISION_CHANNEL : COMMUNICATION_CHANNEL;
```

To invoke the entry of the RADIO_CHANNEL task we would write

```
RADIO_CHANNEL.INPUT (INFORMATION);
```

Task types can also be used to activate tasks dynamically by using access types and the **new** operation.

```
type LINK_TO_TASK is access COMMUNICATION_CHANNEL;
type GROUP_OF_TASK_TYPE is array (1..20) of LINK_TO_TASK;
GROUP_OF_TASKS : GROUP_OF_TASK_TYPE;

for I in GROUP_OF_TASKS'RANGE loop
  GROUP_OF_TASKS (I) := new COMMUNICATION_CHANNEL;
end loop;
```

PROBLEMS

1. Write a message in each task body of the airline program. Do you think you can predict the order of the messages? Run the program to see the actual order of the messages.

2. Rewrite the airline program to put all the tasks in a package.

3. Define some small procedures for the avionics program so that the slow cycle outputs a message " In slow cycle," and the fast cycle outputs a message " In fast cycle." If your computer does not have a clock that you can access via an interrupt, make the main program a pseudo-clock by having it loop 10 times in a busy loop for one tick of the fast clock and 100 times for one tick of the slow clock. Have your error diagnostics program check that

```
(sine (angle)) ** 2 + (cosine (angle)) ** 2 = 1 within 0.001.
```

4. Restructure the optional communication package so that the COMPUTE task is the server task and the RECEIVE and TRANSMIT tasks are user tasks.

5. Rewrite the telephone communication package to contain a TRANSMIT_ PROCESS task. Write a main program to test the package.

CHAPTER
❖ 19 ❖
EXCEPTIONS

❖ You may already have encountered exceptions as a result of programming errors. Ada intends exceptions to be used for handling abnormal conditions; in this chapter you will learn that exceptions are more useful than for just detecting errors—they can help prevent errors as well. This use of exceptions, called *software fault tolerance,* requires the use of exception handlers that execute when some abnormal situation occurs.

Tasking introduces additional complications with exceptions and will be covered separately.

The designer of an Ada program has several options when using exceptions. The major choices are

- ◆ abandon execution of the program,
- ◆ retry the program,
- ◆ use another approach,
- ◆ clean up, or
- ◆ continue execution.

ABANDON OR CONTINUE EXECUTION

You need do nothing at all to abandon execution. Ada will automatically abandon execution of a subprogram or task unless you write your own exception handler. We will learn to write exception handlers in this chapter so that you will not have to settle for having your program automatically terminated on an exception.

The last choice, continue execution, is also a simple option to use although it can be a dangerous one. To continue execution in the presence of exception conditions, you can suppress exceptions. This approach is not recommended, because you are turning off a valuable error-detection mechanism. You turn off exceptions with the SUPPRESS **pragma.**

There are five exceptions that an Ada program can raise. These exceptions are declared in package STANDARD (Appendix F) as

```
CONSTRAINT_ERROR :  exception;
NUMERIC_ERROR    :  exception;
PROGRAM_ERROR    :  exception;
STORAGE_ERROR    :  exception;
TASKING_ERROR    :  exception;
```

Each of these exceptions can arise due to checks that are made during the execution of an Ada program. To prevent the exceptions from occurring, the exceptions can be suppressed with a series of **pragma** statements. Each check must be suppressed individually. The checks are organized by the exception that they cause in the SUPPRESS **pragma** table.

SUPPRESS PRAGMAS

TO SUPPRESS CONSTRAINT_ERROR

```
-- suppress check for non null access value
pragma SUPRESS (ACCESS_CHECK);

-- suppress check that discriminant value and record component agree
-- and suppress check that discriminant value exists
pragma SUPPRESS (DISCRIMINANT_CHECK);

-- suppress check that bounds of an array are not exceeded
pragma SUPPRESS (INDEX_CHECK);

-- suppress check that assignments across arrays are for arrays of
-- the same length
pragma SUPRESS (LENGTH_CHECK);

-- suppress check that the value is within the range constraint
pragma SUPPRESS (RANGE_CHECK);
```

TO SUPPRESS NUMERIC_ERROR

```
-- suppress check that a division by zero is not attempted
-- can occur only with the operations /, rem, and mod
pragma SUPPRESS (DIVISION_CHECK);

-- suppress check that a numeric operation does not overflow
pragma SUPPRESS (OVERFLOW_CHECK);
```

TO SUPPRESS PROGRAM_ERROR

```
    -- suppress check that a subprogram or task entry exists
    -- when invoked
    pragma SUPPRESS (ELABORATION_CHECK);
```

TO SUPPRESS STORAGE_ERROR

```
    -- suppress check that enough space is available
    -- for data, a subprogram, or a task
    pragma SUPPRESS (STORAGE_CHECK);
```

Some time-critical programs may turn off exceptions in order to eliminate the extra time that the computer takes to determine if exceptions should occur. In most cases you will not want to turn off exceptions. When you do want to suppress exceptions, place the **pragma** SUPPRESS in the declaration part of a package or subprogram. In a package, the **pragma** applies to the entire package; in a subprogram, the **pragma** extends to the end of the subprogram including any nested subprograms.

It is also possible to suppress exceptions for a particular object or type or even a particular subprogram if the name is available in a declaration. In this form of the **pragma,** the individual entity is named. For example, to suppress range checking for the array HEIGHT_ARRAY, the statement

```
    pragma SUPPRESS (RANGE_CHECK, HEIGHT_ARRAY);
```

can be used.

The CONSTRAINT_ERROR exception is the one that you have probably encountered most often. As you can see in the table, it can arise from a variety of conditions. The most common occurrence is when a variable goes beyond the bounds of values defined for the type.

The NUMERIC_ERROR exception will be raised if you attempt to divide by zero or one of your arithmetic operations causes an overflow.

The PROGRAM_ERROR exception will occur if the subprogram or task entry you invoke does not exist.

The STORAGE_ERROR exception will be raised if you run out of memory or try to access memory out of the bounds of your program.

The TASKING_ERROR exception occurs when you invoke a terminated task. There is no corresponding **pragma** to suppress the TASKING_ERROR exception. You should be sure to make a test that a task is not terminated with the 'CALLABLE attribute before invoking a task entry.

Naming and Raising Exceptions

You can name your own exceptions by declaring exceptions in your program. Examples of such declarations are

```
-- for the status bit not set to ready
DEVICE_NOT_READY : exception;
-- for the number of columns in the first matrix
-- unequal to the number of rows in the second matrix
MATRICES_NOT_CONFORMABLE : exception;
-- when the temperature times the pressure is too large
DATA_BAD : exception;
```

Once such declarations have been made, the exceptions can be raised by statements such as

```
if STATUS = NOT_READY then
   raise DEVICE_NOT_READY;
end if;
if A'RANGE(2) /= B'RANGE(2) then
  raise MATRICES_NOT_CONFORMABLE;
else
  C := A * B; -- matrix multiplication
end if;

if RAW_TEMPERATURE * RAW_PRESSURE > 500_000.0 then
  raise DATA_BAD;
end if;
```

Such exceptions result in the same actions as the five predefined exceptions.

EXCEPTION HANDLERS

To make use of the fault tolerance features available to Ada programs, an exception handler is written for each possible exception that can occur. At the very least you can write an exception handler that will display the name of the subprogram that caused the error. Other possible options are the retry option, the take another approach option, and the clean up and continue option.

An exception handler is placed at the end of the subprogram unit for which the handler applies. For example, the simple notification handler for a constraint error in a tiny program could be

```
with TEXT_IO; use TEXT_IO;
procedure EXCEPTION_EXAMPLE is
  subtype SMALL is INTEGER range 1..10;
  S : SMALL;
begin
  S := 20;   -- constraint_error --
exception
  when CONSTRAINT_ERROR =>
    PUT (" Constraint error in exception example ");
  when others =>
    PUT (" Exception in exception example ");
end EXCEPTION_EXAMPLE;
```

The keyword **exception** starts off the exception handler for the program. The exception being handled is named in a **when** clause, although it is also possible to use a global **when others** to apply to any unnamed exceptions. The statements following the $=>$ are then executed. In the example, all that happens in the handler is that a message is displayed naming the subprogram that contained the exception. After the exception handler executes, the program unit is exited. Since we had only a main program in this example, the program exits.

Normally exception handlers are associated with subprograms that cause a main program to take more action than merely notification, although notification is a minimal action that should be taken if you can think of nothing else to do.

RETRY

A common type of exception handler is one that retries a subprogram if an exception occurs. In order to avoid an infinite loop set up by exception conditions, a limit is placed on the number of retries. The following example shows one approach to retrying input up to ten times.

In the RETRY_INPUT, a loop is set up which can execute up to ten times. The input procedure is placed in a block containing an exception handler. If the input is successful because an *N* or *Y* is received, the loop will exit and the program can continue as normal. If some other input is received, a CONSTRAINT_ERROR will be raised. As a result the message in the PUT statement will be displayed and the loop will continue to try to input another value. If ten exceptions have been handled, the exception handler raises the exception named FATAL_ERROR for which no handler has been defined. This will cause the program to terminate.

```
with TEXT_IO; use TEXT_IO;
procedure RETRY_INPUT is
   type INPUT_ANSWER_TYPE is (N, Y);
   package INPUT_IO is new TEXT_IO.ENUMERATION_IO (INPUT_ANSWER_TYPE);
   use INPUT_IO;
   INPUT_ANSWER : INPUT_ANSWER_TYPE;
   FATAL_ERROR : exception;
begin
   for I in 1..10 loop -- try up to 10 times to input
      PUT ( " Answer the question with a 'Y' or a 'N' ");
      NEW_LINE;
      begin           -- start block for exception handler
        GET (INPUT_ANSWER);
        exit;         -- exit loop if successful
      exception
        when others =>
          if I = 10 then
              raise FATAL_ERROR;
```

```
        else
          PUT (" Let's try again, I got an erroneous answer ");
          NEW_LINE;
        end if;
    end;              -- exception block
  end loop;
end RETRY_INPUT;
```

USE ANOTHER APPROACH

The most interesting use of exception handlers is to execute another program when the first program has an error. This alternate program could have been written by another group of people who, it is assumed, will not have committed the same error that caused the original exception. Such an approach is true software fault tolerance.

In the next example there are two programs that perform the same function. The programs are independently written and can start to take over from the invocation of the top programs named GROUP_1 and GROUP_2. The program starts off with the GROUP_1 program, and if it fails with an unhandled exception, the GROUP_2 program will take over. Last, if the GROUP_2 program fails with an unhandled exception, the GROUP_1 program will take over again.

```
with PACKAGES_OF_PROGRAMS; use PACKAGES_OF_PROGRAMS;
procedure MAIN is
begin
<<START>>
  loop
    begin
      GROUP_1_PROGRAM;
      exit; -- exit from successful program
    exception
      when others =>
        begin
          GROUP_2_PROGRAM;
          exit; -- exit from successful program
        exception
          when others =>
            goto START; -- start all over again
        end;                    -- exception handler end
    end;                        -- exception block
  end loop;
end MAIN;
```

A **goto** statement cannot be used to transfer into an exception handler or from an exception handler back into the block in which the exception was raised. However, since the program that raises the exception is in a loop, we can transfer outside the loop to start over again.

In a program with several levels of subprograms, a subprogram may want to do some local corrections in the subprogram handler and then propagate the exception to a higher level. This is done by the use of the **raise** statement in the handler itself. For example,

```
exception
  when CONSTRAINT_ERROR =>
    RESULT : = 0;
    raise;
end SUBPROGRAM;
```

will cause the variable RESULT to be cleared and the exception named CONSTRAINT_ERROR to be propagated to the invoking procedure for further handling. This propagation can continue all the way to the top of the program.

CLEAN UP

The clean up approach to exception handlers allows a legitimate data value to be put in the variable causing the exception to let the program continue. For example, if the data being read are out of bounds, some legitimate value is given the variable. This value could be a running average of previous input data or it could be just a reasonable value to keep the program going. We can alter the loop in our retry example to incorporate a clean up approach by changing the part of the program that raises the fatal error to set the answer to Y, which lets the program continue.

The next example shows the clean up approach for a situation where a sensor intermittently provides bad data. A running average of the sensor data are kept for the times when the data are good. When a CONSTRAINT_ERROR occurs on the input of the data, a substitute of the average value is made and the operator is notified that a substitute has been made—when the intermittent data becomes very prevalent, more corrective action can be taken.

```
with TEXT_IO, INPUT_PACKAGE;
use TEXT_IO, INPUT_PACKAGE;
procedure CLEAN is
  INPUT_DATA : INPUT_DATA_TYPE;
  RUNNING_AVERAGE : INPUT_DATA_TYPE : = 100; -- expected value
  FATAL_ERROR : exception;
begin
  loop
    begin -- start block for exception handler
      INPUT (INPUT_DATA);
      RUNNING_AVERAGE := (7*RUNNING_AVERAGE + INPUT_DATA)/8;
      exit;           -- exit if successful
    exception
      when CONSTRAINT_ERROR =>
        INPUT_DATA : = RUNNING_AVERAGE;
        PUT (" Error in input from sensor ");
        NEW_LINE;
    end;              -- exception block
    -- rest of program which uses input data
  end loop;
end CLEAN;
```

EXCEPTIONS AND TASKS

A task can be thought of as a subprogram unit, but because of the parallel nature of tasks, there are special cases for handling exceptions with tasks.

If a task handles its own exceptions, and it should whenever possible, the task will continue to operate normally. However, if a task does not handle its exceptions, then it will terminate execution, and all other tasks that try to invoke an entry point in the task will receive an exception named TASK-ING_ERROR.

A task can also receive a TASKING_ERROR exception from another task during a rendezvous. If the **accept** statement in the invoked task has an un-handled exception or an **abort** statement, the invoking task will receive the TASKING_ERROR exception. The task should have a handler for this exception that takes priority over all other exceptions and is meant to allow a task to restart itself in some clean manner. If a task receives one of these exceptions, then it is recommended to give it some time to recover through a **delay** statement before requesting a rendezvous. If it does not respond to the rendezvous, then the task should probably be terminated or aborted.

Protection is given in tasking for the rendezvous point in Ada so that if an invoking task fails during a rendezvous, the server task will continue. This is because a task may serve more than one task. However if the server task fails during a rendezvous, both the server and the user task may fail (in the case where neither handles the exception). This is one reason for making the statements in the **accept** statement as simple and as short as possible.

WHAT HAVE YOU LEARNED?

Exceptions are an Ada feature for handling out-of-the-ordinary situations. You can use exceptions to

- abandon execution of the program,
- retry the program,
- use another approach,
- clean up, or
- continue execution.

To implement the first choice, abandon execution, you need do nothing at all. The last choice, while dangerous, can be taken by using SUPPRESS **pragmas.**

To suppress the five predefined exceptions:

```
TO SUPPRESS CONSTRAINT_ERROR

    -- suppress check for non null access value
    pragma SUPPRESS (ACCESS_CHECK);
```

```
    suppress check that discriminant value and record component agree
-- and suppress check that discriminant value exists
pragma SUPPRESS (DISCRIMINANT_CHECK);

-- suppress check that bounds of an array are not exceeded
pragma SUPPRESS (INDEX_CHECK);

-- suppress check that assignments across arrays are for arrays of
-- the same length
pragma SUPPRESS (LENGTH_CHECK);

-- suppress check that the value is within the range constraint
pragma SUPPRESS (RANGE_CHECK);

TO SUPPRESS NUMERIC_ERROR

-- suppress check that a divison by zero is not attemped
-- can occur only with the operations /, rem, and mod
pragma SUPPRESS (DIVISION_CHECK);

-- suppress check that a numeric operation does not overflow
pragma SUPPRESS (OVERFLOW_CHECK);

TO SUPPRESS PROGRAM_ERROR

-- suppress check that a subprogram or task entry exists
-- when invoked
pragma SUPPRESS (ELABORATION_CHECK);

TO SUPPRESS STORAGE_ERROR

-- suppress check that enough space is available
-- for data, a subprogram, or a task
pragma SUPPRESS (STORAGE_CHECK);
```

You can declare your own exceptions.

```
DEVICE_NOT_READY : exception;
MATRICES_NOT_CONFORMABLE : exception;
DATA_BAD : exception;
```

When exceptions have been declared, they can be raised by the **raise** statement.

```
raise DEVICE_NOT_READY;
raise MATRICES_NOT_CONFORMABLE;
raise DATA_BAD;
```

An exception handler is placed at the end of the subprogram unit for which the handler applies. The exception handler begins with the keyword **exception.** The exception being handled is named in a **when** clause. It is also possible to use a global **when others** to apply to any unnamed exceptions, and the statements following the => are executed. After the exception handler executes, the program unit is exited.

The general form of a procedure with an exception handler is

```
procedure procedure name is
  -- declarations
begin
  -- sequential statements
exception
  when exception name =>
    -- statements to be executed on exception
end procedure name;
```

An exception handler that retries a subprogram if an exception occurs is placed in a loop to prevent an infinite number of exceptions. The retried program is placed in a block containing an exception handler. If the subprogram executes successfully, the loop exits and the program continues as normal. If an exception occurs, the exception handler statements will execute and then the loop will continue. After some number of retries the handler should raise another exception.

A general structure for a retry approach is

```
procedure RETRY_PROCEDURE is
  FATAL_ERROR : exception;
begin
  for I in 1.. 10 loop   -- try up to 10 times to input
    begin               -- start block for exception handler
      GET (INPUT_ANSWER);
      exit;                 -- exit if successful
    exception
      when others =>
        if I = 10 then
          raise FATAL_ERROR;
        end if;
    end; -- exception block
  end loop;
end RETRY_PROCEDURE;
```

Exception handlers can be used to execute another approach to a problem.

```
with PACKAGES_OF_PROGRAMS; use PACKAGES_OF_PROGRAMS;
procedure MAIN is
begin
<<START>>
  loop
    begin
      GROUP_1_PROGRAM;
      exit;  -- exit from successful program
    exception
      when others =>
        begin
```

```
            GROUP_2_PROGRAM;
            exit; -- exit from successful program
            exception
            when others =>
              goto Start; -- start all over again
            end;              -- exception handler end
          end;                -- exception block
       end loop;
  end MAIN;
```

A **goto** statement cannot be used to transfer into an exception handler or from an exception handler back into the block in which the exception was raised. However, if the program raising the exception is in a loop, we can transfer outside the loop to start over again.

In a program having several levels of subprograms, a subprogram may want to do some local corrections in the subprogram handler and then propagate the exception to a higher level. This is done by the use of the **raise** statement in the handler itself. For example,

```
    exception
      when CONSTRAINT_ERROR =>
        RESULT := 0;
        raise;
    end SUBPROGRAM;
```

will cause the variable RESULT to be cleared and the exception named CONSTRAINT_ERROR to be propagated to the invoking procedure for further handling. This propagation can continue all the way to the top of the program.

The clean up approach to exception handlers allows a legitimate data value to be put in the variable causing the exception to let the program continue.

If a task handles it own exceptions, the task will continue to operate normally. However, if a task does not handle its exceptions, then it will terminate execution and all other tasks that try to invoke an entry point in the task will receive the exception TASKING_ERROR.

Protection is given in tasking for the rendezvous point in Ada so that if an invoking task fails during a rendezvous, the server task will continue.

PROBLEMS

1. Take any program which inputs data from the keyboard and alter it to allow erroneous data to be input.

2. Prepare an INPUT_PACKAGE for the CLEAN_UP procedure.

3. Write a function which performs integer division such that if the denominator is zero, the result will be zero. Use an exception rather than an **if** statement.

4. Write a square root function, using an approximation function. Raise an exception if the operand is less than zero.

5. Rewrite the program in chapter 17 which creates an employee data file to handle erroneous inputs with an exception handler.

6. Write a program to calculate

$$N! = 1 \cdot 2 \cdot 3 \cdots N$$

and display the result. Stop the program when an exception is raised. Then display a message indicating the largest value of N which can be calculated by the computer.

CHAPTER
❖ 20 ❖

REAL-TIME INTERFACES

❖ Real-time interfaces allow computers to send information, to receive information, and to control equipment. An *interface* attaches some other piece of equipment to a computer; *real-time* means that the computer must complete some task within a specified amount of time. Computers are attached to many kinds of equipment: automobiles—the computer provides the driver with information on the state of the engine and the progress of a long trip, including the estimated time of arrival; airplanes—the computer guides and even lands the aircraft; ovens—the computer can sequence a temperature cycle and shut off the oven when the food is ready; and videotape recorders—the tape recorder can be programmed to record your favorite shows, turning the recorder on and off at the appropriate days and times. You can probably think of many other instances of computers adding functions to equipment that would have been thought impossible just a few years ago.

Computers that are part of a piece of equipment serve no other purpose than to perform the operations for that equipment. Sometimes these computers are called *process control computers* because they control something, or *dedicated computers* because they are dedicated to the task at hand, or *embedded computers* because they are embedded in the equipment. In almost all cases, such computers are microcomputers and lack facilities for the development of large computer programs. Until recently most of these computers were programmed using assembly language.

Ada was designed and developed primarily to allow these types of computers to be programmed in a high-level language. To be able to do this, Ada has many of the system-level programming features that assembly language programmers use to control computers in a real-time environment.

The facilities that Ada offers as a system-level programming language are very suitable for real-time programming. With Ada you can

- ◆ specify word formats,
- ◆ control the internal representation of data,
- ◆ control where data are placed,
- ◆ specify register locations and formats, and
- ◆ specify the underlying representation of user-defined types.

Ada gives you access to machine features:

- ◆ machine code,
- ◆ interrupts,
- ◆ interfaces to other languages,
- ◆ unscheduled access to shared variables, and
- ◆ unchecked type conversion.

These features may not all be necessary to write a real-time program. Remember, you do not have to use every feature of a language just because it is there. However, some of the features are very necessary, and we will cover each one of them in this chapter.

The ANSI standard for Ada made some of these features optional. This is unfortunate because it means that Ada is not 100% standardized. Today, there is no compiler that will execute all the programs in this chapter. The examples have been checked for correct syntax, but cannot be checked for correct operation because of the omission of these optional features in current compilers.

WORD FORMATS

Word formats describe the layout in a computer word of the interface to an external piece of equipment. It is a description of how the information in the computer is transferred out of a computer or into a computer. Very often an external piece of equipment is built with no thought to the kind of computer to which it is going to be attached. The designer of the equipment will draw the word format for the device as shown in figure 20.1.

In this case the designer has specified a sixteen-bit interface, which is contained in two words. Each bit position in the word can take on the value 0 or 1. The first word contains information on time and status. The second word contains information on pressure and temperature. Very often, certain values in part of a word are assigned special meaning. In this case the designer has stated that the status field of the word format has these meanings:

◆ 000 means off

◆ 001 means low

◆ 010 means normal

◆ 100 means high

If you know the binary number system, you will recognize that not all the possible values of the status field have been assigned meanings. This is often done in word formats and is handled by Ada.

The first thing to do when faced with a word format such as shown here is to define the types that go in each field. We will define four such types, one for each field.

```
type STATUS_TYPE is (OFF, LOW, NORMAL, HIGH);
subtype TIME_TYPE is INTEGER range 0..2**13-1;
subtype TEMPERATURE_TYPE is INTEGER range 0..2**10-1;
subtype PRESSURE_TYPE is INTEGER range 0..2**6-1;
```

In this definition we give names to the four values that can fall in the status field. Our only restriction in Ada is that the order of the names must follow the numeric order found in the status field. That is, we cannot have the OFF value, 000, listed after the high value, 100.

For the other three fields, we assign an integer data type ranging between 0 and the maximum number (2^{**} number of bits in the field $-$ 1) that can be placed in the field. This is the usual treatment for data formats that do not have specified limits on the range of numbers that can be placed in the word format. In such cases you should ask the designer if the equipment really can put out legitimate values of temperature in the range of 0 to 1023.

The next step in the word format declaration is to define a record data type that contains all the fields in the word format.

```
type SENSOR_WORD_FORMAT is
   record
      STATUS       : STATUS_TYPE;
      TIME         : TIME_TYPE;
      TEMPERATURE  : TEMPERATURE_TYPE;
      PRESSURE     : PRESSURE_TYPE;
   end record;
```

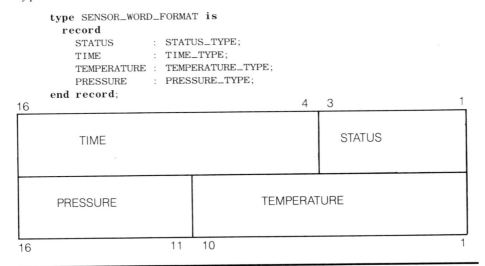

Figure 20.1 Sensor word format

At this point in the definition, we have a *machine-independent* description of the word format—we have described a data record that can be used on any computer. In fact, it is probably a good point to write the package specifications for the subprograms that are to operate on the data.

Our next step in the word format description is to make the word format machine dependent. First, we control the internal representation of the data in the status field by defining the meaning of each bit pattern in the enumeration. This specification is called a *representation specification,* and it has several uses that we will encounter in this chapter. The representation specification is not a loop, and it is not required in all Ada compilers.

```
for STATUS_TYPE use  (OFF      => 2#000#,
                      LOW      =>'2#001#,
                      NORMAL   => 2#010#,
                      HIGH     => 2#100#);
```

Without the representation specification, it is necessary to define the status type as just another integer field. The representation specification allows us to assign more meaningful names to the status field values.

The next step is also machine dependent. There may be two ways to achieve this step, which is to define the placement of each field in the computers memory. The first method uses the representation specification. It places the status field in word 0, bits 1 to 3; the time field in word 0, bits 4 to 16; the temperature field in word 1, bits 1 to 10; and the pressure field in word 1, bits 11 to 16.

```
for SENSOR_WORD_FORMAT use
   record
      STATUS       at 0 range 1..3;    -- word 0 bits 1 to 3
      TIME         at 0 range 4..16;   -- word 0 bits 4 to 16
      TEMPERATURE  at 1 range 1..10;   -- word 1 bits 1 to 10
      PRESSURE     at 1 range 11..16;  -- word 1 bits 11 to 16
   end record;
```

Now we have defined the word format in its machine-dependent form. We say machine dependent because computer designers are very inconsistent in numbering their bits. Some number the bits in a sixteen-bit machine from 1 to 16 and some from 0 to 15. Some number the bits from left to right and some number the bits from right to left. Thus this definition cannot be used on all machines without change. Any time you see a **for use** statement in an Ada program, you know the program is machine dependent and thus may not operate the same way on a different computer.

The other way of handling this word format is to use a **pragma**. Pragma's in Ada give directions to the compiler, but do not generate code.

```
pragma PACK (SENSOR_WORD_FORMAT);
```

tells the compiler to pack the words in the computer as tightly as possible with the fields specified in the machine-independent version of the sensor record. The danger in this method is that you have given the compiler the power to assign the placement of the bits and it may or may not coincide with where they should be placed. So although the PACK **pragma** seems a more readable way of defining where the data are to be placed, I would suggest you use the representation specification to define exactly where the data are to go.

CONVERTING DATA

There are three types of data conversions. The first is when the data are scaled. For example, in the sensor record, temperature comes in as an integer between 0 and 1023 in value. Very often these values must be converted to represent the actual physical temperature in some measure of temperature such as degrees Celsius. The designer of the equipment might have stated that each step in the temperature input represents 0.25 degree Celsius and that a zero input represents -50 degrees.

Thus, to convert the temperature information, we need to multiply the input value by 0.25 and to subtract 50 degrees. This can be done by converting the input information to a floating point type and then performing the calculations in an assignment statement. For example,

```
INPUT : SENSOR_WORD_FORMAT;
TEMPERATURE_IN_CELSIUS := 0.25 * FLOAT (INPUT.TEMPERATURE) - 50.0;
```

The second form of data conversion is most often used and requires that we manipulate the bits to represent a different code. In the most extreme case, all the bits will need to be altered, and in the next example, this is the case. Unfortunately, it is a common situation and will remain so until computer interfaces become standardized.

The interface in figure 20.2 is an eight-bit interface. ASCII data come into this computer at a specified address A040 (in base 16). When bit 8 is FALSE, the data are all there and can be used, but they are of the opposite polarity than will be used in the computer. That is, all the TRUES must be changed to FALSES and bit 8 must be set to indicate that the data have been read.

In specifying the data types for this problem, we can use representation specifications, but we will use another method, the binary bit string, useful for handling groups of bits as a unit. It is not a predefined type in Ada, so you will have to define it.

```
type BINARY_STRING is array (POSITIVE range <>) of BOOLEAN;
```

Figure 20.2 Eight bit interface

An object of type BINARY_STRING is treated as a single unit with regard to the logical operators such as **and** and **or**. This is very convenient in handling bits in an input word such as in our example. To handle the input data, we will define an eight-bit object at location A040. This can be done by

```
INPUT_DATA : BINARY_STRING (1..8);
pragma PACK (BINARY_STRING);
for INPUT_DATA use at 16#A040#;
```

The object declaration for INPUT_DATA assigns eight bits to the object. The **pragma** PACK puts the bits next to each other. The PACK **pragma** is probably safe to use when there is only one field of data to describe.

The form of the representation specification used in this declaration places the data object INPUT_DATA at the desired location A040.

for *object_name* **use at** *address*;

allows the user to place data at any location in the computer's memory. Of course, this is machine dependent just as the other forms of the **for use** statement.

The following program puts the data declarations together with a **while** statement, which tests the eighth bit. The program changes all the bits at once with the **not** statement before storing the data. The new statement shows how to convert data from binary bit strings to one of the predefined data types. To do this conversion, we use a generic function that is available in Ada, the UNCHECKED_CONVERSION. It does not actually perform a conversion, but it moves the data from an object of one data type to another data type without requiring that the types match. In our example, the data is ASCII data, so the values are correct, but the values must be moved from the BINARY_STRING data type to the normal character data type before being operated on by the ordinary Ada operations.

```
with UNCHECKED_CONVERSION;
package DATA_CONVERSION is
  procedure GET_DATA (C : out CHARACTER);
end DATA_CONVERSION;
with UNCHECKED_CONVERSION;
package body DATA_CONVERSION is
  procedure GET_DATA (C : out CHARACTER) is
    type BINARY_STRING is array (POSITIVE range <>) of BOOLEAN;
    INPUT_DATA : BINARY_STRING (1..8);
    TEMPORARY  : BINARY_STRING (1..8);
    pragma PACK (BINARY_STRING);
    for INPUT_DATA use at 16#A040#;
    function UNCHECKED_CONVERSION is new
              UNCHECKED_CONVERSION (BINARY_STRING, CHARACTER);
  begin
    while INPUT_DATA (8) loop -- busy loop on bit 8
      null;
    end loop;
```

```
    INPUT_DATA  : = not INPUT_DATA;    -- changes all bits
                                       -- bit 8 is set
    TEMPORARY  : = INPUT_DATA and (FALSE, others => TRUE);
    C  : = UNCHECKED_CONVERSION (TEMPORARY);
  end GET_DATA;
end DATA_CONVERSION;
```

The statement that *and*'s the input data and the binary string (FALSE, **others** => TRUE) eliminates the eighth bit, which is not used in the Ada character data type.

A third type of data conversion uses derived types with different underlying representations of the data values. To demonstrate this method of conversion, we will use a binary coded decimal (BCD) display device to present numbers. The internal code of the machine is ASCII. We will discover how to convert the data.

A BCD code is a four-bit code that uses 0000 to represent the character 0, 0001 to represent the value 1, and so forth up to 1001 to represent 9. You can check in Appendix B to see the ASCII codes for the characters 0 to 9. To do this problem, we define two data types, one of which is derived from the other.

```
type ASCII_NUMBER is (ZERO, ONE, TWO, THREE, FOUR, FIVE,
                      SIX, SEVEN, EIGHT, NINE);
type BCD_NUMBER is new ASCII_NUMBER;
```

The first definition is just a standard definition of the ASCII characters for 0 to 9. The second definition states that the type BCD_NUMBER is derived from the type ASCII_NUMBER. This means that BCD_NUMBER shares the same values and operations with the type ASCII_NUMBER, but that it may have a different underlying data representation. This is just what we want to do. To specify the different data representation, we use the representation specification once again.

```
for BCD_NUMBER use
      (ZERO  => 2#0000#,
       ONE   => 2#0001#,
       TWO   => 2#0010#,
       THREE => 2#0011#,
       FOUR  => 2#0100#,
       FIVE  => 2#0101#,
       SIX   => 2#0110#,
       SEVEN => 2#0111#,
       EIGHT => 2#1000#,
       NINE  => 2#1001#);


for ASCII_NUMBER use
      (ZERO  => 16#30#,
       ONE   => 16#31#,
       TWO   => 16#32#,
       THREE => 16#33#,
```

```
FOUR  => 16#34#,
FIVE  => 16#35#,
SIX   => 16#36#,
SEVEN => 16#37#,
EIGHT => 16#38#,
NINE  => 16#39#);
```

This establishes the underlying values for BCD_NUMBER and for ASCII_NUMBER. If we declare two objects in the program, one of data type ASCII_NUMBER and one of data type BCD_NUMBER, we can use a standard conversion between the two data types.

```
procedure CONVERT is

    type ASCII_NUMBER is (ZERO, ONE, TWO, THREE, FOUR, FIVE,
                          SIX, SEVEN, EIGHT, NINE);

    type BCD_NUMBER    is new ASCII_NUMBER;

    for BCD_NUMBER use
        (ZERO  => 2#0000#,
         ONE   => 2#0001#,
         TWO   => 2#0010#,
         THREE => 2#0011#,
         FOUR  => 2#0100#,
         FIVE  => 2#0101#,
         SIX   => 2#0110#,
         SEVEN => 2#0111#,
         EIGHT => 2#1000#,
         NINE  => 2#1001#);

    for ASCII_NUMBER use
        (ZERO  => 16#30#,
         ONE   => 16#31#,
         TWO   => 16#32#,
         THREE => 16#33#,
         FOUR  => 16#34#,
         FIVE  => 16#35#,
         SIX   => 16#36#,
         SEVEN => 16#37#,
         EIGHT => 16#38#,
         NINE  => 16#39#);

    DATA : ASCII_NUMBER;

    DISPLAY_DATA : BCD_NUMBER;

begin

    DATA := NINE;    -- just to assign some value to data

    DISPLAY_DATA := BCD_NUMBER (DATA);

end CONVERT;
```

Interrupts

Almost all real-time programs have interrupts, which are signals that stop the computer, have the computer do something else, and then let the computer go back to its original tasks. In many cases the interrupt signals that it is time to input some information into the computer. Other interrupts can signal that the external device is ready to receive more data or that it is time for the computer to perform some computation.

Ada provides for interrupts by assuming that the interrupt is a *vector interrupt,* that is, the interrupt has a particular location in the computer's memory to which a transfer of control takes place as a result of the interrupt.

To write an interrupt program in Ada, it is necessary simply to write a special program, called a *task,* with the interrupt location specified as an entry to that task. First we name the task and the entry for the interrupt:

```
task GET_TEMPERATURE is
  entry READ_DATA;
  for READ_DATA use at 16#0020#;
end GET_TEMPERATURE;
```

This specification for the task GET_TEMPERATURE states that the interrupt location 20 (base 16) will cause the statements in the entry named READ_DATA to be executed. Usually there are only a few statements in such an entry. For example, the statements in an entry may transfer information in from an interface to an internal data location. Other parts of the program will then process the stored data.

In our example for the interrupt entry, we will read a temperature value into location 2000 (base 16) each time the interrupt occurs.

```
procedure INTERRUPT is
  TEMPERATURE : INTEGER range 0..1024 := 0;
  INPUT_TEMPERATURE : INTEGER := 0;
  AVERAGE_TEMPERATURE : FLOAT := 0.0;
  for INPUT_TEMPERATURE use at 16#2000#;
  task GET_TEMPERATURE is
    entry READ_DATA;
    for READ_DATA use at 16#020#;
  end GET_TEMPERATURE;
  task body GET_TEMPERATURE is
  begin
    loop
      accept READ_DATA do
        TEMPERATURE := INPUT_TEMPERATURE;
      end READ_DATA;
    end loop;
  end GET_TEMPERATURE;
begin
-- keep running average temperature
  loop
    AVERAGE_TEMPERATURE := 0.9 * AVERAGE_TEMPERATURE
                         + 0.1 * FLOAT (TEMPERATURE);
  end loop;
end INTERRUPT;
```

This program consists of two programs: An infinite loop in the main program keeps a running average of the temperature by adding only 0.1 of the current temperature to 0.9 of the old average temperature. In the interrupt program there is also an infinite loop, but the program executes only to the **accept** statement and becomes blocked until an interrupt occurs. At that time the information in location 2000 is transferred into the object named TEM-PERATURE, which is used by the main program, and then the main program continues as before.

The task in Ada can go on in parallel with the main program as we saw in chapter 18.

MACHINE CODE

In Ada we can access machine code, which can be very useful if it helps a computer to execute a program an order of magnitude faster when a special instruction on the computer is used. In fact, some computers today do have special instruction sets that are far more powerful than a standard instruction set. Examples of these instructions are the ability to calculate a square root in one machine instruction. Normally it is inadvisable to use this feature in Ada programs because it is very machine dependent.

To use machine code in Ada, it is necessary to define a procedure that uses a predefined library package named MACHINE_CODE. This package will have all the mnemonics for the compiler that is being used with machine code. This package will be documented in Appendix F of the reference manual that comes with the compiler. For example, if our machine code instruction had the name SQROOT and it operated on a register named X to return the value of the square root of X in the same register, we can define a procedure such as

```
with MACHINE_CODE;
package SPECIAL_INSTRUCTIONS is
  X : MACHINE_CODE.X_REGISTER_TYPE;
  procedure SQ_ROOT;
  pragma  INLINE (SQ_ROOT);
end SPECIAL_INSTRUCTIONS;
with MACHINE_CODE;
package body SPECIAL_INSTRUCTIONS is
  procedure SQ_ROOT is
    use MACHINE_CODE;
  begin
    INSTRUCTION_TYPE'(CODE => SQROOT);
  end SQ_ROOT;
end SPECIAL_INSTRUCTIONS;
```

This type of procedure is very restricted. It can have only the single **use** clause in the declaration part of the procedure and it can have only one record definition in the executable part of the procedure. It also needs the **pragma** INLINE to denote to the compiler that the procedure is to be expanded inline in the program where it is used. Inline procedures eliminate the overhead normally associated with procedures. With all these restrictions, you will probably want to avoid machine code in Ada. But if you find the need for it, it is there to use.

Most register locations and formats will be defined for you in the package named MACHINE_CODE. However, just so you have the opportunity to see how a register can be defined in Ada for a hypothetical machine, see figure 20.3.

Note that the figure used with the register format looks just like the figure we looked at in the beginning of the chapter with word formats. In fact, the same method is used to describe register formats as word formats.

First we describe the types for each field:

```
subtype OP_CODE_TYPE is INTEGER range 0 .. 2**6 - 1;
subtype INDEX_TYPE   is INTEGER range 0 .. 7;
subtype ADDRESS_TYPE is INTEGER range 0 .. 2**21 - 1;
```

Next we describe the register as a record:

```
type INSTRUCTION_TYPE is
  record
    OP_CODE : OP_CODE_TYPE;
    INDEX   : INDEX_TYPE;
    ADDRESS : ADDRESS_TYPE;
  end record;
```

Then we either use the PACK **pragma** or specify the bit locations for each field.

```
for INSTRUCTION_TYPE use
  record
    OP_CODE at 0 range 25 .. 32;
    INDEX   at 0 range 22 .. 24;
    ADDRESS at 0 range 1 .. 21;
  end record;
```

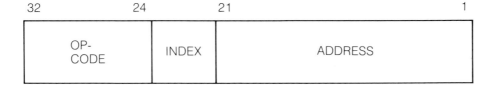

Figure 20.3 Machine register format

Finally, we declare a register name to be of this type

```
INSTRUCTION_REGISTER : INSTRUCTION_TYPE;
```

and assign an address to the register.

```
for INSTRUCTION_REGISTER use at 0;
```

All these declarations should be brought together in a single package, especially if you do not have a MACHINE_CODE package for your compiler.

```
package MY_MACHINE_CODE is
   subtype OP_CODE_TYPE   is INTEGER range 0..2**6-1;
   subtype INDEX_TYPE     is INTEGER range 0..7;
   subtype ADDRESS_TYPE   is INTEGER range 0..2**21-1;
   type INSTRUCTION_TYPE is
     record
       OP_CODE : OP_CODE_TYPE;
       INDEX   : INDEX_TYPE;
       ADDRESS : ADDRESS_TYPE;
     end record;

   for INSTRUCTION_TYPE use
     record
       OP_CODE at 0 range 25..32;
       INDEX   at 0 range 22..24;
       ADDRESS at 0 range 1..21;
     end record;
   INSTRUCTION_REGISTER : INSTRUCTION_TYPE;
   for INSTRUCTION_REGISTER use at 0;
end MY_MACHINE_CODE;
```

INTERFACE TO OTHER LANGUAGES

Even though Ada has many features that make it unnecessary for you to use assembly language in real-time programs, there may be the need for a subprogram to be written in assembly language or some other language such as Fortran. Ada handles this much better than it does the machine code program. If you have the need to use machine code, it might be better to write a program in assembly language and use the **INTERFACE pragma** along with the **INLINE pragma.**

Let us take our previous example of the super-fast square root instruction. We will now define a function that takes the square root of an argument just as though it was an Ada function.

```
function SQROOT (X : FLOAT) return FLOAT;
pragma INTERFACE (ASSEMBLER, SQROOT);
pragma INLINE (SQROOT);
```

The only restriction here is that the function name be the same as the assembler function. You use the function in the same way that you would an Ada function. If, instead, the function was a Fortran program named SQRT, all you write is SQRT.

```
pragma INTERFACE (FORTRAN, SQRT);
```

A MODEM INTERFACE

Ada has specified that there will be two procedures and appropriate data types in a package named LOW_LEVEL_IO so that control data can be sent to and received from an external device such as a disk, modem, or tape unit.

The name of the two procedures are SEND_CONTROL and RECEIVE_CONTROL. They will be overloaded for a variety of devices. The next program uses the SEND_CONTROL procedure to set up a modem for data transfer at 1200 baud. The data type MODEM_CONTROL_DATA will be a predefined data type to allow the fields for speed, parity, and number of bits to be set in a readable manner. Each important device such as a modem will have its own data types, which will be sent to the device to control it and received from the device to check on the device's status.

The dumb terminal program is made up of an infinite loop that reads a character from the keyboard and, when read, sends it out to the modem. It also reads a character from the terminal and displays it on the screen. Line feed characters are eliminated from the display so that extra lines do not appear on the screen.

```
-- A program for a dumb terminal
with TEXT_IO, LOW_LEVEL_IO;
use  TEXT_IO, LOW_LEVEL_IO;
procedure DUMB_TERMINAL is
   SET_UP_DATA : MODEM_CONTROL_DATA;
   SEND_C, RECEIVE_C : CHARACTER;
begin
   -- send setup data for 1200 baud, even parity, 7 data bits
   SET_UP_DATA := (SPEED => TWELVE_HUNDRED, PARITY=> EVEN,
                   BITS  => SEVEN);
   SEND_CONTROL (SMART_MODEM, SET_UP_DATA);
   -- infinite loop for modem
   loop
   -- send keyboard data
      GET (SEND_C);
      PUT (SMART_MODEM, SEND_C);
   -- read contents of modem buffer
      GET (SMART_MODEM, RECEIVE_C);
   -- eliminate line feeds to avoid double spaces when input
   -- is displayed on screen
      if RECEIVE_C = ASCII.LF then
         RECEIVE_C := ' ';
      end if;
   -- display received characters
      PUT (RECEIVE_C);
   end loop;
end DUMB_TERMINAL;
```

WHAT HAVE YOU LEARNED?

With Ada you can

◆ specify word formats,

◆ control the internal representation of data,

◆ control where data are placed,

◆ specify register locations and formats, and

◆ specify the underlying representation of user-defined types.

Ada gives you access to machine features, including

◆ machine code,

◆ interrupts,

◆ interfaces to other languages,

◆ unscheduled access to shared variables, and

◆ unchecked type conversion.

The first thing to do when faced with a word format is to define the types that go in each field. For example, we can define four data types, one for each field.

```
type STATUS_TYPE is (OFF, LOW, NORMAL, HIGH);
subtype TIME_TYPE   is INTEGER range 0..2**13-1;
subtype TEMPERATURE_TYPE is INTEGER range 0..2**10-1;
subtype PRESSURE_TYPE is INTEGER range 0..2**6-1;
```

The next step in the word format declaration is to define a record data type containing all the fields in the word format. This is the machine-independent description.

```
type SENSOR_WORD_FORMAT is
  record
    STATUS      : STATUS_TYPE;
    TIME        : TIME_TYPE;
    TEMPERATURE : TEMPERATURE_TYPE;
    PRESSURE    : PRESSURE_TYPE;
end record;
```

Next, make the word format machine dependent by using representation specifications.

```
-- to define the values in an enumeration type
for STATUS_TYPE use (OFF     => 2#000#,
                     LOW     => 2#001#,
                     NORMAL  => 2#010#,
                     HIGH    => 2#100#);
```

Finally, use the representation specification to place the status field in word 0, bits 1 to 3; the time field in word 0, bits 4 to 16; the temperature field in word 1, bits 1 to 10; and the pressure field in word 1, bits 11 to 16.

```
for SENSOR_WORD_FORMAT use
  record
    STATUS       at 0 range 1..3;    -- word 0 bits 1 to 3
    TIME         at 0 range 4..16;   -- word 0 bits 4 to 16
    TEMPERATURE  at 1 range 1..10;   -- word 1 bits 1 to 10
    PRESSURE     at 1 range 11..16;  -- word 1 bits 11 to 16
  end record;
```

The PACK **pragma** can also be used to pack the fields in a record as tightly as possible

```
pragma PACK (SENSOR_WORD_FORMAT);
```

The binary bit string data type is useful for manipulating individual bits and groups of bits with the logical operations.

```
type BINARY_STRING is array (POSITIVE range <>) of BOOLEAN;
```

An object of type BINARY_STRING is treated as a single unit with regard to the logical operators such as **and** and **or**. This is very convenient in handling bits in an input word.

Data conversions of input data can be handled with the UNCHECKED_CONVERSION generic procedure or derived types. For UNCHECKED_CONVERSION, it is necessary to instantiate the function

```
function UNCHECKED_CONVERSION is
           new UNCHECKED_CONVERSION (BINARY_STRING, CHARACTER);
```

For derived types, the new type must be defined with a representation specification and then the normal method of conversion between related types can be used.

```
type ASCII_NUMBER is (ZERO, ONE, TWO, THREE, FOUR, FIVE,
                      SIX, SEVEN, EIGHT, NINE);

type BCD_NUMBER    is new ASCII_NUMBER;

for BCD_NUMBER use
        (ZERO  => 2#0000#,
         ONE   => 2#0001#,
         TWO   => 2#0010#,
         THREE => 2#0011#,
         FOUR  => 2#0100#,
         FIVE  => 2#0101#,
         SIX   => 2#0110#,
         SEVEN => 2#0111#,
         EIGHT => 2#1000#,
         NINE  => 2#1001#);

for ASCII_NUMBER use
        (ZERO  => 16#30#,
         ONE   => 16#31#,
         TWO   => 16#32#,
         THREE => 16#33#,
         FOUR  => 16#34#,
```

```
FIVE   => 16#35#,
SIX    => 16#36#,
SEVEN  => 16#37#,
EIGHT  => 16#38#,
NINE   => 16#39#);
```

```
-- data conversion between derived types
```

```
DISPLAY_DATA := BCD_NUMBER (DATA);
```

Ada provides for interrupts by assuming that the interrupt is a *vector interrupt*. The interrupt has a particular location in the computer's memory to which a transfer of control takes place as a result of the interrupt.

To write an interrupt program in Ada, write a task with the interrupt location specified as an entry to that task.

```
task GET_TEMPERATURE is
  entry READ_DATA;
  for READ_DATA use at 16#0020#;
end GET_TEMPERATURE;
```

This specification for the task named GET_TEMPERATURE states that the interrupt location 20 base 16 will cause the statements in the entry named READ_DATA to be executed.

To use machine code in Ada, define a procedure that uses a predefined library package named MACHINE_CODE. This package has all the mnemonics for the compiler being used with machine code:

```
with MACHINE_CODE;
package SPECIAL_INSTRUCTIONS is
  X : MACHINE_CODE.X_REGISTER_TYPE;
  procedure SQ_ROOT;
  pragma  INLINE (SQ_ROOT);
end SPECIAL_INSTRUCTIONS;
with MACHINE_CODE;
package body SPECIAL_INSTRUCTIONS is
  procedure SQ_ROOT is
    use MACHINE_CODE;
  begin
    INSTRUCTION_TYPE'(CODE => SQROOT);
  end SQ_ROOT;
end SPECIAL_INSTRUCTIONS;
```

The INTERFACE **pragma** can be used to interface Ada programs to programs written in other languages. For example,

```
function SQROOT (X : FLOAT) return FLOAT;
pragma INTERFACE (ASSEMBLER, SQROOT);
pragma INLINE (SQROOT);
```

The only restriction here is that the function name be the same as the assembler function. You use the function in the same way that you would an Ada function. If the function was a Fortran program, all you write is

```
pragma INTERFACE (FORTRAN, SQRT);
```

Ada has two procedures, SEND_CONTROL and RECEIVE_CONTROL, and appropriate data types in a package named LOW_LEVEL_IO so that control data can be sent to and received from an external device such as a disk, modem, or tape unit.

```
SET_UP_DATA := (SPEED => TWELVE_HUNDRED, PARITY => EVEN,
                BITS => SEVEN);
SEND_CONTROL ( SMART_MODEM, SET_UP_DATA);
```

FIXED POINT

The fixed-point type is one of the two approximate data types in Ada. We have seen the use of the floating-point type, especially the predefined FLOAT type, which is an approximate data type. In most cases, the floating-point types are preferable to use; the fixed-point types require you to manage the scaling after each multiplication or division. Fixed point has its use in very small computers that lack floating-point arithmetic or that perform floating-point operations too slowly for a particular application.

There is no predefined data type for the fixed-point types. You specify the absolute error for the type by the general form

```
type type name is delta error bound;
```

For example,

```
type MY_FIXED_TYPE is delta 0.001;
type MONEY_TYPE is delta 0.01;
```

The **delta** specifies that the absolute error bound. The compiler can provide more accuracy, but is required to supply at least that amount. The fixed-point type has the operations of +, −, *, /, and **abs**.

Adding and subtracting fixed-point types is done as with other data types. If the following declarations are made

```
X, Y, Z : MY_FIXED_TYPE;
ACCOUNT, DEPOSIT, WITHDRAWAL : MONEY_TYPE;
X := Y − Y + 0.2;
ACCOUNT := ACCOUNT + DEPOSIT;
```

are legal.

If you multiply or divide fixed-point types, you need to specify the scaling at each operation. For example,

```
X := MY_FIXED_TYPE (0.1 * Y);
ACCOUNT := ACCOUNT + MONEY_TYPE (0.06 * ACCOUNT);
```

Note that the fixed-point-type definition is similar to the floating-point-type definition

```
type type name is digits number of places;
```

where the *number of places* refers to the number of places after the decimal point. You will normally use the predefined FLOAT type which is on your computer, but you may specify a new data type if you want a different accuracy or if you want to provide a different data type for purposes of strong typing.

Problems

1. List three everyday objects that contain computers today.

2. Write a representation specification to perform the same result as **pragma** PACK (BINARY_STRING);

3. Write another version of the SQ_ROOT procedure. Do it by altering the MY_MACHINE_CODE package to have an op code that performs a square root.

4. Write a package specification for the word format in figure 20.4.

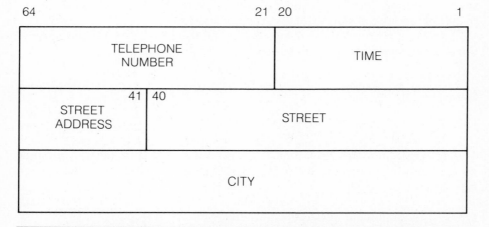

Figure 20.4 Word format

5. Write a package specification for the word format in figure 20.5 where the status and signal fields are defined as

status		signal	
off	000	low	100
battery low	001	medium	010
battery strong	010	high	001

6. Write a program to convert numeric input data received in field data code to ASCII code. In field data code the numbers are represented in six bits:

number	code
0	110000
1	110001
2	110010

| 0 | 13 | 14 | 16 | 17 | 31 |

| AZIMUTH ANGLE | SIGNAL | DISTANCE |

| 0 | 2 | 3 | 16 | 17 |

| STATUS | TIME | ELEVATION ANGLE |

Figure 20.5 Sensor word format

3	110011
4	110100
5	110101
6	110110
7	110111
8	111000
9	111001

7. Write a program to convert two ASCII characters into BCD characters and place them in one eight bit word as shown in figure 20.6.

8. Write a program that responds to a timing interrupt at location 20 (base 16). On every interrupt add 1 to a variable named CLOCK_COUNTER located at location 120 (base 16). When the CLOCK_COUNTER reaches a value of 2**15, reset it to 1 on the next interrupt.

9. Write a program that uses the Fortran program named SQRT to take the square root of an input number. SQRT is a Fortran function that returns the square root of the input value. For example, SQRT(4.0) is 2.0.

10. Write a program to reverse the order of bits in an 8 bit variable defined as a binary bit string with a range of 1..8.

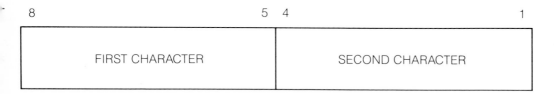

| 8 | 5 | 4 | 1 |

| FIRST CHARACTER | SECOND CHARACTER |

Figure 20.6 BCD character format

❖ 21 ❖

THE ADA ENVIRONMENT

There is more to using a computer than just learning to use the compiler. To learn Ada you may have been using an environment containing the editor you used to prepare your programs. You also used a command language to invoke the compiler, to link your program with other programs, and to execute your program. If you were fortunate you may have had other tools to help you such as a symbolic debugger.

Unless you used an Ada environment, it is quite likely that when you go to another computer system, you will have to learn how to use a different editor and a different command language. You will find a set of tools different from the tools you are used to.

In an attempt to remove these differences and provide a more powerful set of tools to work with Ada, an effort is underway to develop an Ada Programming Support Environment or APSE (rhymes with asp). APSE may eventually be standard across all computers.

TOOLS IN THE ADA ENVIRONMENT

At the heart of the Ada environment is the Kernel Ada Programming Support Environment, called the KAPSE. The KAPSE has two important functions:

- ◆ It hides the host computer system from the rest of the APSE.
- ◆ It provides a minimal set of tools upon which to build other tools.

In one document, Stoneman,[1] the KAPSE tools were specified to be

◆ operator interface routines,

◆ operating system interface routines, and

◆ data base routines to store and process source and object programs.

It is the operator interface routines that will let you use the same set of commands, to perform an Ada compile no matter what computer you are using as long as the KAPSE tools are present. When this has been accomplished in the KAPSE, programmers will no longer have to be retrained when a new computer system is purchased. The operating system interface routines will make it possible to transport tools more easily between computers than has been done in the past. This should make software tools more reusable and shared between computer installations.

Most software tools use some kind of data base to save and operate on the program in either its source or object form. The set of KAPSE data base programs are intended to be a useful set of programs that will be installed on every computer. Such a set of routines will make the task of every tool writer simpler and remove duplication of effort.

On top of the KAPSE, a set of tools has been defined to make up the Minimal Ada Programming Support Environment (MAPSE). The MAPSE is intended to contain an initial set of tools that every installation should have for preparing computer programs. Figure 21.1 shows the tools that are planned for the MAPSE. Besides the Ada compiler and linkage editor, the MAPSE will contain an editor, a formatter, a symbolic debugger, a configuration manager, and a command language interpreter.

The Ada editor may not be your favorite editor, but you will be guaranteed that every computer will have this editor. This is an advantage when you need to use more than one computer.

The symbolic debugger will allow you to test your program under the control of a program that lets you run part of your program, stop execution at selected points, or step through the program one statement at a time. At the points where execution is halted, you can examine or alter the values in variables and then continue execution. This is a very nice tool to use when testing a module in a program.

The configuration manager is a very valuable tool and assists in the development of large systems. There are a few configuration management tools available, but most configuration management is still done manually. Configuration management controls the versions of subprograms that make up a complete program. It also controls changes to that system by the orderly introduction of new modules that have undergone extensive testing before being incorporated in a new version of the complete system.

[1]*Requirements for Ada Programming Support Environments: STONEMAN*, US Dept. of Defense, Washington, DC, Feb. 1980.

John N. Buxton and Larry E. Druffel, "Requirements for an Ada Support Environment: Rationale for Stoneman," *Proc. Computer Software and Applications Conf.*, Oct. 1980, pp. 66–72.

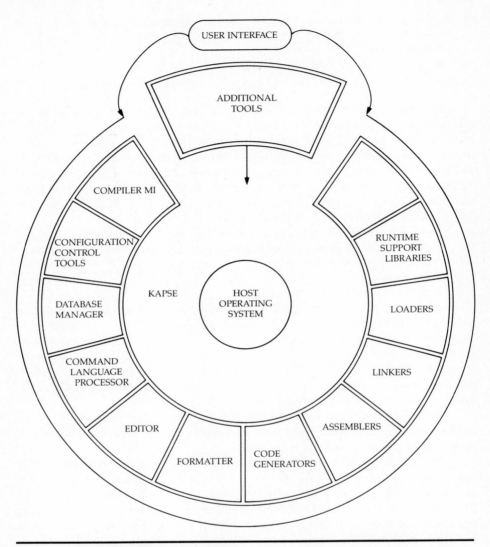

Figure 21.1 The ADA Environment

Once a MAPSE is available to develop programs, a full APSE will be developed with a more complete set of tools to support the complete life-cycle of a computer program. The full APSE will contain tools to support the production of requirements, program designs, program specifications, test plans, and software documentation. The APSE will also contain test tools and software management tools.

It is the combination of Ada together with portable tools in a powerful environment that will make Ada a powerful language to use.

APPENDIX A

PREDEFINED IDENTIFIERS

AMPERSAND
ASCII
AT_SIGN
BACK_SLASH
BAR
BOOLEAN
CALENDAR
CHARACTER
CIRCUMFLEX
COL
COLON
CONSTRAINT_ERROR
CREATE
CURRENT_INPUT
CURRENT_OUTPUT
DATA_ERROR
DELETE
DEVICE_ERROR
DIRECT_IO
DOLLAR
DURATION
END_ERROR
END_OF_FILE
END_OF_LINE

END_OF_PAGE
EXCLAM
FALSE
FLOAT
FORM
GET
GET_LINE
GRAVE
INDEX
INTEGER
IO_EXCEPTIONS
L_BRACE
L_BRACKET
LINE
LINE_LENGTH
LOW_LEVEL_IO
MODE
MODE_ERROR
NAME
NAME_ERROR
NATURAL
NEW_LINE
NEW_PAGE
NUMERIC_ERROR

MACHINE_CODE
OPEN
PAGE
PERCENT
POSITIVE
PROGRAM_ERROR
PUT
PUT_LINE
QUERY
QUOTATION
R_BRACKET
R_BRACE
READ
RESET
SEMICOLON
SEQUENTIAL_IO
SET_COL
SET_INDEX
SET_LINE

SET_PAGE
SHARP
SIZE
SKIP_LINE
SKIP_PAGE
STANDARD
STANDARD_INPUT
STANDARD_OUTPUT
STORAGE_ERROR
STRING
SYSTEM
TEXT_IO
TILDE
TRUE
UNDERLINE
UNCHECKED_CONVERSION
UNCHECKED_DEALLOCATION
USE_ERROR
WRITE

APPENDIX
❖ B ❖
ASCII
CHARACTER SET

THE ASCII SYMBOLS

VALUE	SYMBOL	ALTERNATE SYMBOL	COMMON NAME
0	NUL		Null
1	SOH		Start of heading
2	STX		Start of text
3	ETX		End of text
4	EOT		End of transmission
5	ENQ		Enquiry
6	ACK		Acknowledge
7	BEL		Bell
8	BS		Backspace
9	HT		Horizontal tabulation
10	LF		Line feed
11	VT		Vertical tabulation
12	FF		Form feed
13	CR		Carriage return
14	SO		Shift out
15	SI		Shift in
16	DLE		Data link escape
17	DC1		Device control #1
18	DC2		Device control #2
19	DC3		Device control #3
20	DC4		Device control #4
21	NAK		Negative acknowledge
22	SYN		Synchronous idle
23	ETB		End of transmission block
24	CAN		Cancel
25	EM		End of medium

26	SUB		Substitute
27	ESC		Escape
28	FS		File separator
29	GS		Group separator
30	RS		Record separator
31	US		Unit separator
32	' '		Space (blank)
33	'!'	EXCLAM	Exclamation mark
34	'"'	QUOTATION	Quote
35	'#'	SHARP	Pound sign
36	'$'	DOLLAR	Dollar sign
37	'%'	PERCENT	Percent sign
38	'&'	AMPERSAND	Ampersand
39	'''		Prime (single quote)
40	'('		Left parenthesis
41	')'		Right parenthesis
42	'*'		Multiplication sign (asterisk)
43	'+'		Plus sign
44	','		Comma
45	'-'		Minus sign (hyphen)
46	'.'		Period
47	'/'		Divide sign (slash)
48	'0'		Zero
49	'1'		One
50	'2'		Two
51	'3'		Three
52	'4'		Four
53	'5'		Five
54	'6'		Six
55	'7'		Seven
56	'8'		Eight
57	'9'		Nine
58	':'	COLON	Colon
59	';'	SEMICOLON	Semicolon
60	'<'		Less than sign
61	'='		Equal sign
62	'>'		Greater than sign
63	'?'	QUERY	Question mark
64	'@'	AT_SIGN	At sign
65	'A'		
66	'B'		
67	'C'		
68	'D'		
69	'E'		
70	'F'		
71	'G'		
72	'H'		
73	'I'		
74	'J'		
75	'K'		
76	'L'		

77	'M'		
78	'N'		
79	'O'		
80	'P'		
81	'Q'		
82	'R'		
83	'S'		
84	'T'		
85	'U'		
86	'V'		
87	'W'		
88	'X'		
89	'Y'		
90	'Z'		
91	'['	L_BRACKET	Left bracket
92	'\'	BACK_SLASH	Back slash
93	']'	R_BRACKET	Right bracket
94	'^'	CIRCUMFLEX	Caret
95	'_'	UNDERLINE	Underscore
96	'`'	GRAVE	Open single quote
97	'a'	LC_A	
98	'b'	LC_B	
99	'c'	LC_C	
100	'd'	LC_D	
101	'e'	LC_E	
102	'f'	LC_F	
103	'g'	LC_G	
104	'h'	LC_H	
105	'i'	LC_I	
106	'j'	LC_J	
107	'k'	LC_K	
108	'l'	LC_L	
109	'm'	LC_M	
110	'n'	LC_N	
111	'o'	LC_O	
112	'p'	LC_P	
113	'q'	LC_Q	
114	'r'	LC_R	
115	's'	LC_S	
116	't'	LC_T	
117	'u'	LC_U	
118	'v'	LC_V	
119	'w'	LC_W	
120	'x'	LC_X	
121	'y'	LC_Y	
122	'z'	LC_Z	
123	'{'	L_BRACE	Left brace
124	'|'	BAR	Bar
125	'}'	R_BRACE	Right brace
126	'~'	TILDE	Tilde
127	DEL		Delete

APPENDIX C

INPUT/OUTPUT PACKAGES

```
with IO_EXCEPTIONS;
package TEXT_IO is

   type FILE_TYPE   is limited private;

   type FILE_MODE   is (IN_FILE, OUT_FILE);

   type COUNT   is range 0 .. IMPLEMENTATION_DEFINED;
   subtype POSITIVE_COUNT is COUNT range 1 .. COUNT'LAST;
   UNBOUNDED : constant COUNT := 0; -- line and page length

   subtype FIELD        is INTEGER range 0 .. IMPLEMENTATION_DEFINED;
   subtype NUMBER_BASE is INTEGER range 2 .. 16;

   type TYPE_SET is (LOWER_CASE, UPPER_CASE);

   -- File management

   procedure CREATE (FILE  : in out FILE_TYPE;
                     MODE  : in FILE_MODE := OUT_FILE;
                     NAME  : in STRING := "";
                     FORM  : in STRING := "";

   procedure OPEN   (FILE  : in out FILE_TYPE;
                     MODE  : in FILE_MODE;
                     NAME  : in STRING;
                     FORM  : in STRING := "");
```

314

```
procedure CLOSE    (FILE  :  in out FILE_TYPE);
procedure DELETE   (FILE  :  in out FILE_TYPE);
procedure RESET    (FILE  :  in out FILE_TYPE; MODE :  in FILE_MODE);
procedure RESET    (FILE  :  in out FILE_TYPE);

function  MODE     (FILE  :  in FILE_TYPE) return FILE_MODE;
function  NAME     (FILE  :  in FILE_TYPE) return STRING;
function  FORM     (FILE  :  in FILE_TYPE) return STRING;

function  IS_OPEN  (FILE  :  in FILE_TYPE) return BOOLEAN;

-- Control of default input and output files

procedure SET_INPUT  (FILE : in FILE_TYPE);
procedure SET_OUTPUT (FILE : in FILE_TYPE);

function  STANDARD_INPUT  return FILE_TYPE;
function  STANDARD_OUTPUT return FILE_TYPE;

function  CURRENT_INPUT   return FILE_TYPE;
function  CURRENT_OUTPUT  return FILE_TYPE;

-- Specification of line and page lengths

procedure SET_LINE_LENGTH  (FILE : in FILE_TYPE; TO : in COUNT);
procedure SET_LINE_LENGTH  (TO : in COUNT);

procedure SET_PAGE_LENGTH  (FILE : in FILE_TYPE; TO : in COUNT);
procedure  SET_PAGE_LENGTH  (TO : in COUNT);

function  LINE_LENGTH (FILE :  in FILE_TYPE) return COUNT;
function  LINE_LENGTH return COUNT;

function  PAGE_LENGTH (FILE :  in FILE_TYPE) return COUNT;
function  PAGE_LENGTH return COUNT;

-- Column, Line and Page Control

procedure NEW_LINE   (FILE :  in FILE_TYPE; SPACING :  in POSITIVE_COUNT : = 1);
procedure NEW_LINE   (SPACING :  in POSITIVE_COUNT : = 1);

procedure SKIP_LINE  (FILE :  in FILE_TYPE; SPACING :  in POSITIVE_COUNT : = 1);
procedure SKIP_LINE  (SPACING :  in POSITIVE_COUNT : = 1);

function  END_OF_LINE  (FILE :  in FILE_TYPE) return BOOLEAN;
function  END_OF_LINE  return BOOLEAN;

procedure NEW_PAGE    (FILE :  in FILE_TYPE);
procedure NEW_PAGE;

procedure SKIP_PAGE   (FILE :  in FILE_TYPE;
procedure  SKIP_PAGE;

function  END_OF_PAGE  (FILE :  in FILE_TYPE) return BOOLEAN;
```

```
function    END_OF_PAGE  return BOOLEAN;

function    END_OF_FILE  (FILE : in FILE_TYPE) return BOOLEAN;
function    END_OF_FILE  return BOOLEAN;

procedure   SET_COL  (FILE : in FILE_TYPE; TO : in POSITIVE_COUNT);
procedure   SET_COL  (TO   : in POSITIVE_COUNT);

procedure   SET_LINE (FILE : in FILE_TYPE; TO : in POSITIVE_COUNT);
procedure   SET_LINE (TO   : in POSITIVE_COUNT);

function    COL  (FILE : in FILE_TYPE) return POSITIVE_COUNT;
function    COL  return POSITIVE_COUNT;

function    LINE (FILE : in FILE_TYPE) return POSITIVE_COUNT;
function    LINE return POSITIVE_COUNT;

function    PAGE (FILE : in FILE_TYPE) return POSITIVE_COUNT;
function    PAGE return POSITIVE_COUNT;

-- Character Input-Output

procedure   GET (FILE : in  FILE_TYPE; ITEM : out CHARACTER);
procedure   GET (ITEM : out CHARACTER);
procedure   PUT (FILE : in  FILE_TYPE; ITEM : in CHARACTER);
procedure   PUT (ITEM : in  CHARACTER);

-- String Input-Output

procedure   GET (FILE : in  FILE_TYPE; ITEM : out STRING);
procedure   GET (ITEM : out STRING);
procedure   PUT (FILE : in  FILE_TYPE; ITEM : in  STRING);
procedure   PUT (ITEM : in  STRING);
procedure   GET_LINE (FILE : in FILE_TYPE;
                      ITEM : out STRING;
                      LAST : out NATURAL);
procedure   GET_LINE (ITEM : out STRING;
                      LAST : out NATURAL);
procedure   PUT_LINE (FILE : in FILE_TYPE;
                      ITEM : in STRING);
procedure   PUT_LINE (ITEM : in STRING);

-- Generic package for Input-Output of Integer Types

generic
  type NUM is range <>;
package INTEGER_IO is

  DEFAULT_WIDTH  : FIELD := NUM'WIDTH;
  DEFAULT_BASE   : NUMBER_BASE := 10;

  procedure GET (FILE  : in  FILE TYPE;
                 ITEM  : out NUM;
                 WIDTH : in  FIELD := 0;
  procedure GET (ITEM  : out NUM;
                 WIDTH : in  FIELD := 0);
```

```
   procedure PUT (FILE  :  in  FILE_TYPE;
                  ITEM  :  in  NUM;
                  WIDTH :  in  FIELD := DEFAULT_WIDTH;
                  BASE  :  in  NUMBER_BASE := DEFAULT_BASE);
   procedure PUT (ITEM  :  in  NUM;
                  WIDTH :  in  FIELD := DEFAULT_WIDTH;
                  BASE  :  in  NUMBER_BASE := DEFAULT_BASE);

   procedure GET (FROM  :  in   STRING;
                  ITEM  :  out  NUM;
                  LAST  :  out  POSITIVE);
   procedure PUT (TO    :  out  STRING;
                  ITEM  :  in   NUM;
                  BASE  :  in   NUMBER_BASE := DEFAULT_BASE);

end INTEGER_IO;

-- Generic packages for Input-Output of Real Types

generic
  type NUM is digits <>;
package FLOAT_IO is

  DEFAULT_FORE  :  FIELD := 2;
  DEFAULT_AFT   :  FIELD := NUM'DIGITS-1;
  DEFAULT_EXP   :  FIELD := 3;

  procedure GET (FILE  :  in   FILE_TYPE;
                 ITEM  :  out  NUM;
                 WIDTH :  in   FIELD := 0);
  procedure GET (ITEM  :  out  NUM;
                 WIDTH :  in   FIELD := 0);

  procedure PUT (FILE  :  in  FILE_TYPE;
                 ITEM  :  in  NUM;
                 FORE  :  in  FIELD := DEFAULT_FORE;
                 AFT   :  in  FIELD := DEFAULT_AFT;
                 EXP   :  in  FIELD := DEFAULT_EXP;
  procedure PUT (ITEM  :  in  NUM;
                 FORE  :  in  FIELD := DEFAULT_FORE;
                 AFT   :  in  FIELD := DEFAULT_AFT;
                 EXP   :  in  FIELD := DEFAULT_EXP);

  procedure GET (FROM  :  in   STRING;
                 ITEM  :  out  NUM;
                 LAST  :  out  POSITIVE);
  procedure PUT (TO    :  out  STRING;
                 ITEM  :  in   NUM;
                 AFT   :  in   FIELD := DEFAULT_AFT;
                 EXP   :  in   FIELD := DEFAULT_EXP);

end FLOAT_IO;

generic
  type NUM is delta <>;
package FIXED_IO is
```

```
  DEFAULT_FORE    : FIELD := NUM'FORE;
  DEFAULT_AFT     : FIELD := NUM'AFT;
  DEFAULT_EXP     : FIELD := 0;

  procedure GET (FILE  : in  FILE_TYPE;
                 ITEM  : out NUM;
                 WIDTH : in  FIELD := 0);
  procedure GET (ITEM  : out NUM;
                 WIDTH : in  FIELD := 0);

  procedure PUT (FILE  : in  FILE_TYPE;
                 ITEM  : in  NUM;
                 FORE  : in  FIELD := DEFAULT_FORE;
                 AFT   : in  FIELD := DEFAULT_AFT;
                 EXP   : in  FIELD := DEFAULT_EXP);
  procedure PUT (ITEM  : in  NUM;
                 FORE  : in  FIELD := DEFAULT_FORE;
                 AFT   : in  FIELD := DEFAULT_AFT;
                 EXP   : in  FIELD := DEFAULT_EXP);

  procedure GET (FROM  : in  STRING;
                 ITEM  : out NUM;
                 LAST  : out POSITIVE);
  procedure PUT (TO    : out STRING;
                 ITEM  : in  NUM;
                 AFT   : in  FIELD := DEFAULT_AFT;
                 EXP   : in  FIELD := DEFAULT_EXP);

end FIXED_IO;

-- Generic package for Input-Output of Enumeration Types

generic
  type ENUM is range (<>);
package ENUMERATION_IO is

  DEFAULT_WIDTH   : FIELD := 0;
  DEFAULT_SETTING : TYPE_SET := UPPER_CASE;

  procedure GET (FILE  : in  FILE_TYPE;
                 ITEM  : out ENUM);
  procedure GET (ITEM  : out ENUM);

  procedure PUT (FILE  : in  FILE_TYPE;
                 ITEM  : in  ENUM;
                 WIDTH : in  FIELD    := DEFAULT_WIDTH;
                 SET   : in  TYPE_SET := DEFAULT_SETTING);
  procedure PUT (ITEM  : in  ENUM;
                 WIDTH : in  FIELD    := DEFAULT_WIDTH;
                 SET   : in  TYPE_SET := DEFAULT_SETTING);

  procedure GET (FROM  : in  STRING;
                 ITEM  : out ENUM;
                 LAST  : out POSITIVE);
  procedure PUT (TO    : out STRING;
```

```
                              ITEM  :  in  ENUM;
                              SET   :  in  TYPE_SET := DEFAULT_SETTING);

end ENUMERATION_IO;

-- Exceptions

STATUS_ERROR  :  exception renames IO_EXCEPTIONS.STATUS_ERROR;
MODE_ERROR    :  exception renames IO_EXCEPTIONS.MODE_ERROR;
NAME_ERROR    :  exception renames IO_EXCEPTIONS.NAME_ERROR;
USE_ERROR     :  exception renames IO_EXCEPTIONS.USE_ERROR;
DEVICE_ERROR  :  exception renames IO_EXCEPTIONS.DEVICE_ERROR;
END_ERROR     :  exception renames IO_EXCEPTIONS.DEVICE_ERROR;
DATA_ERROR    :  exception renames IO_EXCEPTIONS.DATA_ERROR;
LAYOUT_ERROR  :  exception renames IO_EXCEPTIONS.LAYOUT_ERROR;

private
  -- implementation-dependent

end TEXT_IO;

with IO_EXCEPTIONS;
generic
  type ELEMENT_TYPE is private;
package SEQUENTIAL_IO is

  type FILE_TYPE  is limited private;

  type FILE_MODE  is (IN_FILE, OUT_FILE);

  -- File management

  procedure CREATE  (FILE  :  in out FILE_TYPE;
                     MODE  :  in FILE_MODE := OUT_FILE;
                     NAME  :  in STRING := "";
                     FORM  :  in STRING := "");

  procedure OPEN    (FILE  :  in out FILE_TYPE;
                     MODE  :  in FILE_MODE;
                     NAME  :  in STRING;
                     FORM  :  in STRING := "");

  procedure CLOSE   (FILE  :  in out FILE_TYPE);
  procedure DELETE  (FILE  :  in out FILE_TYPE;
  procedure RESET   (FILE  :  in out FILE_TYPE; MODE : in FILE_MODE);
  procedure RESET   (FILE  :  in out FILE_TYPE);


  function MODE     (FILE  :  in FILE_TYPE) return FILE_MODE;
  function NAME     (FILE  :  in FILE_TYPE) return STRING;
  function FORM     (FILE  :  in FILE_TYPE) return STRING;


  function IS_OPEN  (FILE  :  in FILE_TYPE) return BOOLEAN;

  -- Input and output operations
```

```ada
   procedure READ    (FILE : in FILE_TYPE; ITEM : out ELEMENT_TYPE);
   procedure WRITE   (FILE : in FILE_TYPE; ITEM : in  ELEMENT_TYPE);

   function END_OF_FILE (FILE : in FILE_TYPE)  return BOOLEAN;

   -- Exceptions

   STATUS_ERROR  : exception renames IO_EXCEPTIONS.STATUS_ERROR;
   MODE_ERROR    : exception renames IO_EXCEPTIONS.MODE_ERROR;
   NAME_ERROR    : exception renames IO_EXCEPTIONS.NAME_ERROR;
   USE_ERROR     : exception renames IO_EXCEPTIONS.USE_ERROR;
   DEVICE_ERROR  : exception renames IO_EXCEPTIONS.DEVICE_ERROR;
   END_ERROR     : exception renames IO_EXCEPTIONS.END_ERROR;
   DATA_ERROR    : exception renames IO_EXCEPTIONS.DATA_ERROR;

private
   -- implementation-dependent
end SEQUENTIAL_IO;

with IO_EXCEPTIONS;
generic

   type ELEMENT_TYPE is private;
package DIRECT_IO is

   type FILE_TYPE    is limited private;

   type    FILE_MODE is (IN_FILE, INOUT_FILE, OUT_FILE);
   type    COUNT     is range 0 .. IMPLEMENTATION_DEFINED;
   subtype POSITIVE_COUNT is COUNT range 1 .. COUNT'LAST;

   -- File management

   procedure CREATE (FILE : in out FILE_TYPE;
                     MODE : in FILE_MODE := INOUT_FILE;
                     NAME : in STRING := "";
                     FORM : in STRING := "");

   procedure OPEN   (FILE : in out FILE_TYPE;
                     MODE : in FILE_MODE;
                     NAME : in STRING;
                     FORM : in STRING := "");

   procedure CLOSE  (FILE : in out FILE_TYPE);
   procedure DELETE (FILE : in out FILE_TYPE);
   procedure RESET  (FILE : in out FILE_TYPE; MODE : in FILE_MODE);
   procedure RESET  (FILE : in out FILE_TYPE);

   function MODE    (FILE : in FILE_TYPE) return FILE_MODE;
   function NAME    (FILE : in FILE_TYPE) return STRING;
   function FORM    (FILE : in FILE_TYPE) return STRING;

   function IS_OPEN (FILE : in FILE_TYPE) return BOOLEAN;

   -- Input and output operations
```

```
procedure READ      (FILE  : in FILE_TYPE; ITEM : out ELEMENT_TYPE;
                      FROM : POSITIVE_COUNT);
procedure READ      (FILE  : in FILE_TYPE; ITEM : out ELEMENT_TYPE);

procedure WRITE     (FILE  : in FILE_TYPE; ITEM : in  ELEMENT_TYPE;
                      TO : POSITIVE_COUNT);
procedure WRITE     (FILE  : in FILE_TYPE; ITEM : in  ELEMENT_TYPE);

procedure SET_INDEX (FILE : in FILE_TYPE; TO : in POSITIVE_COUNT);

function  INDEX     (FILE  : in FILE_TYPE) return POSITIVE_COUNT;
function  SIZE      (FILE  : in FILE_TYPE) return COUNT;

function  END_OF_FILE (FILE : in FILE_TYPE)  return BOOLEAN;

-- Exceptions

STATUS_ERROR   : exception renames IO_EXCEPTIONS.STATUS_ERROR;
MODE_ERROR     : exception renames IO_EXCEPTIONS.MODE_ERROR;
NAME_ERROR     : exception renames IO_EXCEPTIONS.NAME_ERROR;
USE_ERROR      : exception renames IO_EXCEPTIONS.USE_ERROR;
DEVICE_ERROR   : exception renames IO_EXCEPTIONS.DEVICE_ERROR;
END_ERROR      : exception renames IO_EXCEPTIONS.END_ERROR;
DATA_ERROR     : exception renames IO_EXCEPTIONS.DATA_ERROR;

private
-- implementation-dependent
end DIRECT_IO;

package IO_EXCEPTIONS is

STATUS_ERROR   : exception;
MODE_ERROR     : exception;
NAME_ERROR     : exception;
USE_ERROR      : exception;
DEVICE_ERROR   : exception;
END_ERROR      : exception;
DATA_ERROR     : exception;
LAYOUT_ERROR   : exception;

end IO_EXCEPTIONS;
```

APPENDIX
❖ D ❖

PREDEFINED LANGUAGE ATTRIBUTES

An attribute is a characteristic of a type, a subprogram, package, task, or label. Attributes are always prefixed by the name of the type or object for which the attribute applies. For example, INTEGER'FIRST is an attribute of the INTEGER data type. In the table which follows the attributes are organized without their prefix. Thus to look up INTEGER'FIRST, you turn to the description of 'FIRST. Since INTEGER is a scalar type, the line that states the attribute is the lower bound of the type and the type of the attribute will be the type of the prefix applies. Hence the type of INTEGER'FIRST is INTEGER.

--DECLARATIONS FOR EXAMPLES --

- *DISCRETE TYPE*
  type AUTHOR **is** (CHARLES, MARY, DICK, NANCY);
- *DISCRETE SUBTYPE*
  subtype OLD_AUTHORS **is** AUTHOR **range** CHARLES..MARY;
- *FIXED POINT TYPE*
  type MONEY_TYPE **is delta** 0.001;
- *FIXED POINT SUBTYPE*
  subtype DOLLAR_TYPE **is** MONEY_TYPE **range** 0.0..1000000.0;

- *TASK TYPE*
  task type KEYBOARD_TYPE;

- *TASK WITH ENTRY*
  task KEYBOARD **is**
     entry KEY_INTERRUPT;
     for KEY_INTERRUPT **use at** 16#42#;
  end KEYBOARD;

- *UNCONSTRAINED ARRAY TYPE AND OBJECT*
  type ARRAY_OF_NAMES **is array** (INTEGER **range** <>) **of** AUTHOR;
  SHORT_LIST : ARRAY_OF_NAMES (1..4);
  LONG_LIST : ARRAY_OF_NAMES (1..100);

- *FLOATING POINT TYPE*
  type REAL **is digits** 6;

- *FLOATING POINT SUBTYPE*
  subtype MY_REAL **is** REAL **range** 0.0..10000.0;

- *MULTIDIMENSIONAL ARRAY TYPE AND ARRAY*
  type MATRIX_TYPE **is array** (1..2, 0..3) **of** FLOAT;
  MATRIX : MATRIX_TYPE;

- *RECORD TYPE AND RECORD*
  type COMPLEX **is**
    record
      REAL_PART : FLOAT;
      IMAGINARY_PART : FLOAT;
    end record;
  C : COMPLEX;

- *ACCESS TYPE*
  type POINTER_TYPE **is access** COMPLEX;

ATTRIBUTE	TYPE OF PREFIX	RESULT TYPE	DEFINITION
'ADDRESS	Object, program unit, label, entry	ADDRESS	Beginning address of prefix. If the prefix is a subprogram package, task, or label, the address is the location of the body or statement. If the prefix is an entry to which an address clause has been attached (with a **for use** statement), the value refers to the corresponding hardware interrupt.
example: KEYBOARD'ADDRESS gives value 42(base 16)			
'AFT	Fixed point subtype	Universal Integer	Number of decimal digits needed for specified precision of the subtype.
example: DOLLAR_TYPE'AFT gives value 3			
'BASE	Type or subtype	Base type	Base type of prefix. Used in name of another attribute such as P'BASE'FIRST.
example: DOLLAR_TYPE'BASE'FIRST gives value 0.0			
'CALLABLE	Task	BOOLEAN	FALSE when the task is completed or terminated or abnormal. TRUE when the task is active.
example: KEYBOARD'CALLABLE should be TRUE			
'CONSTRAINED	Object of a type with discriminants	BOOLEAN	TRUE when a discriminant constraint applies to the object or if the object is a constant (including a formal parameter of mode **in**). FALSE otherwise. If the prefix is a formal parameter of mode **in out**, the value of the attribute comes from the actual parameter.

ATTRIBUTE	TYPE OF PREFIX	RESULT TYPE	DEFINITION
example: SHORT_LIST'CONSTRAINED gives value TRUE			
'CONSTRAINED	Private type or subtype	BOOLEAN	FALSE when the prefix stands for an unconstrained nonformal private type with discriminants. FALSE when the prefix stands for a generic formal private type and the actual subtype is unconstrained. TRUE otherwise.
example: SHORT_LIST'CONSTRAINED is TRUE			
'COUNT	Task entry	UNIVERSAL INTEGER	Number of calls on queue for the entry.
example: KEY_INTERRUPT'COUNT should be a small number such as 0, 1, 2			
'DELTA	Fixed-point subtype	UNIVERSAL REAL	Value of delta in specification for the type.
example: MONEY_TYPE'DELTA gives the value 0.001			
'DIGITS	Floating-point subtype	UNIVERSAL INTEGER	Number of decimal digits in mantissa (fraction part) of the subtype.
example: FLOAT'DIGITS gives the value 6 on my computer			
'EMAX	Floating-point subtype	UNIVERSAL INTEGER	Largest exponent value of the subtype.
example: FLOAT'EMAX gives the value 128 on my computer			

ATTRIBUTE	TYPE OF PREFIX	RESULT TYPE	DEFINITION
'EPSILON	Floating-point subtype	UNIVERSAL REAL	Smallest difference representable above 1.0 for the subtype.
example: FLOAT'EPSILON gives the value $2**(-23)$ on my computer			
'FIRST	Scalar type or scalar subtype	Type of prefix	Lower bound of type.
example: AUTHOR'FIRST gives the value CHARLES			
'FIRST	Array type or constrained array type	Type of first index	Lower bound of first index range.
example: SHORT_LIST'FIRST gives the value 1			
'FIRST (N)	Array type or constrained array type	Type of nth index	Lower bound of nth index range. n is a static expression of type UNIVERSAL INTEGER. n must be positive, nonzero, and within the dimensionality of the array.
example: MATRIX_TYPE'FIRST (2) gives the value 0.			
'FIRST_BIT	Component of a record object	UNIVERSAL INTEGER	Offset in bits from the start of the record to the start of the component.
example: C.IMAGINARY_PART'FIRST_BIT gives the value 32 on my machine			
'FORE	Fixed-point subtype	UNIVERSAL INTEGER	Number of characters needed to represent the integer part of the subtype—includes a space for the sign.

ATTRIBUTE	TYPE OF PREFIX	RESULT TYPE	DEFINITION
example: 　DOLLAR_TYPE'FORE gives the value 8			
'IMAGE (X)	Discrete type or subtype	STRING	Provides string representation of X, also called image of X.
example: 　AUTHOR'IMAGE (Mary) gives value "MARY"			
'LARGE	Real subtype	UNIVERSAL REAL	Largest positive number of the subtype.
example: 　FLOAT'LARGE gives the value $2**127 * (1 - 2** - 24)$			
'LAST	Scalar type or scalar subtype	Type of prefix	Upper bound of type.
example: 　AUTHOR'LAST gives the value NANCY			
'LAST	Array type or constrained array subtype	Type of index	Upper bound of the first index range.
example: 　SHORT_LIST'LAST gives the value 4			
'LAST (N)	Array type or constrained array subtype	Type of nth index	Upper bound of the nth index range. n is a static expression of type UNIVERSAL INTEGER. n must be positive, nonzero, and within the dimensionality of the array.
example: 　MATRIX_TYPE'LAST (2) gives the value 3			
'LAST_BIT	Component of a record object	UNIVERSAL INTEGER	Offset in bits from the start of the record to the end of the component.

ATTRIBUTE	TYPE OF PREFIX	RESULT TYPE	DEFINITION
'LENGTH	Array type or constrained array subtype	UNIVERSAL INTEGER	Number of values in the range of the first index.
example: C.REAL_PART'LAST_BIT is 31 on my machine			
'LENGTH (N)	Array type or constrained array subtype	UNIVERSAL INTEGER	Number of values in the range of the nth index. n is a static expression, positive, nonzero, and within the dimensionality of the array.
example: SHORT_LIST'LENGTH is 4			
'MACHINE_EMAX	Floating-point type or subtype	UNIVERSAL INTEGER	Largest value of the exponent for the machine representation of the base type of the prefix.
example: MATRIX_TYPE'LENGTH(2) is 4			
'MACHINE_EMIN	Floating-point type or subtype	UNIVERSAL INTEGER	Smallest (most negative) value of the exponent for the machine representation of the base type of the prefix.
example: REAL'MACHINE_EMAX gives the value 127 on my machine			
'MACHINE_MANTISSA	Floating-point type or subtype	UNIVERSAL INTEGER	Number of digits in the mantissa for the machine representation of the base type of the prefix.
example: REAL'MACHINE_EMIN gives the value -127 on my machine			
'MACHINE_OVERFLOWS	Real type or subtype	BOOLEAN	TRUE if every predefined operation on the type either provides a correct result or raises the exception NUMERIC_ERRORS in overflow situations. FALSE otherwise.
example: REAL'MACHINE_MANTISSA gives the value 24 on my machine			

ATTRIBUTE	TYPE OF PREFIX	RESULT TYPE	DEFINITION
example: REAL'MACHINE_OVERFLOWS gives the value TRUE on my machine			
'MACHINE_RADIX	Floating-point type or subtype	UNIVERSAL INTEGER	Value of the radix used in the machine representation of the base type of the prefix.
example: REAL'MACHINE_RADIX is 2 on my machine			
'MACHINE_ROUNDS	Real type of subtype	BOOLEAN	TRUE if every predefined arithmetic operation on values of the base type of the prefix returns an exact result or performs rounding. FALSE otherwise.
example: REAL'MACHINE_ROUNDS is FALSE on my machine			
'MANTISSA	Real subtype	UNIVERSAL INTEGER	The number of binary digits in the mantissa (fraction part) for the subtype.
example: REAL'MANTISSA is 24 on my machine			
'POS (X)	Discrete type or subtype	UNIVERSAL INTEGER	X is a value of the prefix type. The result is the position number of X in the enumeration type.
example: AUTHOR'POS (MARY) is 1			
'POSITION	Component of a record object	UNIVERSAL INTEGER	Offset in storage units between the component and the start of the record.
example: C.IMAGINARY_PART'POSITION is 4 Stands for 4 bytes in my machine			
'PRED (X)	Discrete type or subtype	Prefix type	X is the value of the prefix type. The result is the value whose position number is one less than that of X. Also called the predecessor function.

ATTRIBUTE	TYPE OF PREFIX	RESULT TYPE	DEFINITION
example: AUTHOR'PRED (MARY) is CHARLES			
'RANGE	Array type or constrained array subtype	First index range type	Range of first index for the array in the prefix.
example: SHORT_LIST'RANGE is 1..4			
'RANGE (N)	Array type or constrained array subtype	nth index range type	Range of nth index for the array in the prefix.
example: MATRIX_TYPE'RANGE(2) is 0..3			
'SAFE_EMAX	Floating-point type or subtype	UNIVERSAL INTEGER	Value of the largest exponent of safe number for the base type in the prefix.
example: REAL'SAFE_EMAX is 127 on my machine			
'SAFE_LARGE	Real type or subtype	UNIVERSAL REAL	Value of the largest positive safe number for the base type in the prefix.
example: REAL'SAFE_LARGE is $2^{127}(1 - 2^{(-24)})$ on my machine			
'SAFE_SMALL	Real type or subtype	UNIVERSAL REAL	Value of the smallest positive (nonzero) safe number of the base type in the prefix.
example: REAL'SAFE_SMALL is $2^{(-23)}$ on my machine			
'SIZE	Object	UNIVERSAL INTEGER	Number of bits allocated to hold the object.
example: C'SIZE is 64 on my machine			

ATTRIBUTE	TYPE OF PREFIX	RESULT TYPE	DEFINITION
'SIZE	Type or subtype	UNIVERSAL INTEGER	Minimum number of bits the computer needs to hold any object of the type.
example: COMPLEX'SIZE is 64 on my machine			
'SMALL	Real subtype	UNIVERSAL INTEGER	Smallest positive, nonzero model number of the subtype.
example: REAL'SMALL is 2**(−23) on my machine			
'STORAGE_SIZE	Access type or subtype	UNIVERSAL INTEGER	Total number of storage units associated with the type.
example: POINTER_TYPE'STORAGE_SIZE is 4 bytes on my machine			
'STORAGE_SIZE	Task type or task object	UNIVERSAL INTEGER	Number of storage units reserved for each activation of the prefix task.
example: KEYBOARD'STORAGE_SIZE is 132 bytes on my machine			
'SUCC (X)	Discrete type or subtype	Prefix type	Value of the type whose position number is one greater than that of X. X is a value of the prefix type. Also called the successor function.
example: AUTHOR'SUCC (MARY) is DICK			
'TERMINATED	Task	BOOLEAN	TRUE if task is terminated. Otherwise FALSE.

ATTRIBUTE	TYPE OF PREFIX	RESULT TYPE	DEFINITION
example: KEYBOARD'TERMINATED is FALSE			
'VAL (X)	Discrete type or subtype	Prefix type	X is a position number of type UNIVERSAL INTEGER. The result is the value in the type for the specified position.
example: AUTHOR'VAL(1) is MARY			
'VALUE (X)	Discrete type or subtype	Prefix type	X is a STRING. The result is the conversion of the string form of X to the prefix type.
example: AUTHOR'VALUE ("Mary") is MARY			
'WIDTH	Discrete subtype	UNIVERSAL INTEGER	Minimum number of characters needed in an IMAGE' of the type. Leaves a space for the sign.
example AUTHOR'WIDTH is 8			

APPENDIX
❖ E ❖

PREDEFINED LANGUAGE PRAGMAS

Ada provides directions to the compiler by means of the pragmas which appear in the following table. Pragmas are useful for controlling listings with such pragmas as

> **pragma** LIST (OFF);
> and
> **pragma** LIST (ON);

for controlling the compiler optimization techniques with

> **pragma** OPTIMIZE (TIME);
> and
> **pragma** OPTIMIZE (SPACE);

for speeding up execution by suppressing checks and expanding procedures inline with

> **pragma** SUPPRESS
> and
> **pagma** INLINE

for allowing programs written in other languages to be used from an Ada program with

pragma INTERFACE

All the predefined Ada pragmas are listed in the following table along with where the pragmas may be placed and what type of parameters may be passed to the pragma.

PRAGMA NAME AND DEFINITION	TYPE OF PARAMETER	PLACEMENT OF PRAGMA
CONTROLLED (X) Turns off automatic storage reclamation for the type	Access type	After declaration of access type in same declaration part
ELABORATE (X,Y,...) Specifies the library bodies for the specified units which must be elaborated before the following compilation unit	Library units	Immediately after **with** statement
INLINE (X,Y,...) Specifies the code for the subprogram should be expanded inline wherever the subprogram is invoked	Subprogram name or generic subprogram name	Declarative part or after library unit and before compilation unit
INTERFACE (X,Y) Used to notify that the subprogram exists as an object module prepared by another compiler	X is language name Y is subprogram name	Declarative part after the subprogram declaration before any other subprogram
LIST (ON) Resume compiler listing		Anywhere
LIST (OFF) Turn off compiler listing		Anywhere
MEMORY_SIZE (X) Defines the value for the predefined identifier MEMORY_SIZE	Numeric Literal	Start of compilation
OPTIMIZE (TIME) Specifies time is the primary optimization criteria		Declaration part
OPTIMIZE (SPACE) Specifies space is the primary optimization criteria		Declaration part
PACK (X) Storage representation for the type is to be minimized	Name of a record or array type	Declaration part after the name of the record or array type

PRAGMA NAME AND DEFINITION	TYPE OF PARAMETER	PLACEMENT OF PRAGMA
PAGE Compiler listing is to start on a new page		Anywhere
PRIORITY (X) Specifies the priority of the task or the main program	Integer subtype PRIORITY	In the specification of a task unit or in the outermost declarative part of a main program
SHARED (X) Specifies that every read or update of the variable is a synchronization point	Variable name of a scalar or access type	Immediately after the variable declaration
STORAGE_UNIT (X) Specifies the value of the predefined item STORAGE_UNIT	Numeric literal	Start of a compilation
SUPPRESS (X) Omit the specified check	Name of a check	Declarative part
SUPPRESS (X,Y) Omit the specified check for the specified object	X is name of check Y is name of an object, a type, a subtype, a subprogram, a task or a generic unit	Declarative part
SYSTEM_NAME (X) Assigns the literal to the constant SYSTEM_NAME	Enumeration literal of type NAME in package SYSTEM	Start of a compilation

APPENDIX F

PACKAGE STANDARD

```
package STANDARD is

   type BOOLEAN is (FALSE, TRUE);
   -- The predefined relational operators for this type are as follows:

   -- function "="    (LEFT, RIGHT : BOOLEAN) return BOOLEAN;
   -- function "/="   (LEFT, RIGHT : BOOLEAN) return BOOLEAN;
   -- function "<"    (LEFT, RIGHT : BOOLEAN) return BOOLEAN;
   -- function "<="   (LEFT, RIGHT : BOOLEAN) return BOOLEAN;
   -- function ">"    (LEFT, RIGHT : BOOLEAN) return BOOLEAN;
   -- function ">="   (LEFT, RIGHT : BOOLEAN) return BOOLEAN;

   -- The predefined logical operators and the predefined logical
   -- negation operator are as follows:

   -- function "and" (LEFT, RIGHT : BOOLEAN) return BOOLEAN;
   -- function "or"  (LEFT, RIGHT : BOOLEAN) return BOOLEAN;
   -- function "xor" (LEFT, RIGHT : BOOLEAN) return BOOLEAN;

   -- function "not" (RIGHT : BOOLEAN) return BOOLEAN;
```

```
-- The universal type UNIVERSAL_INTEGER is predefined.

type INTEGER is IMPLEMENTATION_DEFINED;

-- The predefined operators for this type are as follows:

-- function "="   (LEFT, RIGHT : INTEGER) return BOOLEAN;
-- function "/="  (LEFT, RIGHT : INTEGER) return BOOLEAN;
-- function "<"   (LEFT, RIGHT : INTEGER) return BOOLEAN;
-- function "<="  (LEFT, RIGHT : INTEGER) return BOOLEAN;
-- function ">"   (LEFT, RIGHT : INTEGER) return BOOLEAN;
-- function ">="  (LEFT, RIGHT : INTEGER) return BOOLEAN;


-- function "+"   (RIGHT : INTEGER) return INTEGER;
-- function "-"   (RIGHT : INTEGER) return INTEGER;
-- function "abs" (RIGHT : INTEGER) return INTEGER;


-- function "+"   (LEFT, RIGHT : INTEGER) return INTEGER;
-- function "-"   (LEFT, RIGHT : INTEGER) return INTEGER;
-- function "*"   (LEFT, RIGHT : INTEGER) return INTEGER;
-- function "/"   (LEFT, RIGHT : INTEGER) return INTEGER;
-- function "rem" (LEFT, RIGHT : INTEGER) return INTEGER;
-- function "mod" (LEFT, RIGHT : INTEGER) return INTEGER;


-- function "**"  (LEFT : INTEGER; RIGHT : INTEGER) return INTEGER;


-- An implementation may provide additional predefined integer
-- types.  It is recommended that the names of such additional types
-- end with INTEGER as in SHORT_INTEGER or LONG_INTEGER.  The
-- specification of each operator for the type UNIVERSAL_INTEGER, or
-- for any additional predefined integer type, is obtained by
-- replacing INTEGER by the name of the type in the specification of
-- the corresponding operator of the type INTEGER, except for the
-- right operand of the exponentiating operator.
```

```
-- The universal type UNIVERSAL_REAL is predefined.

type FLOAT is IMPLEMENTATION_DEFINED;

-- The predefined operators for this type are as follows:

-- function "="    (LEFT, RIGHT : FLOAT) return BOOLEAN;
-- function "/="   (LEFT, RIGHT : FLOAT) return BOOLEAN;
-- function "<"    (LEFT, RIGHT : FLOAT) return BOOLEAN;
-- function "<="   (LEFT, RIGHT : FLOAT) return BOOLEAN;
-- function ">"    (LEFT, RIGHT : FLOAT) return BOOLEAN;
-- function ">="   (LEFT, RIGHT : FLOAT) return BOOLEAN;


-- function "+"    (RIGHT : FLOAT) return FLOAT;
-- function "-"    (RIGHT : FLOAT) return FLOAT;
-- function "abs"  (RIGHT : FLOAT) return FLOAT;


-- function "+"    (LEFT, RIGHT : FLOAT) return FLOAT;
-- function "-"    (LEFT, RIGHT : FLOAT) return FLOAT;
-- function "*"    (LEFT, RIGHT : FLOAT) return FLOAT;
-- function "/     (LEFT, RIGHT : FLOAT) return FLOAT;


-- function "**"   (LEFT : FLOAT; RIGHT : INTEGER) return FLOAT;

-- An implementation may provide additional predefined floating
-- point types.  It is recommended that the names of such additional
-- types end with FLOAT as in SHORT_FLOAT or LONG_FLOAT.  The
-- specification of each operator for the type UNIVERSAL_REAL, or
-- for any additional predefined floating point type, is obtained by
-- replacing FLOAT by the name of the type in the specification of
-- the corresponding operator of the type FLOAT.

-- In addition, the following operators are predefined for
-- universal types:

-- function "*"   (LEFT : UNIVERSAL_INTEGER;   RIGHT : UNIVERSAL_REAL)
                   return UNIVERSAL_REAL;
-- function "*"   (LEFT : UNIVERSAL_REAL;      RIGHT : UNIVERSAL_INTEGER)
                   return UNIVERSAL_REAL;
-- function "/"   (LEFT : UNIVERSAL_REAL;      RIGHT : UNIVERSAL_INTEGER)
                   return UNIVERSAL_REAL;

-- The type UNIVERSAL_FIXED is predefined.  The only operators declared
-- for this type are

-- function "*" (LEFT : ANY_FIXED_POINT_TYPE; RIGHT : ANY_FIXED_POINT_TYPE)
                 return UNIVERSAL_FIXED;
-- function "/" (LEFT : ANY_FIXED_POINT_TYPE; RIGHT : ANY_FIXED_POINT_TYPE)
                 return UNIVERSAL_FIXED;
```

```
-- The following characters form the standard ASCII character
-- set.  Character literals corresponding to control characters are
-- not identifiers;  they are indicated in italics in this definition.

type CHARACTER is

   (nul,     soh,     stx,     etx,      eot,     enq,     ack,     bel,
    bs,      ht,      lf,      vt,       ff,      cr,      so,      si
    dle,     dc1,     dc2,     dc3,      dc4,     nak,     syn,     etb,
    can,     em,      sub,     esc,      fs,      gs,      rs,      us,

    ' ',     '!',     '"',     '#',      '$',     '%',     '&',     ''',
    '(',     ')',     '*',     '+',      ',',     '-',     '.',     '/',
    '0',     '1',     '2',     '3',      '4',     '5',     '6',     '7',
    '8',     '9',     ':',     ';',      '<',     '=',     '>',     '?',

    '@',     'A',     'B',     'C',      'D',     'E',     'F',     'G',
    'H',     'I',     'J',     'K',      'L',     'M',     'N',     'O',
    'P',     'Q',     'R',     'S',      'T',     'U',     'V',     'W',
    'X',     'Y',     'Z',     '[',      '\',     ']',     '^',     '_',

    '`',     'a',     'b',     'c',      'd',     'e',     'f',     'g',
    'h',     'i',     'j',     'k',      'l',     'm',     'n',     'o',
    'p',     'q',     'r',     's',      't',     'u',     'v',     'w',
    'x',     'y',     'z',     '{',      '|',     '}',     '~',     del);

for CHARACTER use   -- 128 ASCII character set without holes
     (0, 1, 2, 3, 4, 5, ..., 125, 126, 127);
-- The predefined operators for the type CHARACTER are the same
-- as for any enumeration type.

package ASCII is

-- Control characters:

NUL     : constant CHARACTER := nul;    SOH   : constant CHARACTER := soh;
STX     : constant CHARACTER := stx;    ETX   : constant CHARACTER := etx;
EOT     : constant CHARACTER := eot;    ENQ   : constant CHARACTER := enq;
ACK     : constant CHARACTER := ack;    BEL   : constant CHARACTER := bel;
BS      : constant CHARACTER := bs;     HT    : constant CHARACTER := ht;
LF      : constant CHARACTER := lf;     VT    : constant CHARACTER := vt;
FF      : constant CHARACTER := ff;     CR    : constant CHARACTER := cr;
SO      : constant CHARACTER := so;     SI    : constant CHARACTER := si;
DLE     : constant CHARACTER := dle;    DC1   : constant CHARACTER := dc1;
DC2     : constant CHARACTER := dc2;    DC3   : constant CHARACTER := dc3;
DC4     : constant CHARACTER := dc4;    NAK   : constant CHARACTER := nak;
SYN     : constant CHARACTER := syn;    ETB   : constant CHARACTER := etb;
CAN     : constant CHARACTER := can;    EM    : constant CHARACTER := em;
SUB     : constant CHARACTER := sub;    ESC   : constant CHARACTER := esc;
FS      : constant CHARACTER := fs;     GS    : constant CHARACTER := gs;
RS      : constant CHARACTER := rs;     US    : constant CHARACTER := us;
DEL     : constant CHARACTER := del;
```

```
    -- Other characters:

    EXCLAM     : constant CHARACTER := '!';   QUOTATION  : constant CHARACTER := '"'
    SHARP      : constant CHARACTER := '#';   DOLLAR     : constant CHARACTER := '$'
    PERCENT    : constant CHARACTER := '%';   AMPERSAND  : constant CHARACTER := '&'
    COLON      : constant CHARACTER := ':';   SEMICOLON  : constant CHARACTER := ';'
    QUERY      : constant CHARACTER := '?';   AT_SIGN    : constant CHARACTER := '@'
    L_BRACKET  : constant CHARACTER := '[';   BACK_SLASH : constant CHARACTER := '\'
    R_BRACKET  : constant CHARACTER := ']';   CIRCUMFLEX : constant CHARACTER := '^'
    UNDERLINE  : constant CHARACTER := '_';   GRAVE      : constant CHARACTER := '`'
    L_BRACE    : constant CHARACTER := '{';   BAR        : constant CHARACTER := '|';
    R_BRACE    : constant CHARACTER := '}';   TILDE      : constant CHARACTER := '~'

    -- Lowercase letters:

    LC_A : constant CHARACTER := 'a';
    ...
    LC_Z : constant CHARACTER := 'z';

end ASCII;

    -- Predefined subtypes:

    subtype NATURAL  is INTEGER range 0 .. INTEGER'LAST;
    subtype POSITIVE is INTEGER range 1 .. INTEGER'LAST;


    -- Predefined string type:

    type STRING is array (POSITIVE range <>) of CHARACTER;

    pragma PACK (STRING);

    -- The predefined operators for this type are as follows:

    -- function "="  (LEFT, RIGHT : STRING) return BOOLEAN;
    -- function "/=" (LEFT, RIGHT : STRING) return BOOLEAN;
    -- function "<"  (LEFT, RIGHT : STRING) return BOOLEAN;
    -- function "<=" (LEFT, RIGHT : STRING) return BOOLEAN;
    -- function ">"  (LEFT, RIGHT : STRING) return BOOLEAN;
    -- function ">=" (LEFT, RIGHT : STRING) return BOOLEAN;

    -- function "&" (LEFT : STRING;     RIGHT : STRING)    return STRING;
    -- function "&" (LEFT : CHARACTER;  RIGHT : STRING)    return STRING;
    -- function "&" (LEFT : STRING;     RIGHT : CHARACTER) return STRING;
    -- function "&" (LEFT : CHARACTER;  RIGHT : CHARACTER) return STRING;
```

```
type DURATION is delta IMPLEMENTATION_DEFINED range IMPLEMENTATION_DEFINED;

-- The predefined operators for the type DURATION are the same as
-- for any fixed point type.

-- The predefined exceptions:

CONSTRAINT_ERROR    : exception;
NUMERIC_ERROR       : exception;
PROGRAM_ERROR       : exception;
STORAGE_ERROR       : exception;
TASKING_ERROR       : exception;

end STANDARD;
```

APPENDIX
◈ G ◈
PACKAGES SYSTEM AND CALENDAR

```
package SYSTEM is
    type ADDRESS      is IMPLEMENTATION_DEFINED;
    type NAME         is IMPLEMENTATION_DEFINED_ENUMERATION_TYPE;

    SYSTEM_NAME       : constant NAME   := IMPLEMENTATION_DEFINED;

    STORAGE_UNIT      : constant := IMPLEMENTATION_DEFINED;
    MEMORY_SIZE       : constant := IMPLEMENTATION_DEFINED;

    -- System-Dependent Named Numbers:

    MIN_INT           : constant := IMPLEMENTATION_DEFINED;
    MAX_INT           : constant := IMPLEMENTATION_DEFINED;
    MAX_DIGITS        : constant := IMPLEMENTATION_DEFINED;
    MAX_MANTISSA      : constant := IMPLEMENTATION_DEFINED;
    FINE_DELTA        : constant := IMPLEMENTATION_DEFINED;
    TICK              : constant := IMPLEMENTATION_DEFINED;

    -- Other System-Dependent Declarations

    subtype PRIORITY is INTEGER range IMPLEMENTATION_DEFINED;

    -- IMPLEMENTATION_DEPENDENT

end SYSTEM;
```

```
package CALENDAR is
  type TIME is private;
  subtype YEAR_NUMBER    is INTEGER    range 1901 .. 2099;
  subtype MONTH_NUMBER   is INTEGER    range 1 .. 12;
  subtype DAY_NUMBER     is INTEGER    range 1 .. 31;
  subtype DAY_DURATION   is DURATION   range 0.0 .. 86_400.0;

  function CLOCK return TIME;

  function YEAR    (DATE  : TIME) return YEAR_NUMBER;
  function MONTH   (DATE  : TIME) return MONTH_NUMBER;
  function DAY     (DATE  : TIME) return DAY_NUMBER;
  function SECONDS (DATE  : TIME) return DAY_DURATION;

  procedure SPLIT  (DATE     : in  TIME;
                    YEAR     : out YEAR_NUMBER;
                    MONTH    : out MONTH_NUMBER;
                    DAY      : out DAY_NUMBER;
                    SECONDS  : out DAY_DURATION);

  function TIME_OF (YEAR     : YEAR_NUMBER;
                    MONTH    : MONTH_NUMBER;
                    DAY      : DAY_NUMBER;
                    SECONDS  : DAY_DURATION := 0.0) return TIME;

  function "+"  (LEFT : TIME;      RIGHT : DURATION) return TIME;
  function "+"  (LEFT : DURATION;  RIGHT : TIME)     return TIME;
  function "-"  (LEFT : TIME;      RIGHT : DURATION) return TIME;
  function "-"  (LEFT : TIME;      RIGHT : TIME)     return DURATION;

  function "<"  (LEFT, RIGHT : TIME) return BOOLEAN;
  function "<=" (LEFT, RIGHT : TIME) return BOOLEAN;
  function "> " (LEFT, RIGHT : TIME) return BOOLEAN;
  function ">=" (LEFT, RIGHT : TIME) return BOOLEAN;

  TIME_ERROR : exception;  -- can be raised by TIME_OF, "+", and "-"

private
  -- IMPLEMENTATION_DEPENDENT
end;
```

GLOSSARY

Accept statement   Specifies the actions to be performed when a task entry is called. Keyword: **accept**.

Access type   An access type can dynamically create objects during execution. Keyword: **access**.

Access value   Provides the location of an object created by an allocator. If no object can be accessed, the access value is null. Keywords: **access**, **null**.

Actual parameter   The parameter used in a subprogram call, entry call, or generic instantiation.

Accuracy constraint   Specifies the relative or absolute error bound of values of a real type. Keywords: **delta**, **digits**.

Aggregate   A written form denoting a composite value. An array aggregate denotes a value of an array type; a record aggregate denotes a value of a record type. The components of an aggregate may be specified using either positional or named association.

Allocator   Creates a new object of an access type and returns an access value designating the location of a created object.

Ancestor compilation unit   An ancestor compilation unit of a compilation unit currently being compiled is a member of the following set: a. a unit mentioned in a **with** clause of the compilation unit currently being compiled; b. an outer, textually nested unit containing the unit currently being compiled, if that unit is a subunit; c. the specification part of a subprogram or package body currently being compiled; d. one of the units mentioned in a **with** clause of the ancestor compilation units defined in parts (b) and (c) above; and e. package STANDARD. In short, any compilation unit made visible to a compilation unit currently being compiled is an ancestor compilation unit, not including the unit currently being compiled itself.

Attribute   A predefined characteristic.

Block statement   A single statement that can contain other statements. Block statements are useful for declaring local variables in the executable part of a program and for isolating exception handlers. Keywords: **declare**, **begin**, **end**.

Body A program unit defining the executable portion or implementation of a subprogram, package, or task.

Body stub A replacement for a body that is compiled separately.

Collection The entire set of allocated objects of an access type.

Compilation unit A program unit compiled independently from any other text. It is preceded by a specification naming other compilation units on which it may depend. A compilation unit may be the specification or the body of a subprogram, task, or package.

Complete program A program with no unresolved external references.

Component Denotes a part of a composite object. An indexed component is a name containing expressions denoting indices, and names a component in an array or an entry in an entry family. A selected component is the identifier of the component, prefixed by the name of the entity of which it is a component.

Composite type An object of a composite type comprises several components. An array type is a composite type, all of whose components are of the same type and subtype; the individual components are selected by their indices. A record type is a composite type whose components may be of different types; the individual components are selected by their identifiers. Keywords: **array**, **record**.

Composite value The values that make up the components of a composite type.

Constant An object the value of which cannot be changed. Keyword: **constant**.

Constraint A restriction on the set of possible values of a type. A constraint specifies the lower and upper bounds of the values for a type. Range constraints are placed on scalar types; index constraints are for array indices, and discriminant constraints constrain the discriminants of a record of a private type. Keyword: **range**.

Context clause Defines additional compilation units upon which a following compilation unit depends.

Declaration Provides an association between a name and an Ada entry. This association is valid over the scope of the declaration.

Declarative part A sequence of declarations and related information such as subprogram bodies and representation specifications that apply over a region of a program text.

Delimiter A separator such as a comma, semicolon, parentheses, or a colon.

Derived type A type with operations and values taken from an existing type. Keyword: **new**.

Direct visibility A name is directly visible if the name is known at that part of the program.

Discrete type   The enumeration and integer types. A discrete type has an ordered set of distinct values. Discrete types may be used for indexing and iteration and for choices in case statements and record variants.

Discriminant   A specially designated component of a record that allows the record to take on various sizes and/or shapes. The variations of the record may depend on the value of the discriminant.

Discriminant constant   A restriction on the possible values of the discriminant in a record.

Elaboration   The process of assigning memory to a declaration. During elaboration, this memory may be initialized.

Entity   Anything that has a name is an Ada entity: Objects, types, values, and program units are all entities.

Entry   The points in a task that communicate with other tasks are entry points. These points have names and may have parameters. In a task, an entry is called just as a subprogram is called. Keyword: **entry**.

Enumeration type   An enumeration type has discrete values specified in the declaration of the type. These values can be identifiers, integers, or characters.

Exception   An exception is an event that causes the termination of normal program execution. It is expected that an exception is the result of a software or hardware error. Users can define and cause exceptions to occur that are meaningful to their application. Keywords: **exception, raise**.

Exception handler   That part of a program that will be executed when an exception occurs. If no exception handler is provided and an exception occurs, the program will be abnormally terminated.

Expression   Anything that has a value is an expression. The term is mostly applied to formulas that have a numeric or logical value.

Fixed-point type   Fixed-point types have an absolute error bound expressed in terms of the precision of the number. Keyword: **delta**.

Floating-point type   Floating-point types have a relative error bound expressed in terms of the number of significant digits. Keyword: **digits**.

Formal parameter   A subprogram has formal parameters that are declared in the subprogram specification.

Function   A subprogram that has a value and is treated as an expression. Keyword: **function**.

Generic unit   A subprogram that can process parameters of more than one type. The classes of parameters that are acceptable to the subprogram are specified in a generic clause. Before using a generic program unit, the types that it is to process are specified during generic instantiation. Keyword: **generic**.

Incomplete program   A program with some unresolved external references.

Index   Each component in an array is distinguished by an index or by a sequence of indices. Each index must be a value of a discrete type.

Indexed component   Names a component in an array or an entry in a family of task entries.

Index constraint   Specifies the lower and upper bounds of an array index.

Instantiation   Causing a generic program unit to be created for the specified parameter types. Keyword: **new**.

Introduce   A declaration introduces an identifier.

Lexical unit   An identifier, number, character literal, string, delimiter, or comment.

Limited type   Neither assignment nor the test for equality is automatically available for the limited type. Task types are limited. Private types may be limited. Although the assignment operator can not be defined for limited types, the equality tests can be declared for limited types.

Literal   States the value for a type. Examples of literals are numbers, enumeration values, characters, or strings.

Main subprogram   The subprogram that initially executes.

Mode   The mode of a formal parameter specifies if the actual parameter is to provide a value to the formal parameter (mode **in**), if the formal parameter is to provide a value to the actual parameter (mode **out**), or if both are to occur (mode **in out**). Keywords: **in**, **out**.

Model number   An exact representation of a floating-point data type. Arithmetic operations on floating-point numbers are defined in terms of operations on model numbers. These operations will be the same on all implementations of Ada.

Object   A variable or constant. An object can stand for any type of data—scalar, composite, or access.

Operation   An elementary function associated with one or more types. It is either implicit to the type or is available from a subprogram declared for the type.

Operator   An operation with one or two operands. Many operators are implicitly declared for the predefined types. Other operators can be declared as functions for each type.

Overloading   Overloading allows operators, identifiers, and literals to have more than one meaning or function. An overloaded operator is one a user has defined to have special meaning depending on the types it receives. An overloaded subprogram identifier allows the definition of several subprograms with the same name. The one chosen to execute is the one whose parameters match the invocation. An overloaded enumeration literal is one that appears in more than one definition of an enumeration type. Ada uses type information to select the correct literal.

Package   A package is a separately compilable program unit that should contain related data types, data objects, and subprograms that operate on objects with the defined data type. The visible part contains names that can be used external to the package. The private part of the package contains internal data that complete the package specification but are hidden from the user. The body of a package contains the implementations of subprograms that have been specified in the visible part of the package. Other compilation units may use the names introduced in the package by listing the package name in a **use** clause. Keywords: **package, use**.

Parameter   Subprograms, task entries, and generic programs have parameters. A formal parameter is a parameter that defines the parameter in the compilation of the subprogram, task, or generic program. An actual parameter is the name of the identifier used in a subprogram or task invocation or in a generic instantiation. The mode of the parameter specifies whether the parameter is used for input, output, or input and output to a program. A positional parameter is an actual parameter whose association with a formal parameter is a result of its position in the invocation. A named parameter is an actual parameter whose association with a formal parameter is handled by naming the corresponding formal parameter.

Parent type   The existing type from which a derived type is taken.

Positional association   Positional association associates an item with its position in a list.

Pragma   A pragma instructs the compiler to perform some action such as compiler optimization. Keyword: **pragma**.

Private type   A type a user may use without knowing its internal data structure. A private type is known by its discriminants and by the set of operations that are defined for it. A private type and operations are defined in the visible part of a package. Assignment and inequality are defined for private types unless the private type is also limited. Keywords: **private, limited**.

Procedure   A subprogram that specifies a sequence of actions. A procedure is invoked by a procedure call statement. Keyword: **procedure**.

Program   A program is a collection of one or more compilation units that have all been compiled relative to each other. One of the subprograms will be designated to be the main subprogram.

Program library   The compilation units that make up a program belong to a program library. A program library has a name specified in a **with** clause at the start of compilation. Keyword: **with**.

Qualified expression   A qualified expression further specifies an identifier by adding the name of the type or subtype to the name. Occasionally it is necessary to qualify expressions with their type in order to remove ambiguities caused by overloading.

Raising an exception   An exception can be raised to cause the program to abandon normal program execution and to signal that an error has taken place. Keyword: **raise**.

Range A contiguous set of values of a scalar type. A range is specified by giving the lower and upper bounds for the values. Keyword: **range**.

Range constraint Specifies the lower and upper bound of the values of a scalar type. Keyword: **range**.

Real type Fixed-point types and floating-point types are real types. Both these types have values approximating the real numbers. Keywords: **digits, delta**.

Record type A record type is made up of components usually of different types or subtypes. Each component has a name. Keyword: **record**.

Renaming declaration Provides another name for an Ada entity. Keyword: **renames**.

Rendezvous The interaction that occurs between two parallel tasks when one task has called an entry of the other task and the other task is executing an **accept** statement to perform an action on behalf of the calling task. Keyword: **accept**.

Representation specification A representation specification specifies the underlying bit patterns and/or addresses for data and programs. Keywords: **for, use, at**.

Scalar type A scalar type is a type the values of which have no components. Integer types, enumeration types, and real types are scalar types.

Scope The scope of a type or an identifier is the region of text over which the name can be used.

Selected component The identifier of the component together with the name of the structure of which it is a component.

Statement Specifies one or more actions to be performed during the execution of a program.

Static expression An expression the value of which does not depend on the execution of a program.

Subprogram An executable program unit that may have parameters for communication between the subprogram and its invoking program. A subprogram declaration specifies the name of the subprogram and its formal parameters. A subprogram body specifies its execution. A subprogram can be either a procedure, which performs an action, or a function, which returns a result. Keywords: **procedure, function**.

Subtype A subtype of a type has the same operations of the parent type but has a constrained set of values. Keyword: **subtype**.

Task A program unit that may operate in parallel with the main program. A task specification defines the name of the task and the names and parameters of its entries. A task body defines the implementation of the task. A task type is a specification that allows the subsequent declaration of similar tasks. Keyword: **task**.

Type A type has both a set of values and a set of operations for those values. A type definition is a language construct that defines a type. A type is either an access type, an array type, a private type, a record type, a scalar type, or a task type. Keyword: **type**.

Use clause   A **use** clause adds the names of the visible part of a package to the names that a program can use. Keyword: **use**.

Variant   The variant part of a record specifies alternative record components, depending on a discriminant of the record. Each value of the discriminant establishes a particular alternative of the variant part.

Visibility   At a given point in a program text, the declaration of an entity with an identifier is said to be visible if the entity has meaning at that point in the text.

INDEX